D1550268

Breaking Out of the Middle-Age Trap

Other books by the author

THE SECOND TIME AROUND: Remarriage in America

FROM NOW TO ZERO: Fertility, Contraception
and Abortion in America

Breaking Out
of the
Middle-Age Trap

Leslie Aldridge Westoff

NEW AMERICAN LIBRARY

TIMES MIRROR

The author wishes to thank the following sources for
permission to quote material in this book:

Journal of Marriage and the Family, May 1978, for material from "Are Working
Women Really More Satisfied? Evidence from Several National Surveys,"
by James D. Wright, Copyright © 1978.

Little, Brown & Co., for material from *Adaptation to Life,*
by George Vaillant, © 1977 by George Vaillant.

The Viking Press, for material from *The Portable Dante,* trans.
by Laurence Binyon, copyright 1947,
copyright renewed 1969 by Nicolete Gray.

Copyright © 1980 by Leslie A. Westoff
All rights reserved. For information address The New American Library, Inc.

NAL BOOKS TRADEMARK REG. U.S. PAT. OFF. AND FOREIGN COUNTRIES
REGISTERED TRADEMARK—MARCA REGISTRADA
HECHO EN CRAWFORDSVILLE, INDIANA, U.S.A.

SIGNET, SIGNET CLASSICS, MENTOR, PLUME, MERIDIAN and
NAL BOOKS
are published by The New American Library, Inc.,
1633 Broadway, New York, New York 10019

Designed by Eve Kirch
First Printing, May, 1980

1 2 3 4 5 6 7 8 9
PRINTED IN THE UNITED STATES OF AMERICA

Library of Congress Cataloging in Publication Data

Westoff, Leslie Aldridge.
Breaking out of the middle-age trap.

Bibliography: p.
1. Middle aged women—United States. 2. Women—
Psychology. 3. Women—Employment—United States.
I. Title.
HQ1221.W4   301.41'2   79-20518
ISBN 0-453-00374-5

REV.

*For my middle-aged husband
And my aging son.*

ACKNOWLEDGMENTS

Many thanks to my editor, Joan Sanger, for her enthusiastic response to this book. Her editorial acumen at polishing and perfecting, and even cutting a favorite word or page to help the reader, rather than cater to my vanity, is much appreciated. Magnums of praise also to Roz Siegel whose astuteness helped the editing along.

Thanks to Barbara Burn for aiding in the initial concept. And warm thanks to all the women, friends and strangers, who told me about their lives and helped me describe what it means to be middle-aged today.

Grateful appreciation to Alison Hankinson who offered occasional helpful comments and typed the manuscript with such ferocious rapidity that it was all I could do to keep up with her.

Thanks to my son, Geoffrey, whom I always thank for not driving me totally out of my mind, as teenagers can so expertly do.

A fond thank-you to my friends Sally and Peter Kunstadter for lending their idyllic, vine-tangled Hawaiian beach cottage where I could sleep and work to the thunder of surf and finish this book. For their selfless offerings of good fellowship, food and a desk-with-a-view, I offer continued gratitude.

Finally, profoundest thanks to my husband, Charlie, for being that rare bird—a hardworking, hard-playing companion who keeps me going in so many ways, who doesn't mind reading a manuscript and making suggestions, and who infuses our life with large pleasures, humor and his special love.

Contents

PART I—LOOKING INTO MIDDLE AGE

1. A Time to Grow   17

*The Four Revolutions • The New Middle Age • When Is
Middle Age? • Productivity and Denial*

2. How Do I Know It When I See It?   33

*An Added Bonus • My Trip Back to Youth • Taking a
Close Look*

3. Physical Stresses   46

*The Outer Shell—Skin and All • The Games We
Play • Cooling the Calories • Why I Won't Get a Face-
Lift—Yet • The Menopause • The Awful Illnesses*

4. The Inevitable Tensions   65

*Is There a Mid-Life Crisis? • Time and Terms •
The Adolescent Analogy • To Work or Not to Work •*

*The Children • The Empty Nest • Divorce and
Widowhood • The Widow Sarah*

5. Breakdowns and Breakups   83

*Reacting with Drugs and Drink • Carrie and the
Bottle • Suicide • Carol and Her Nervous
Breakdown • Why Agnes Ran Away*

6. Finding the Skills and the Self   102

*Visit with a Career Counselor • A Weekend of Transition
Planning • At a Buddhist Retreat with Maggie*

7. Back to School   129

*Continuing Education and Matriculation • Pressures of
Returning to School • Back to School with
Pat • Graduate School for Annie, the English
Major • The Fears • Kathy and the Guilt of Law
School • Cora, Her Law Degree and Her Divorce • Cindy
and Her Route to School—Medical School • Noreen and
the Mother's Residency*

8. How to Find a Job   156

*Where the Jobs Are • What Salary to Ask For • How the
Personnel Interviewer Sees You • Job Hunting with Pat*

PART II—THE WOMEN WHO WORK

9. Women Who Need to Work   173

*Women's Job Status • The New Jobs • Does a Working
Mother Damage Her Kids? • Divorcées Who Have to
Work • Virginia, Who Got Dumped at Forty-seven • More
of Cora, the Black Lawyer • Martha, Divorced
Housewife, Makes Good • The Widows—Another Form
of Having to Work • Katharine Graham, the Most
Powerful Widow • Working and Single*

10. The Vanishing Volunteers   198

*Enough Volunteering for Betty • The End of Volunteering
for Connie • Other Volunteers*

11. Well, I'll Be Damned—I'm Good at Business 206

*Decorating • Food • How Vicki Started a Lunch
Restaurant With $1,000 • How Angie Became the Plant
Lady • The Lady and the Camera • One Woman and Her
Advertising Business • Real Estate • Consultant in
Human Relations • Urban Planning*

12. Women Who Move Up   230

*Welcome to the Top • Can We Make Her Cry? • Men
Versus Women • Words of Executive Advice • The Vice-
President Who Changed Careers • Demystifying Power*

13. Politics and the Mid-Life Woman   249

*The Scoreboard • What Kind of Women
Run? • Discrimination • Women Versus Men • Alice of
the Township Committee • Barbara Sigmund, the County
Freeholder • Millicent, the Pipe-Smoking
Congresswoman • The Senate's First Elected
Woman • Anne Wexler, the President's Special
Assistant • The Egyptian President's Wife*

14. My Own Way   283

*Portrait of the Artist as a Middle-Aged
Woman • Andrea's Affair • The Woman Who Turned to
Religion • The Woman Who Became a Priest*

PART III—TELLING IT FROM
ALL SIDES

15. Backlash—What The Other Women Say   299

*She Gave Up Business to Be a Housewife • Rachel, the
Washington Housewife • Who Is Happier—the
Housewife or the Working Woman?*

16. Views from Both Sides   312

*The Husband's Perspective • The Lawyer's
Husband • The Restaurant Manager's Husband • The
Divorcée's Former Husband • The Wife's View • How
Women See Their Husbands • The Problem with Men*

17. The Wisdom of the Middle Ages   329

*Mid-Life Surprises • What They All Said • The Advice of
the Middle Ages • Middle-Age Power*

Appendix   343

INFERNO

Canto I

It is Good Friday of the year 1300 and Dante is
thirty-five years old.

Midway life's journey I was made aware
   That I had strayed into a dark forest,
   And the right path appeared not anywhere.
Ah, tongue cannot describe how it oppressed,
   This wood, so harsh, dismal and wild, that fear
   At thought of it strikes now into my breast.
So bitter it is, death is scarce bitterer.
   But, for the good it was my hap to find,
   I speak of the other things that I saw there.
I cannot well remember in my mind
   How I came thither, so was I immersed
   In sleep, when the true way I left behind.
But when my footsteps had attained the first
   Slope of a hill, at the end of that drear vale
   Which with such terror had my spirit pierced,
I looked up, and beheld its shoulders pale
   Already in clothing of that planet's light
   Which guideth men on all roads without fail.

DANTE ALIGHIERI

.

PART ONE

Looking into Middle Age

1

A Time to
Grow

It was a warm, glittering winter day on the big island of Hawaii. My husband and I were enjoying a week's vacation from his business, and we were staying at what surely must be one of the world's most beautiful hotels. Its shutters and halls were open to the sea, and it sat on a winding curve of beach like a washed-up, sun-bleached shell, a part of the environment rather than a refuge from it.

Lunch was over, a tempting display of mouth-watering edibles which we always skipped because it was not included in the American plan of two meals a day and, more to the point, we were always trying to lose weight and needed to leave some caloric credit for dinner. Regardless of whether the motive was frugality or the shedding of a few pounds of real flesh, forgetting to eat at midday in the tropics wasn't too much of a hardship. So it was after our nonlunch that we made our way along the sea path to the tennis courts. We had both signed up for the round-robin tournament arranged so that tennis-playing guests could meet one another, and I was soon hard at work banging forehands and backhands to my female opponent on a far court hidden in lush, flowered foliage.

My husband, feeling smart in his new powder blue shorts, was playing on a court near the pro shop. I had watched him warm up just for a moment with his doubles partner, a man they had randomly teamed him with, someone neither of us had met before. He seemed to be about forty-eight, which was my husband's age. They were beginning what promised to be a pretty good match as I walked over to my court. I won't stop here to analyze why the women were playing out in the bush while the men were on the number one, two and three courts with shade and chairs around them; it was certainly one aspect of life that was not going to bother anyone that afternoon.

I remember hitting with my usual amateur enthusiasm, winning all the impossible points and losing all the easy ones. Perhaps I was intimidated by the surroundings, but the often frantically played shot at 40–30 to take the game didn't seem nearly as crucial as simply moving in the ceaseless breeze, feeling the warmth soak into my skin, catching the glint of sun bouncing off my bronzing shoulders. I lack the killer instinct to win.

I think I was serving when we heard someone in the distance ask if there was a doctor around. We must have thought it was a joke, because the twang and ping of tennis continued all around us, and tennis players are constantly moaning about sprains and pains, knees and elbows. It might have been five minutes later when we heard the siren and saw the ambulance go down the flower-bordered road near our court. Still nothing seemed wrong until we saw people suddenly drop their racquets and start running.

"What is it?" we called.

"That fellow in the blue shorts. He's had a heart attack," someone called back to us.

I think I was completely paralyzed for several moments. My partner, who had met my husband on the way to the courts, could only look at me, her mouth half open. We dropped our racquets too and ran down the path toward court number one, and there he lay at the far end near the fence, a speck of powder blue on the red clay. Someone was rhythmically pounding his chest, hoping to trigger the heartbeat which must have stopped. There was a flurry of people surrounding the upper portion of his body, busy with life-saving medical paraphernalia. I could feel terror choke me. I felt instantly hot in the face, cold in the hands. Blood pounded. Adrenaline jerked my stomach. Tears blinded my eyes. I fought to control myself. I had to sit down. Right away. My world was splintering away into nothing.

Minutes later a pair of flappy-sneakered, skinny legs stood in front of me. I began to look up past the bony knees and then I saw the powder blue shorts, and my husband was standing in the pathway near the court.

"I . . . I thought it was you, damn it." I jumped up and kissed him, and he put an arm around me. "Squeeze me tighter . . . tighter." I almost wanted him to hurt me with his living strength. Then I finally asked who it was in that other pair of powder blue shorts.

My husband was visibly shaken. "My doubles partner. God! He was my partner till just a few minutes ago." We looked at the rescue team pounding away on his chest. Then I saw his wife nearby, crying, and his two sons standing helpless and watching.

"What happened?" I asked, sniffling and drying my eyes.

"We were playing our matches of four games each. We had won the first one, split the second, and in the third we had beaten his twenty-year-old sons 4–0 and were feeling very proud of ourselves. We were playing our fourth match and were up against a stronger team. My partner's game was a bit erratic, and I wasn't doing too well. We were behind, and I was serving. . . ." He paused to look over at the body still motionless on the court except for the periodic shudders that wracked it every time a hand pressed down onto the chest, one TWO, three four. By now his brain would be gone even if they could start his heart.

"Go on. . . . What happened?"

"I was serving, and we were behind, and one of our opponents lobbed the ball back over my partner's head. He turned and chased the lob but couldn't get to it in time. Then it happened. He was slowing down and making the turn near the fence, and he stumbled. I was looking at him, and I could see his head go back and his eyes roll away in their sockets. He fell. The fence broke his fall a bit, but his head hit the court as he dropped.''

"How horrid," I said, looking over at the rescue team, still working. I could see tubes attached to the body through which flowed an intravenous solution from a bottle being held up by one of the men. Then tension finally hit one of the sons who realized that it was too late but refused to abandon hope. "Can't anybody do something?" he screamed. His brother went over to comfort him.

"You know," my husband went on, "it was almost like a bad Western, with the bad guy being shot down in a barroom brawl. It was that sudden, and that phony looking. I got to him within seconds, and all I could think of was asking him whether he was all right. Only the whites of his eyes showed, and he was making strange gurgling sounds and vomiting his lunch slightly. I thought perhaps it was an epileptic fit and yelled for his sons to come from the next court where they were playing."

People had gathered around us to hear the story, and we all looked ashen and felt nauseated. My husband continued. "They ran over, and the older son managed to pry open his jaw, and the young woman running the tournament who had some first-aid training applied mouth-to-mouth resuscitation while one son pressed on his chest and the other knelt near his father crying and praying out loud. I got him to run back to the hotel for his mother. Someone had called the ambulance which arrived, and one of the hotel officers came running down. They managed to get his heart beating again for a few seconds. But then it faltered and stopped."

It had been some time since the attack, and we knew he must by now have died. For him it had all ended in the corner of a tennis court at age forty-eight, after an exotic lunch, playing a sport reputed to exercise the heart and keep it in good working order. My husband leaned his face against his sleeve and wiped his forehead. I felt extremely depressed watching the man and thinking that everything he had done that day had been for the last time: the last breakfast, the last lunch, the last game, the last point, the last time he would wear powder blue shorts. He had reached middle age and stopped forever.

I had seen only one other dead body. It had been my mother-in-law. She had been lying there, all made up, in the funeral parlor, looking better than in life because of the liquids that had been pumped into her arteries and veins, fleshing out her face, much fuller and firmer than it had been in a long time. It was only the year before, and I had expected to get sick seeing death for the first time, but I didn't. Her friends were all sitting there in the room staring at her as she lay in her coffin in front of a large cross. I walked up to see her for the last time. I felt her arm and was startled at the cool, solid sensation. She looked so peaceful, had been ill and was fairly old, all of which made it easier for me to accept what had happened. But this was different. This was the first time I had seen the frantic fight to keep hold of life, and the man was my husband's age, only halfway along in his years and the end had come, not in the morbid atmosphere of a nursing home, but on a great and balmy afternoon when fun and laughter were all around us.

Watching, I had been forced into being part of his death. I was an unwilling witness. And this time I was sick. I wanted no part of this kind of experience. We all stood around, not knowing what to do, feeling grateful to have been spared, to be alive. The girl who ran the tournament was showing people the bite marks on her hand where the man had nipped her as she tried to keep his mouth open in order to breathe air into his lungs. It was his last act of life, ironically, biting the hand that was trying to save him.

Because my husband and I were in our forties, I understood that this is normally a time of life when one adds up the pluses. Whatever had been struggled for was paying off now. A business, a profession, a creative life, a family—this was the time to draw the various strands of life together, total up the assets, enjoy the accomplishment, and if a final grand achievement was forthcoming, a culmination of all the strivings made over the last years, this is when it would happen. I felt my husband could accomplish the best work of his life now, he was so expert and comfortable with what he did. I could write things that I hadn't been experienced enough to write before. There was much to be done and to enjoy in middle age. And for one endless moment I thought I had been robbed of part of my own destiny.

There are tragedies like this in the lives of most middle-aged men and women which shake them up and make them realize that they are not only no longer young, but that they are not immortal. Traveling a route that once seemed to go on unendingly because we were adolescent for so long, we now see clearly at this age, for the first time ever, that there is a definite and foreseeable end.

But when did we leave youth behind and advance so boldly on this path into sudden middle age? It's a hard question to ask, let alone answer, and many would deny that middle age exists at all. There seems to be a universal dread of this period of life, as though it were the last gasp before the end, something to be stayed away from and denied—as though if we deny it, it will just never happen. Somehow, in many minds, middle age stands for a dull, uninteresting vegetable period. It may just be that this is because certain things begin to happen then—like the death of someone of the same age on a tennis court. Fear of middle age may be another name for fear of debility and death. For many, it also means the more immediate death of aspiration.

It's hard to admit that life does not necessarily allow all our dreams to come true. Middle age is the time when we have to acknowledge that we will probably not fly a Concorde airplane to Bahrain or sail a hot-air balloon around the world or swim between Cuba and Miami or write the great American novel. More realistically, we may have to confront the possibility of not making even that company vice-presidency or sales manager's position. It may be a plaintive cry we utter when we face the fact that life is not long enough to make all the efforts we had in mind when we were growing up and there was time to do absolutely anything because time was forever. For some of us there just isn't enough time.

The Four Revolutions

I began to think about writing a book on women in middle age when I became one myself. The idea grew more compelling to me as a clutch of books on middle-aged males began to appear. None of the professional studies had included women, and I could not find my own experiences in these or the more popular books I looked at. What was a middle-aged woman really like? What were women my age feeling, thinking and doing? What was happening to all of us? How men are supposed to react at ages twenty, thirty, forty and so on, and what crises they will experience, has been described in detail. But how is a woman supposed to respond to changes in her own life? Her problems are, in most cases, totally different from those of her husband or a man of equal age; and, as usual, she is being given the short end of the stick. So far, there were no books probing her crises, looking into her transitions, examining her life stages, except as an adjunct to a man. There was no documentation on how women who marry differ from those who do not; on how those who have children early differ from those who have them late in life—or those who don't have them at all; or on how women who work all their lives differ from those who break out at forty and go to work later, or who never work outside the home. Any study of the life stages of women would have to involve many more options and combinations than the equivalent studies of men. A man may marry or not, have children or not, but his career is what his life is centered on from the beginning. And his life will not be changed as much by marrying and having children, for example, as will the life of a woman.

My purpose in this book was to examine one small aspect of the drastic changes in the American social structure. There seem to be at least four simultaneous and interconnected revolutions taking place. Revolution One is the shrinking of the American family which is primarily due to Revolution Two— the universal use of effective methods of birth control—and

Revolution Three, the continuing force of women's lib and the seriousness with which women now take their new career opportunities and economic independence. This all results in Revolution Four—the lengthening of middle age—a stage of life that never existed before recent years.

Interacting with one another, these stages are having a more dramatic impact on all women, particularly on the middle-aged woman, than ever before in history. There is an enormous upheaval, a total defection from the past. Women are marrying much later, or not at all. They are having fewer or no children. And children are becoming less important to them, whereas once they seemed to be the whole purpose of life and marriage. More and more women are going out to work because of financial need and the psychic pressure to fulfill themselves. They are growing more interested in getting out of the house and finding out who they are. Shunning the domestic life seems fairly logical on the part of young college women who have an investment in expensive educations and are feeling the pinch of the increasing cost of living. But even for less well educated young women, the chance to earn needed money and to get ahead is equally appealing. The insurrection against past ideals and traditions is most dramatic, however, in the situation of the middle-aged woman for whom accepting these new values often means a change in life style.

One reason why the concept of middle age is so confused and fuzzy, even abhorrent, to many is that this period of life never really existed before. People married, had a lot of children, and by the time the young ones were grown and ready to leave home, these parents were old or had died. The present long, post-parental stage after the children are gone is completely new to society. Women today are having fewer children—an average of only 1.8 per woman in 1977 compared with 3.5 between 1960 and 1964. The period of their lives when they are needed as housewives and mothers is therefore diminishing. According to the U.S. Census Bureau, in 1976 almost all women aged thirty-five to thirty-nine believed they had already had all the children they were ever going to have. In 1955, only 75 percent of them had said this. In the past, women not only had more children, but they died earlier and were less well educated. So there was not nearly so long a period after raising their families when they were free, or so many outlets for this freedom. The average couple in 1900 had only two years left to live alone after the last child left home permanently. In 1970 this had increased to an average of thirteen years.

Many of today's women who are having only one or two children will say goodbye to their last child when they are forty or forty-five, and because they can expect to live, on the average, to age seventy-five or eighty, they have forty years of life ahead of them. Most of these years are the busy, productive, newly discovered, expanding middle years which small families and the women's movement have made possible. The fact that couples spend more and more of the post–child-rearing years in this "completion phase" of the family cycle has been called by two researchers from Duke University, "perhaps the most radical change experienced by the family in the twentieth century." They point out that with a longer life expectancy, children born close together in age, and a low birth rate, almost half of all families in America consist of only a husband and wife with no children living at home. This new development coupled with economic opportunity is the cause of all the ferment.

The New Middle Age

The middle-aged woman today is the one who is caught between changing values, and she is the one whose response to the new standards cherished by society at this moment is so explosive and unbelievable. Because of her age, her past experience and her new career opportunities she, more than any other group of women, seems to be proving what women are capable of doing if given the chance. Such an about-face in mid-life—never before attempted by so many women—explains how and why women are entering doors that can never be closed to them again.

I am interested in knowing not only how today's middle-aged woman is changing her life, but also how she is reacting to the inevitable strains as society around her sets about reordering its social code. Specifically, what is she doing in response to these stresses, and how can she make her life work? And I want to know in detail. I want to find a large-scale map of middle age as seen by the woman in it, a map that anyone can follow.

Until recently, concern with human development began with child psychology and ended in a complacent way, right there. The adult was supposed to be permanently formed, his future indelibly programmed once he finished adolescence. Of course he went through the changing stages of parenthood, middle and old age (often one and the same), but whatever problems he faced were considered his own individual worries, and no one evaluated and charted them. Now, because of studies of the life cycle of adult males by such professionals as Daniel J. Levinson, Roger Gould and George E. Vaillant, and the popularization of their work by the journalist Gail Sheehy in her best-selling book *Passages,* more is being said about the stages of adult life and how we adjust to them.

For women, experiencing life's stages openly is something completely new. Before women's lib we were not allowed by society to acknowledge that we were going through periods in which the pressures confronting us were incompatible with the life we were living. In the past, activities beyond the domestic sphere were supposed to be suppressed as abnormal, bizarre or, at best, deviant. Housework, shopping and tea parties were, in so many cases, the only outlets to fill the lives of women who had nothing to live for because they could not live for themselves. Now the lid is off and many formerly unsaid things about this age are being said, and undone things are being done. The stages a woman goes through in her life are, for the first time, becoming clearer.

What do we know about the woman who begins her career in middle age? She usually startles her unsuspecting husband by breaking out at this midpoint in her life, perhaps going back to college, and looking outside of the home and outside of his influence to explore a second set of interests. Why does she do it? And where does she get the courage? Then there is the woman who starts a career after college, gets it firmly established, takes a year or two off around age thirty-five to have a child before it's too late and goes back to work as soon as she can. What is she searching for? These women, because of a late start or taking time off, lingering discrimination, lower salaries or lengthening waits for promotions, will probably find that it takes them many more years to reach their career goals than it does men. A woman may be ten or fifteen years behind a man, especially if she starts a career in mid-life or if she takes a long time to advance in her field. What are her goals and why is she so anxious to work? We need to know more about what motivates middle-aged women today and, in particular, how they find out what they can do and precisely how they go about doing it.

Realizing that this is indeed a landmark time for the mid-life woman, I started talking to people in California, Washington, Connecticut, Washington, D.C., Chicago, New Jersey, Virginia, North Carolina, Honolulu, New York and wherever else I happened to be. I tried to meet women, some of whose experiences are not unique, but all of whom are examples of the many possible directions women are taking and the many possible solutions they are finding to cope with middle age and its pressures. I looked for women in school, women who were working hard for money and to be doing something, women who were gutsy enough to start businesses of their own, though they had never managed more than their own houses and budgets, women of my age who were going to law school and medical school and women who had to work because they became widows or were divorced. I found women who turned to travel, religion, politics and sculpture to express themselves, and women who had always worked who reached for the top of their fields in middle age like Anne Wexler, Special Assistant to President Carter. And I tried to find out how it's done, how a woman begins when she feels thwarted in terms of doing more with her life but doesn't know where to turn to find direction and support. I spent a weekend at a life-planning seminar in Philadelphia and went to see a career counselor in New York. I spoke with the wife of a former member of the President's Cabinet who has chosen to stay at home and make her career there. I asked working women what they get out of it, what problems they find, how they solve them and what they think women in general must do to succeed. And I spoke to several women vice-presidents whose aspirations reach as high as any man's but who believe women have something special to offer.

When is Middle Age?

At first when I began a conversation with a woman, I would explain, "I'm doing a book on middle-aged women, and I want to talk to you." They all kind of looked over their shoulders as though I were talking to someone else. They were acting out the national repugnance toward middle age.

"Who me? Me . . . middle-aged?" And they would shriek, giggle or protest, regardless of how old they were. So I learned to circumvent the need to accuse any one of them of being middle-aged, and instead I said I'm doing a book on women between the ages of forty and sixty-five. That was okay. They would sooner admit they were forty-five or fifty-five than that they were middle-aged. It got to be rather funny. A woman who was going to be forty in one month looked horrified when I asked her if she was middle-aged.

"No," she said.

"When will you be?" I asked.

"Never," she replied.

This is rather like what one female in *A Chorus Line* said when she was asked, "What do you want to be when you grow up?"

"Young," she replied.

Bette Davis also once remarked, "Anybody who tells you it's the most attractive thing in life to get older is crazy. I don't agree that life begins at forty. My birthday will be horrible. I shall probably dig a big hole, get in it and not appear all day. On my fortieth birthday I thought life was over. [It obviously wasn't.] I went into deepest depression."

Another woman I spoke to said about becoming forty, "I

wish it were otherwise, but as they say, it's better than the alternative.''

Middle age was defined as anywhere up to sixty-five, and I recently read that with mandatory retirement disappearing and men and women now able to work until seventy, the upper limits of middle age may even go that high. At the other extreme, someone of twenty-four told me she often wakes up and feels ancient.

A woman I know looked bemused when I asked her when middle age begins. She replied, ''When you suddenly feel closer to your parents than you do to the younger people you meet.''

''When is that?'' most women ask when I mention middle age, as though it were somewhere very distant and they had no part of it. Women seem to prefer going from youth right into old age, both of which are incontrovertible. Middle age is too vague. It's too easy to stretch youth, too tempting to say you are young until you have to say you are old. The fact is that these women are no longer part of youth and they know it, they are bothered by it, they react to it, they challenge it, they defy it, some accept it, most deny it.

One of the surest ways to be forced into accepting one's place in the age hierarchy is to lose one's parents. While they were alive, you were always their child, and it made you feel younger. When they are gone you know that you are no longer a kid. You've suddenly, in your own family at least, become the older generation. Recently Helen, a friend of mine, was telling me about the exciting family reunion she had had last summer in the country with children, grandchildren and great-grandchildren. ''We were twenty-two altogether with my mother sitting at the head of the table beaming at us. She's eighty-five, and I suddenly realized that when she dies, I'll be the oldest member of the family. I'll be the matriarch and I'm only a little over fifty. It really was a shock.''

As I was growing up, I remember all my relatives and parents' friends seemed middle-aged or old (the two were synonymous in my mind), and they were all rather repulsive to me because they made me recite poetry or play the piano, slobbered their kisses all over my face and never understood me. I firmly resolved never to become the older generation—never to have wrinkled skin and bad breath and a bulging tummy and laugh at nothing. And now they are old or dead, and I am middle-aged, I think.

When is chronological middle age? Some people calculate that because we are children until about age twenty when we really begin to be aware of what's happening to us, we should properly take that age and subtract it from the life expectancy of about eighty to achieve the length of grown-up life. That leaves an adult lifetime of sixty years. Half of that is thirty. Therefore twenty plus thirty equals fifty, and that would be the midpoint of adult life. By surrounding this midpoint with fifteen years at either end, we figure that middle age would span the period from thirty-five to sixty-five. The five years from thirty-five to forty would be transition years into middle age, and those from sixty to sixty-five, into old age.

It's a nebulous time of life, difficult to pin down because it comes at different times for different people, as I discovered talking to the approximately 120 women I interviewed. It begins sooner for a woman who has one child rather than two, or who goes through the menopause earlier, or whose parents die younger.

I think the answer is that for most, middle age is an attitude that evolves over several years in response to stresses that people must deal with at this time of life. For some it begins while their children are still at home but in school. For others it arrives when the children go to college or work, leaving behind their empty, silent rooms. It comes at different ages, not only because people at the same age behave and think differently, but because people start families and careers at different ages and proceed along their life tracks at different speeds. Some women at forty are living like those of thirty if they had children late in life. Some at fifty are living like others at thirty-five if they are active, young-looking people. I don't think anyone would have thought of the exuberant anthropologist Margaret Mead, who died recently at seventy-six, as old.

Although there is no specific age signifying the end of youth and beginning of the middle years, most people agree that for a woman who has children, the time when the young ones leave home for school or work is the beginning of a new era, the point at which her mothering role is pretty well over. She is no longer needed at home to hover over her children and is free to move on to other things. One type of problem ends and new ones take its place. The concerns of middle age seem to arrive prepackaged like unasked-for giveaway gifts in the mail. They often come in a bunch at the same time, and everyone in this age range begins to be aware of a series of new stresses, which I will discuss in the next chapters. These stresses, rather than any particular chronological age, may be the only way people know that they have really reached the middle years.

Productivity and Denial

If we can get around all the stereotypes of when middle age is and what it looks like, it becomes obvious that this period of life is probably the most important and productive of any of the phases we go through. Expert in whatever we do, we are surrounded by other middle-aged experts running things, from the President of the United States to corporation presidents, from lawyers, professors, jet pilots and physicians to businesspeople and diplomats. These are the leaders who make the decisions that affect all of us.

It is true that young people may have such advantages as better health, but they also have a good many problems that mid-life people have already solved. So why all the envy? Why the denial? At the bottom of this reluctance to reach the middle years is the sense that for a long time, it seems, we have felt young and favored, and everyone else seemed older. Then, suddenly, in our forties, we realize that most people in the country are younger than we, that the average age is around twenty-eight and that we are now in what is thought of as a less-fortunate category. We may also just be reacting against our parents' image.

There is no status attached to being middle-aged. The young

have status, and the senior citizens are beginning to build status and political power, but the middle-aged, despite the fact that they are the ones with the power, don't have a strong public image. They simply haven't been written about and talked about in terms of their age group. Because youth today tends to glorify youth, and because middle-aged people join in this adulation of the young and try to remain youthful, there is no one left to glorify middle age. Those in "middlescence" appear as an amorphous, slightly paunchy group who are neither young nor old, like someone with one foot on the dock and the other on a moving boat—a very uncomfortable position.

So, whatever we call it, in 1980 there was a total of almost twenty-nine million women between the ages of forty and sixty-five. And most of them probably consider themselves still young, knowing that this youth, however long they stretch it, will be followed by a mid-life period they prefer not to name. Much of this image of youth that they still try to project is real. These women are healthier and physically more attractive and active than people of comparable age ever were before. They jog, they play tennis, ski and travel. They go braless and wear youthful clothing. They speak in the latest clichés, knowing what is "in," and go to discos and "hustle" along with everyone else—even at sixty-five. For them, middle age is whenever they want it to be.

2

How Do I Know It When
I See It?

My friend Ginny and I are standing in the crush of a cocktail party and talking. She is looking exceptionally well and I ask her if she doesn't worry about middle age. She surprises me by being one of the few women I've spoken to who doesn't mind at all. She is not shrinking from it or hiding it. She knows what it is and she likes it. Ginny says, "I love being forty-four. I have more freedom now with my children in school and a better income." She tells me that she married and had children while still in college and then had to leave school. She finally went back at night but didn't finish until she was thirty-five. Here are two examples she gave me of what middle age means to her. First, she has been teaching sociology and American Studies in high school and last year was made the chairman of her department. "I was surprised that running a home prepared me to run this department. A lot of the skills were transferable to administration work. I wouldn't have had this organizing ability before." Second, she is free enough to try things she has always wanted to do. When she was young she never had the money, the time or the nerve. A couple of summers ago she applied to Earthwatch, a group that puts laymen in touch with scientists, and obtained a fellowship to go on an archaeological dig for three weeks. In the past she had been limited to reading about archaeology in books. "I was a spectator, but you can't learn about archaeology solely from a book," she said. So she flew down to New Mexico where she joined a group of eighty people of all ages who were digging in a pueblo that American Indians had originally built in the eleventh century. Ginny spent the boiling hot days with her small team, sifting through the dirt looking for eight-hundred-year-old artifacts, then taking group showers with the other women, difficult for someone who is accustomed to absolute privacy. She lugged heavy pails of dirt up ladders from the digs, explored the use of stone tools, found which desert vegetation could be eaten, learned to work with Navajo Indians and to use the metric system, all things she had never done before. "I survived it and I enjoyed it," was Ginny's comment. She remembered a rather enlightening conversation she had had with one of the other women on her team who said, "I've never been out on my own. I never knew you could have a great time with a group of women. I thought you needed a man around." For Ginny, middle age is not at all depressing. On the contrary, it is exciting, a time of freedom and experimentation, of turning dreams into realities.

An Added Bonus

What, then, is middle age? It's a vast sea of newly released time women never knew they would have. It's an extra bonus, an opportunity to restart the motor, rekindle the old fantasies. It's a time that has often been wasted by those who assumed that whatever choices they made were irrevocable—as in many cases they were, especially for women who married, had a lot of children and found themselves bogged down in domestic chores. Larger families took longer to evacuate the nest. When the children were gone, there were no opportunities for career training or further study, and there was little to occupy a woman's mind. Because of this, we have not, in the past, imagined this portion of life as having any shape or purpose. And women hardly ever planned for it or devoted much thought to it.

The crucial point about middle age today is the extraordinary way a large portion of an entire generation of women is changing goals in mid-life—as though all the salmon rushing upstream suddenly stopped and said, "Hey, wait a minute, why am I rushing upstream? What will I have when I get there? Is this all there is going to be to my life? To spawn and die upstream? Hell, no," and they all turn around and start rushing downstream again, and some go out to the ocean and some go off into tributary streams. It's quite a phenomenon and quite a sight.

The fact is that this is the first time that women who were brought up under one set of rules are suddenly turning around in mid-life and behaving under another set. Women who are now middle-aged grew up with the expectations only of marrying and having children. They married right out of college, moved to the suburbs, had their children and felt they had married into security: children, husband, the institution of the family that would shelter and protect them forever. But the values didn't hold. The women's movement jarred their complacency, if they were really feeling that way, and it gave voice to many of their frustrations. Divorce became rampant. At the current rate, half of all marriages now are destined to break up. Marriage, which had supplanted any thought of jobs and careers, was now something women found that they couldn't count on. Being "just" a wife, in addition, was suddenly frowned upon by society as being unimportant, whereas when they had married it was the only thing that was accepted. Now, they suddenly find in their middle years that they are supposed to be living a life that is totally different from the one for which they prepared. Nothing, for them, held together.

This book is primarily about those women who are facing the challenge, breaking out of their used up past and doing what they have secretly always wanted to do. For that is what is happening. In increasing numbers, middle-aged women everywhere, but particularly in metropolitan areas, are breaking away from those husbands who have kept them trapped, away from children who held their time and energies captive, breaking out of boredom and into a future as individuals. Life styles and expectations are reversing overnight and the results are incredible. Women who spent their years performing automatic, routine household jobs are now involved in every imaginable business and activity. Never in the history of women has there been such an explosion of vigor and self-improvement. Middle-aged women are becoming an amazing force to deal with as they find out who they really are—and a surprising source of talent for prospective employers. Regardless of what they call those years, this middle period for women is being recognized as an era of renewed purpose, growth, renaissance. Even in families in which only the husband has a job, women are becoming more independent. They are asking to be a greater part of what he does. A group of Ivy League college presidents' wives, for example, recently asked their husbands to let them sit in on meetings so they could be better informed about the decisions their husbands have to make. Rosalynn Carter sits in on Cabinet meetings with the President so she can stay informed. Women want a bigger part in running their total lives, and bigger means equal.

The irony for many men is that, now that they are slowing down to enjoy whatever rewards their labor has earned them, their wives who have postponed this part of their lives, helping to push their husbands up, are breathing a sigh of relief that it's all over and are ready to devote themselves to increasing the tempo of their own lives. While the husband may be thinking of buying a retirement home before the prices get too high, she's thinking of going back to college. While he's thinking of taking an extra-long vacation, she's thinking of getting a full-time job in advertising and eventually working her way up to executive levels.

This middle life is a time for a second chance, a second career (homemaker was the first), and even more, it's a time for concentrating on YOU, and what you need. Not what HE needs (the button sewn on mornings when you are barely awake) or what THEY need (pick me up at school and take me to ballet or

Little League baseball, don't forget). But who you are. It's a time of internal inventory-taking. This is not an easy task if you were one of the women who bought the old ideas so long ago. But this is a time of recycling, the moment of ultimate focus, the final chance to rethink and revitalize the entire self.

And nobody can do it for you. That's the really scary part of middle age. It's up to each person to remake herself. When, as a woman, you get bored enough, insulted enough or feel useless enough, you will make the move out of laziness and inertia and break out. You will make sense out of all the pieces of your life that have come before and didn't add up to anything.

It's a true point of discovery. Finding out who you've always wanted to be before you automatically took the path society had picked out for you. Your discovery is bound to be stimulating. Some of the excitement will come from a new confidence in recently discovered abilities. It is gratifying to find you can be recognized for skills you never realized you had. Imagine finding out that you're really terrific at business, or that you can manage an office or interest corporations in what you have to sell. A woman I know says, "When I was twelve, I thought of middle-aged people as fat, and not intelligent, because intelligent people were never middle-aged. Now that I'm that age, I have to do things. I can't sit around like a mashed potato." She is finding that she can breed horses, have children, bake bread, grow her own flowers and vegetables and more besides.

Some of the good feeling will come from being able at last to be assertive. The man in your life will finally have to consider and understand your needs, something he never had to do before. He has to accept the fact that his wife is a real person, not just the mother of his kids. It won't be easy for him, and a lot of men crack under the effort. But for most women, there's no turning back.

I was talking to the person beside me one day as we both were finishing our chicken lunches and waiting to speak to a college fund-raising group.

She said, "I've thought a lot about becoming middle-aged and what it means. I know I am. My body tells me. I see the flab. I used to be lean and athletic. Thirty-five is a milestone. Now I'm an adult. I've really grown up. I'm not a kid. I'm not the young married couple. There are all those couples out there younger than I am. I see where I'm going. Where I've been. I feel quieter, not as frenetic about things. Calmer, more comfortable. I feel more mature, physically and mentally. I think of myself as a woman not a girl. When I was young I used to go into a store and people would ignore me. They knew I wasn't going to make a major purchase. Now they treat me differently. Or I'd answer the door when I was married and people would ask me if my mother was home. Now they don't. I think middle age is a state of mind, an attitude, and women are refusing to accept it.

"Most women today want to do something—but what? They think, 'If only the kids were in school I would do this—or that —' You make a mental checklist. Suddenly they are in school and you have to make some concrete choices. All this time I knew there was a me. A *me* in relation to my kids, a *me* in relation to my husband. I wanted to know, who was the *me* in relation to ME? I had to find out. That hit me. I knew I'd entered a different phase of life."

My Trip Back to Youth

My own awareness of what middle age is came upon me gradually. Like most women, I always said I was young and thought I was young, and looked young, and therefore I WAS young. But things changed in my life and I changed with them. Take for example my recent trip to Chicago on a writing assignment. During this time I met a much older man in uniform whose close-shaven head and muscular arms held up pounds of gold braid. He was staying at the same hotel, and I found myself staring at him, thinking how fantastic he looked. Perhaps it was because I was too young during World War II to be involved with men in uniform, but I felt a sudden violent attraction for this person I didn't even know. I made up an excuse to have a drink with him. I even contemplated sleeping with him. And when I returned home to the man I actually love, I missed this image in uniform. What could have happened to me?

I was obviously trying to fall in love with a uniform, with romance, not with a person, but with a concept. Ironically, I think this happened because I know I am happily married and not likely to fall in love or marry again.

Edith Luray, an NBC television producer, and I were discussing affairs among middle-aged women one day, and she pointed out that "women at forty have put aside romance. We don't think about it too much. You think, 'I'm finished with that.' Then something happens. You meet someone, there's a real physical attraction. We middle-aged women are unprotected, inexperienced. We haven't been playing this game for a while. We don't have our guard up. We fall for the idea of romance, for the person—fall like a ton of bricks. We want the excitement of romantic passion again, we want to feel attractive again.''

And I too must have felt that this was one part of life I regretted no longer being able to enjoy, and knew I would miss. That fantastic and youthful sensation of being "in love.'' I subconsciously longed for romance, which had once been such an active and enjoyable part of my life. And that is one way I know I must be middle-aged. I am getting nostalgic about my past.

I look around the room at photographs of friends who in earlier years had come to the house, whom I have fed and laughed with and sometimes loved, and they aren't here anymore. It's the same with old movie stars I can tune to on television and see laughing, breathing, kissing, although they are no longer alive. It's hard to make death seem real enough to understand, encompass and accept. It's like trying to imagine infinity. Imagining yourself going to bed and never waking up. A friend of mine was so frightened of this prospect that he was literally afraid to go to sleep at night, afraid he would never wake up, and there would be no tomorrow. This is another middle-aged concern.

But it's not just a question of photographs. A few years ago the people I knew were appearing in the wedding pages. Then gradually, a few years later, their pictures moved into the news section—they had taken a job in government, the directorship of a museum, become a successful writer, fashion designer, movie producer, TV star . . . now I am finding some of their names in the obituary columns.

Other changes increase my awareness of time. In my forties now, I have a son about to go to college. And where do I think he should apply? The college I went to, of course. There he is an alumni child and will get preference. My son has a girlfriend who comes to the house and looks at me crossly if I want him to do something. He belongs to her. I feel young, but if my son is about to be a freshman in my college, I must not be young. He is now old enough to get married, though it would be extremely foolish of him. He drives a car and fixes it and does all the things that men do, and he can cook some things better than I. He makes me feel older than I am ready to feel.

Middle age is a time when one sees life repeating itself like the seasons. It is now his turn to do the young things: college, first loves, Europe for the first time. All the great things are about to happen to him. And although I would like the feeling of being able to fall in love again with my husband and feel again all the breathless excitement, we can't—because we have already done that, and now we are middle-aged and must look for new pleasures. Not the excitements of first things, but of knowledge and wisdom, of being in control of what's happening to us, of knowing what's important, and what no longer matters.

This past summer I went on a nostalgia trip to Europe to relive my youth. I wanted to show the things I saw when I was eighteen to my son. How can it have been that long ago when I was there? It's so hard to believe. The answer, of course, is that middle age doesn't come very long after youth, and eighteen years in the time continuum, which is my son's age now, is nothing. So here I am wanting to pick up where I left off. It chagrins me to realize that, regardless of how I feel, I must truly be middle-aged. The sight of my six-foot-one-inch son proves this to me every minute. But as I plan the trip back to my youth, I can see through my own motives. One, of course, is to educate him from boy into man, and the other is to demonstrate that time has not passed, though I know it has.

We arrived in England, where I had been on my first trip. We visit London, and I find myself thrilled again at the changing of the guard. I trudge up all the castle stairs once more and try to be as indefatigable as he. We are two young students exploring Europe for the first time. Except I have done it before he was born. And I am not satisfied with student dorms and cheap food, and I need a good night's sleep, or I can't get up in the morning.

We go on to Paris where I have two old friends. I see them and they are once more young and handsome men. One is a top fashion designer who sends me two dozen long-stemmed pink roses, the other is a deputy in the National Assembly. I meet the designer, and his tall figure enters the room and shocks me with his white hair. Is he playing some trick? Has he powdered a wig to wear like some Louis XIV courtier? It is not possible. I see the deputy, and he has colored his white hair almost orange, and I see the white roots peeping out at me. How amusing they are in France, playing games like that, dusting their hair with colored powders.

We go out again together just as we used to, and we are three young, happy people who are just beginning. No one has done anything yet. It's all ahead of us. Except the designer is talking of selling his business and traveling and living in the country surrounded by animals, just relaxing, and the deputy is saying he is disappointed because he sees now he cannot become president of France. He is quiet and his eyes stare at the floor, his orange hair parted so that it falls forward over his balding head. He will have to be satisfied with deputy, or do something entirely different.

I am eating dinner with two American friends who live in Paris. They are both remarried, both middle-aged, and both have careers. We are in a restaurant huddled over a coq au vin. We talk about politics and marriage. Is President Carter a man with ideas or a clever Georgia politician? Is remarriage as good as it seems to be? I ask what they think middle age really is and why. The man says, "It is a time when you're interested in high yield rather than high appreciation of long-term investments. It's horrible to have to 'come to terms,' as they say, when you feel you don't have any future ahead of you, that you won't change except for the worse, that you're not evolving anymore. You're just geared to survival.''

His wife prefers to point out the positive side. "But," she says sitting straight, perhaps frightened at the picture her husband has drawn. "There is another side of that coin. The fact that you are not trying to get ahead or evolve anymore means you can enjoy what you have. You don't have to try for promotions. Now you are just interested in being respected, appreciated. Instead of doing new things, you can enjoy the power you have, enjoy what you are.'' I delve into the crème caramel and wonder why I worry about age so much.

The next day I show my son things he enjoys—Notre Dame, the Eiffel Tower, the Sacré-Coeur—but I begin to realize I am getting in his way. I am a chain around his neck. He wants to pick up girls, stay up late. He can't attract people his own age walking around with his middle-aged mother. He has now begun to do the leading. He darts across the busy streets of Paris with a shrug of his shoulders, and I follow in horror or stand on the curb waiting and waiting for a large enough hole in the endless traffic to guarantee a safe crossing. I see the opposite sidewalk. I see the dangers of oncoming cars. He sees dodging the cars as a game. He is leaving me behind in more ways than one. His energy is charging up; mine is running down. I am becoming more and more aware that we are diverging. He is growing impatient and irritable.

My son is looking forward to seeing Italy. I am growing weary of daily attacks on each new city, of locking eyes with Mona Lisa and standing at parade rest beside a red-coated member of the Cold Stream Guard to have my picture taken. I begin to long for my husband, my telephone, my mail, a world I have created. My son, as I once did, is ready to go on, to discover Rome, Naples, Florence, Venice. His ties at home are very few. His world is still out there. I will open his cage reluctantly and let him fly out alone. It is his turn. My son needs to begin. I need to continue.

Sitting in Rome on my hard single bed, in a dreary room found at the last minute, I am incredibly alone and on the verge of tears. I suspect it is more fatigue than anything. But there I am, in Rome to catch my plane, alone after eighteen days of total, engrossing concentration on touring with my son. The scooter horns clamor outside, and voices call from distances, and there I sit on a twilight evening in the Eternal City in my small, bare room, never so strongly aware that my role as mother is eternally over, and whatever must come after motherhood has begun, wrenching my mother's heart as it does. I am beginning the next stage of my growth.

Even my middle-aged husband left at home to fend for himself is feeling changed. It is the first time he has had to do anything domestic for himself. It is the first time he has ever lived alone. (He had gone from the Navy to college and marriage.) He has become helpless and, after living in our new house for four years, still wasn't sure which drawer the silverware was in. Now with me away for three weeks he has followed the instructions and has done the laundry, dried it, done the dishes and cooked breakfast and heated up dinner, remembering to turn the stove off.

It is late August, and my son, having returned home in triumph from Europe, is about to leave for college. I bring up the question of whether I should perhaps go with him. His college is too far away to drive to the way most parents do, cars laden with blankets and pillows, books and footlockers. So I wonder if I should fly out and help get him settled. My husband thinks it's a good idea. There's a special chartered plane leaving from Kennedy Airport. But I don't want to be the only parent along. So I call the man at the University in charge of the flight and ask him whether he thinks I could be of help to my son.

"Well," he says in a patient tone, "I'm sure he's old enough by now to manage everything himself."

"But," I say, "there are a lot of details. Tell me, how many parents come out on that plane?"

"Oh," he estimates, "about 15 or 20 out of 175."

"Are the kids embarrassed?"

"Usually the ones who have both parents with them are pretty embarrassed."

"Oh, I see. Well, I'm not sure what to do."

"Let me say something at the risk of offending you," he finally offers. "I'd say that the parents who fly out with their kids are the ones who can't bear to break the umbilical cord."

"I understand," I say, tensing up inside and wondering if I am one of those. "Well, never mind," I decide, "just make the reservation for him. Thanks."

I hang up a little disturbed. Could that be me despite all my protestations of objectivity? I hope not. But one thing the conversation does for me is to redefine quite accurately where I am in life. And once this is defined in bold, harsh terms and one recognizes and accepts that, yes, one is now in a new mid-life phase, then the growth, the digging up of buried assets can begin.

Taking a Close Look

In the following chapters I want to look at the middle years as they are lived by today's women, examine the stresses of this time of life in this time of history, probe the lives of women who find that they cannot continue living the way they have in the past, or that they don't want to. These can be the hardest years of all for a woman because they are uncharted. There are great spaces of time when she may not feel involved in anything that any longer interests her. Many women find the problem of creating a new purpose in life too great a burden and don't know where to turn. Others seek help and encouragement from counseling services. Most women need to work for economic reasons, to contribute to keeping the children in college or to help support the standard of living in a rising inflation that won't go away. Even those who don't need the money are behaving as though they did. An enormous number of women are refusing to go through the rest of their lives doing the same old thing, or less than they are capable of. They are breaking out in all directions like Chinese fireworks on New Year's Eve.

One of my aims, then, is to tell women between the ages of forty and sixty-five that they are not alone in experiencing the mid-life mutations. Their problems are real and solvable. I want them to know that many women are experiencing this need to escape the traditional woman's role, to break away from their used-up jobs of mother and housewife, to create interesting futures for themselves that express their own capabilities and talents, or simply to enjoy the pleasure of seeing their names on a regular salary check. Women need to read of other women's experiences, to know what problems they had, how they got around them, what satisfactions they found, where they found the courage and guts to do what they did.

Now is the moment for women in middle life to admit to themselves—and to tell their husbands, if it's not already abundantly obvious—that they also want to feel important, that they do have passions that they have suppressed for years and that their expectations are rising. Women must feel free to announce that they are going through a personal as well as societal transition, and that this movement is life-giving, a good and wonderful infusion that will make the second half of their lives even more interesting than the first has been, rather than a downhill sleigh ride to nowhere.

Women readers need to look at the women I will present to them, look at themselves again and answer some pretty tough questions about where they want to go from here. They must learn to think about what comes next, even if all they are aware of is a vague sense of discontent and a lot of confusion. With so much change around us, it's got to be a whole new game. Even if a woman doesn't want to return to school or begin to work or leave the surroundings of her daily world, things can never be the same. For mother, the tide has come in again when the children sail out. And for those without children, the tide rises as well.

3

Physical Stresses

A deepening awareness of one's own mortality and children leaving home are the two major impacts that define middle age. But there are many minor ones that at different times, and in different minds, seem just as major. These are physical and mental stresses that force a reexamination of how we react to those around us and how we see ourselves in the grand design that is our future. Some of them come from within ourselves like a need for identity, a career, or an art form that brings with it ego satisfaction. Others come at us from the impact of society on our private lives, such as divorce or just observing our peers. These pressures are just as difficult to ignore as the fashions of the day. Many of them seem to converge during the middle years, and it is because of their effect upon us that women find themselves making drastic renovations in the most private interiors of their souls. But a word of caution. Because middle age encompasses a large range of at least twenty-five years, the strains and symptoms of that period are felt earlier by some people than others, or a woman may be relatively free of them until she is fairly well along in middle age. But if you are forty, it is not too soon to take a second look at your life. If you expect what is to come and give some thought to what is ahead, you can avoid problem areas in the transition.

The Outer Shell—Skin and All

It is around age forty when we suddenly notice the first small wrinkles on a formerly perfect visage. I think the sight of age slowly creeping along the face during the middle years can be one of the most devastating physical changes for a woman. You can hide your age verbally from anyone by subtracting a couple of years, but when the telltale physical signs begin appearing, there is only one verdict. It's not only a public announcement of true age, but it is a sharply felt statement to each woman who sees herself in the mirror that she is no longer young, that the years are moving on more rapidly than she was aware of and that she is beginning to look more and more like the aged parents and relatives she has always felt sorry for.

In its usual lopsided way, society tends to value age in men far more than in women. When my husband and I were about to be married in our late thirties, his very good friend warned him, "You realize, at her age she has only a few good years left." My husband, who was the same age, appeared, in his friend's male-oriented mind, to be young. I was about to "join the over-the-hill gang," as *Newsweek* once said of a movie star approaching her fortieth birthday. I look over at my husband now sitting there reading, his face decorated with the usual wrinkles and sagging jowls of his age, looking what we all think of as quite distinguished. And here I am sitting near him with my own set of wrinkles and wondering if he's going to want to exchange me for someone twenty years younger who one day will have the same wrinkles but doesn't yet. Why doesn't society think I look distinguished? A man can wear his pot belly comfortably under his tweed jacket. It may even make him look more substantial, more successful. If my belly bulges the slightest bit, society says I am fat. Why should the criteria be different? Why this double standard? Why should there be a separate code for male-female sex roles?

A woman of forty-four who is getting her doctorate in social work made the same observations. "Why, at the same age, do women seem older than men?" she asked me as we sat in her Cape Cod living room. "With women one thinks of attractiveness, fertility, motherhood. One does not evaluate men on the basis of biological and social criteria. And women buy into the image, and benignly accept these definitions. They look at other women to see who's prettier. They use makeup and sexy clothes." Because a woman is judged and valued for her looks rather than what she does, there is an extraordinary pressure on those who begin to see the approach of age. They naturally are concerned that they will no longer be valued or wanted.

One of the cruelest tricks nature plays on us is to make us unaware of aging, to keep us feeling young inside while the external changes are taking place. When we were young, we'd sometimes see a few lines near our eyes when we were tired, but if we went to sleep for ten hours, they'd disappear. We could stay up all night and look like hell the next day but eradicate any damage by sleeping. Now when I look in the mirror and see the lines like cat's whiskers radiating from the corners of my eyes and try to erase them with sleep, it doesn't work. They are there to stay.

The Games We Play

A friend of mine in her mid-thirties noticed a small vertical line between her eyes that became even more pronounced with a sunburn. Now when she sunbathes she lies there with her hands pulling her eyebrows apart so the white indentation will also be burned. I once read a theory that suggested exercising the facial muscles by making weird faces at oneself in the mirror. Often, now, when I drive my car around town, having nothing better to do, I will make the most frightening and distorted expressions I can think of. I pull my jaw to left and right, I laugh violently, I pull my lower lip in, move my jaw up and down and lift and lower my eyebrows. I'm a horror show on wheels. Drivers pulling up beside me for a red light must think I am out of my mind. I ignore them. That part of the body, almost more than any other, needs to have some toning up. And that is probably the part that gets the least exercise, except perhaps in families where there is a lot of fighting going on. Women do not accept aging and its accompanying furrows and creases gracefully, simply because society has told us that aging women are no longer of interest. We allow ourselves to be judged by our appearance just as we accept the fact that we are measured by the particular arrangement of fat on our bones in three vital places. Is a bust, waist and hip of a woman 36–26–36 worth more than one who is 33–28–36? Apparently so. Why not judge men by neck sizes. A 16½ would be more in demand than a 14½. It's just as preposterous.

Heredity plays a large role in this contest with aging, and all we can do is hope that our genes will be kind to us. There is great variety in the way different women grow old, and some faces collapse at forty whereas others make it till fifty. Some people always look younger than their age, and these are supposedly the lucky ones. To look exactly your age is practically unthinkable in the protocol of aging.

Because society compounds the shame of natural aging by telling women they are less valuable as they grow older, women naturally bear the added stress of thinking it vital to expend large amounts of time and money on trying to look younger than they are. The efforts of middle-aged women today to pay their dues to the youth cult are monumental. The attention given, and the almost mystical faith in cosmetics, vitamins, exercise spas, massages, new clothes, hairdressers and face-lifts is incredible. Every hamlet in the land has a cosmetics shop, a vitamin outlet and an exercise clinic somewhere nearby. When Keats wrote poetry, beauty was truth and truth, beauty, and that was all we knew on earth and all we needed to know. Now youth is beauty and beauty is youth and that is all we seem to need to know. Truth has become youth. Everyone wants to be what society values. If they valued women with stretched noses and rings going through them, we'd be paying huge sums to have our noses stretched and ringed. Not only do we pour and smear on what is advertised to help us on the outside, we swallow what we cannot anoint ourselves with. Americans spend $1.2 billion annually (the more education they have, the more they spend) on vitamins and minerals: vitamin C to fight colds; vitamin B to prevent aging; vitamin E to help fertility and restore male potency; and yeast and wheat germ for general good health. In addition some people take lecithin, kelp, alfalfa, zinc, selenium, bone meal, garlic oil, dolomite, bee pollen tablets, inositol, RNA/DNA and iron. Some will eat only natural products, disdaining the synthetic ones. Women with enough money go to Rumania to see Anna Aslan and try her rejuvenation pills and serum injections. But most of us at home make desperate investments in creams that are supposed to make the lines vanish. We try every new kind of formula cream (spelled "creme" when it is really expensive), "vanishing," "moisturizing," "perfection," vitamin, protein, honey, cucumber, egg, milk, turtle. We try face creams, night creams, eye creams, body creams, cleansing creams and creams that go under makeup or under other creams. The list is endless.

Furthermore, we look beyond the face to the "middle-aged spread" the thickening thighs, hips and waist. The need to remain young extends from the face down to the toes. Women join gyms and work out on machines, go on diets which center on large amounts of grapefruit or protein, vegetables or fish. Or they don't eat at all. Because although as youths we could eat and drink what we wanted and our metabolism would burn up the excess calories, now the body is not quite as efficient. The calories linger on and multiply into bulges across the hips, above the hips, down the thighs and across the belly. I go to the gym for a shower after tennis at a university where I play. In the locker room I see the girls, college girls, and I stare shamelessly like a male voyeur comparing the various angles of breast, slope of buttock, girth of thigh.

We know how old we are, but we delude ourselves, because of genetics, the creams, the exercise, into believing that others don't know. When I meet someone new who asks me, "How old are you?" I always answer, "How old do you think I am?"

not wanting to give an outright lie, yet hoping for a guess at least five years below my real age. Something keeps me from giving a straight answer. And that something is simply wanting a better score in his eyes. It's the same motive at work when middle-aged people who go to their college reunions always examine their classmates to see who looks younger or older or if, by chance, they are themselves the youngest looking of them all. Even if you cannot say this, you can at least have a great time talking about those who do look older, how Binki has aged and Finney has gained twenty pounds, all of which results in making you feel that much better.

Television producer Edith Luray told me she makes similar comparisons. "When we go to a restaurant I ask my husband as I look around the room, 'Do I look older than she does? Or the same age?' " She goes on. "I need to know how old I look. Young is good. Old is bad. There is a sadness about chronological age. Inside you feel lively, young, attractive. I feel I should be perceived that way, and I'm not. I know what society thinks of women of my age. I'm an 'older' woman. But I don't feel *middle* (as in middle-aged), I feel *beginning*. I work in an active world, with things happening all the time. I spend my days with a lot of young, attractive people. I've had close relationships with young girls. We laugh, have fun, talk. I don't want to be them. But I don't want to be their grandmothers. I *do* want to look like them. And I don't want to look like a person who is fifty, or what we used to think of as fifty. There's a little self-consciousness about what forty-eight or fifty looks like now. Someone once said to Gloria Steinem, 'You don't look like forty.' She replied, 'Maybe this is what forty looks like.' "

We are having lunch in a crowded restaurant near the NBC-TV studios in New York and we continue to chat. "It's the approach of fifty that's scary," she says. "We've legitimized forty. We look, feel, and act better at forty than our parents did. But we have not yet legitimized fifty. The forty-year-old today has lived through a lot of societal changes, changed images of ourselves. We're the first group to become glamorous, sexy forty-year-olds. But I have a funny feeling that there may be a point between forty-five and fifty when things start emerging, concerns of age and sex. You never felt better, but people look at you as though you're older. It's people's image of you that changes. How can you reconcile how you feel and how they see you?"

Edith points out that today a boy's forty-five-year-old father is scuba diving with him, not just sitting there reading *The Wall Street Journal*. Parents today look and act younger. "What we feel like and what we're supposed to look like. They aren't coming together.

"Goddamn," she says banging her fork down, "I don't want to be fifty—unless being fifty becomes fashionable."

I remark that she is looking great, far better and younger than when I saw her last. She says it's because she has cut her hair and gotten one of those thick body waves so that her head is a mass of curls, and she is wearing contact lenses. Television people are acutely aware of age. And there are, of course, those few cinema exceptions like Fred Astaire, Helen Hayes and George Burns who are famous enough to have transcended age. They are accepted because they are now in their second childhoods, their second go-rounds with youth. She continues, "I have begun to feel anger when I have to go to a party with a lot of people I don't know and not one person comes over and talks to me because at my age I'm not sought after as a woman. At times like that I think, 'Screw the world. This is how I perceive myself. I'm right and you're wrong.' I think women will be in good shape when we get to that point and can say that. Say, 'It's not my problem, it's yours if you don't like the way I look.'"

I remembered a recent conversation with Ginny, my friend who has also thought about the way society views women. She had obviously gained a few pounds since the last time I'd seen her, though she looked happy and healthy. She said she didn't care about the weight. "I'm tired of being wrapped up in what people think. That was what I used to worry about all the time, trying to look like what people thought I should look like, or act like. I was constantly geared toward others' expectations. I don't believe in this Farrah Fawcett-Majors thing, that young is beautiful. I think aging is a natural process and it's the culture that's all hung up. That's their problem, not mine. If they don't like the way I look they don't have to look at me.''

That has pretty much been actress Elizabeth Taylor's response to movie critics who review her weight as often as they do her acting ability. She admits to having the wrinkles and bulges of her forty-six years. She happens to think that what she does, acting or politicking for her husband, is more important than what she looks like. But most women do not have Taylor's money or reputation for beauty, so they are far more vulnerable to the marks of age.

Edith Luray and I are walking through the post-lunch crowds back to her office at NBC, and she is getting more and more annoyed by that fact that looks play such an important part in the way most women are evaluated.

"My husband and I went to the theater," she remembers, "and there was this TV personality, a man with some young blonde. Our conversation went like this.

"She: 'He's always with some young blonde.'

"He: 'Why not?'

"She: 'What do you mean why not? Supposing he were with some middle-aged brunette?'

"You see, the idea is if he can be with some young blonde, of course do it. If you can be with a young person why not? It's preferable." Men seem to agree universally on this subject. My own husband remarked one day that he didn't mind being middle-aged, but he'd hate to imagine himself being married to a middle-aged woman.

She relates another incident. "One time I was on a boat with a middle-aged man and some others. He turned to me and told me he liked women under thirty. So I said: 'You have some goddamned nerve. How do you think saying that makes people like me feel?' And I think, here's this ugly little guy, but he only wants them under thirty. 'What makes you think you are better than some middle-aged woman?' ''

We have by then walked through the halls past the empty, dark, cavernous studios and are sitting in her small office beside a window. We can't talk too much longer because she is getting ready to go out again with one of her young girlfriends to have her ears pierced so she can wear those big gold loops the way young people around the studio do. Besides, they go so well with her young-looking, curly, fluffed-up hair. Even though she is not on camera, she still feels that to be a successful producer she should look young, and so she remakes herself. She is annoyed that the marks of age announce to her that she may not be a TV producer forever, that time is moving her on and future assignments may go to younger people, but she is smart enough to know that she doesn't like that scale of measurement. There are days when I don't like it either.

I wear turtleneck sweaters to hide the neck lines, a dab of color here and there to hide the few forties gray hairs, and I eat any vitamin that promises to keep my skin moist and resilient, my teeth from crumbling, my bones from breaking. I am a coward, like most women, and will do almost anything to stay on the young side of middle age.

Cooling the Calories

But will I go as far as giving up eating and drinking, which now affect me so differently in middle age? I used to be able to share a beautifully iced pitcher of martinis with my husband before dinner. Recently I had a gin and tonic at a garden party. The person who poured my drink gave me what must have been a half glass of pure gin and added some tonic as an afterthought. While drinking it my head went into a spin and I nosedived down in the back of the station wagon for the rest of the party. I had to admit that my body had gotten too old to handle that much gin comfortably. How did Papa Hemingway do it?

Drink also adds calories, and I have to ask myself whether I am prepared at the middle-age point, when calories stick to the bones like adhesive, to drink my calories instead of eating them. I must decide whether to ignore all the restraints about avoiding desserts, and give up those chocolate mousse delicacies, those thick steaks and loaves of French bread, that cheesecake I adore, the fat chestnuts . . . Shall I grow and grow like Elizabeth Taylor who is obviously having a good time, or should I watch it, keep as slim as I was at twenty-five? There comes a point in your life when you ask yourself whom you are trying to stay cardboard thin for, on what market are you offering yourself for appraisal?

Yet, I eat granola and bran muffins and soybeans and fish and chicken, and everything is polyunsaturated with plenty of fiber. I gobble my fifteen vitamin pills a day, and I hope for the best. Fear of age and illness makes me try to stay thin and healthy. So the conscious choice must be made between either gaining weight or changing one's eating and drinking habits. Health as well as looks now become an imperative. I vote to keep to my boring diet and do my boring exercises—some days West Point, some days Canadian Air Force, some days nothing. However, it is not only beauty and health that one need be concerned with. The signs of age may make it more difficult to get certain jobs. So perhaps it makes sense to take advantage of science, as we do when we are sick, and use it when we are well, to stay young, until society learns to look beneath the skin.

Why I Won't Get a Face-Lift—Yet

As the sight of my face began to annoy me with its permanent collection of lines here and there, with its droop and its hint of bumps and lumps, I began to consider a face-lift. I had heard about face-lifts for a long time. Rumor was that certain buxom and youthful-looking movie stars had not only had their faces lifted in order to continue to be attractive to men, even younger men, and to continue to appear on television and in films, but they had also had their breasts filled with silicone bags and had total body lifts. The faces were pulled back, the arms tightened, the thighs pulled up, the buttocks tucked under, the stomach pulled in. The thought of such surgical repair was overwhelming. The cost must have been astronomical. In addition, the thought that anyone would go to such pains, and real pain must have been part of it, to stay young seemed on one level understandable, and on another level preposterous—but on every level unnatural. The person who would emerge from such an operation would simply not be the original package anymore. It seemed like cheating, becoming a plastic surgery imitation of one's former self. But it also made sense. If science can improve upon the crudities of nature, why not allow it to? I think the source of my real resentment, when I heard about it, stemmed from the fact that those particular faces and bodies were "manmade," and it seemed unfair to compare them with others. I wanted the real thing to be worth more than the counterfeit; however, I remained open to a small amount of tinkering, perhaps just a tuck here and there.

So I continued to mull over getting a face-lift to help Nature regain her vitality, and me regain my sense of still being as young as I felt. I was not ready to look any older than my thirties. My husband thought it was a good idea if I could continue to look young, and he backed the proposed lift. I went to see a local plastic surgeon who looked me over and offered to do the job. He photographed me and asked if I wanted to make an appointment. He made it very clear that I would not look younger, just better. I needed more time to think; he was rushing me. Then I got another name from a friend. It was almost like asking for an abortionist in the prelegal days. The names were whispered, and no one cared to admit that she'd had one. My friend didn't tell me she had had her own face lifted, only that she knew of a doctor on Park Avenue in New York. I went to see him, and he too warned me that I had to be sure, and I had to realize I would not look younger—just as though I'd had a long rest and come from a long vacation. Not a bad way to look. The total cost including hospital fees would be $5,000 (costs in smaller cities vary from $1,500 to $3,000). I'd be black and blue for a while and have to hide for a couple of weeks till the coloring disappeared. If I had my skin burned and peeled above my lip to diminish the lines there, I ran the risk of having the skin above the upper lip remain a different color than the rest of my facial skin. He then pulled out his book of before-and-after photos, and we flipped through them. That was his mistake. The before-and-after pictures, taken with the harsh reality of the medical camera, looked so similar that I began to feel sorry for the people whose pictures I was looking at. To spend $5,000 on such slight modifications in appearance seemed hardly worth it.

Then something else happened. About this time my husband and I went on a vacation in the sun. And gradually I developed a smooth, creamy tan. It occurred to me one morning as I did the usual mirror-mirror-on-the-wall routine, that I indeed looked much younger and rested and a lot of the lines didn't show at all. It hit me like a revelation. A vacation, rather than a face-lift would do the trick. Not permanently, but the face-lift isn't permanent either. It's worth only five years, and then everything can plunge, and you have to repeat the operation, again and again. The lines, which the surgeon could only soften but not do away with entirely, would again look harsh. So I finally opted for vacations in the sun rather than surgery to look better.

But the sun was supposed to be an enemy, not a friend. The sun was supposed to age my skin faster. Therefore at the same time that I was masking the lines with suntan, I was also making new ones, making the old ones deeper and adding carotin freckles that weren't cute. I couldn't win. What do other women do, I wondered? I see women of all ages ignoring the warnings of skin doctors and lying for hours in the sun. They all looked fine to me. I finally got up enough nerve to go over to an attractive blond woman in her forties one day and say, "Aren't you afraid of sunning yourself? Aren't you afraid the sun will ruin your skin?" And she gave me the answer that I wanted badly to hear. "I don't care if I get to look like a prune. I love the sun, tennis and swimming and bathing in the sun, and I'm going to do it anyway and enjoy it."

I also noticed something else. When I had carried on the daily appraisal of my face in the mirror and found a new line, like one more gray hair every morning, I had begun to walk around looking sad and wilted. Once I had decided that a suntan and some rest would do it, I brightened up and actually began to look a lot younger. So I discovered that if sleep won't eradicate my new lines, that a smooth, moderate suntan and a huge smile would. Of course I couldn't always have a suntan, and a constant grin would make me look idiotic, but I could smile a lot. And I had just saved $5,000, which made me smile even more. But then I became aware of a rather odd situation. Whether I had a suntan or not, no one seemed to think I looked any different. Others could not possibly see me as I saw myself. People are not very observant in any case. Besides, why did I need to look absolutely smooth-skinned? Didn't I admire the looks of men who had a few creases here and there? Certainly the fortyish Cary Grant had a lot more sex appeal than the Cary Grant of twenty. Didn't I like Walter Cronkite on the news just as much even with his wrinkles? What standards had I been using?

And that is why there are no stitches going up the side of my scalp behind my ear. I decided it wasn't worth it. If some day medicine can eradicate the lines of age permanently and in a more sophisticated way, we all might be interested. But for now, I don't feel I need the $5,000 sewing job on my face. I'd rather smile.

There are some women who will have different opinions about redesigning the face and will have their skin tightened while still quite young. Perhaps when I am older I will think differently, like Betty Ford who recently had her face lifted. Said Betty, "I'm sixty years old and I wanted a nice new face to go with my beautiful new life. I just decided it was about time." The five and one half hours of surgery removed the puffiness from under her eyes and lifted and tightened the skin around the neck. After the operation, Mrs. Ford had to be very quiet for about three days while ice compresses were used. Then she spent five to seven days in the hospital just recovering; it took twelve more days for most of the healing to take place and another week for everything to return to normal. It adds up to a month of recuperation.

I was talking to a woman I know in Boston about our looks one evening, and she stated flatly that some day she intended to have a face-lift. "A woman's internal image of herself depends on her external image. I think of myself as looking like I felt when I was thirty-one. But occasionally I catch a glimpse of myself in the window of a store as I walk by and I'm shocked.

I don't know that lady that I see in the reflection." She also said that looking older influences her actions. "I have to behave differently. I'm more sedate. I'm concerned about behaving incongruously, given my appearance. I can't act like a seventeen-year-old if I look near fifty. That would be ridiculous. I think I'll have a face-lift just to feel more attractive. But for me, it's something you do in desperation. I'm not that desperate yet. But talk to me again in the middle of next winter when I'm pale and feeling lousy. . . ."

The decision whether to have cosmetic facial surgery must be based on how badly a woman's looks deteriorate, and on what kind of life she is living. If you are judged by your looks, you may want the operation, but if you are judged more by your character and personality, you simply may not care. Lauren (Betty) Bacall, who does live by her looks, feels differently. When asked if she had had a face lift, she replied with a vehement no. "I'm never going to have one. I don't have the guts, I suppose. What if they made a mistake, cut a nerve? This is my face and I'm going to live with this face. It's me, Betty Bacall —by myself and part of myself, wrinkles and all." However an estimated forty-five to fifty-five thousand people a year succumb to having their faces lifted.

A young woman in her twenties recently told me that the thing she missed most about being in college was the time to write and think. Now in the business world, working on Wall Street, she finds, "I don't have time to think about where it's all leading, where I am, what I want to do. I just live." Most people, I imagine, go through life in pretty much the same way. One step leads to the next, and we live through them in a sleepwalking, automatic way. Who am I and what is my identity, and what do I want out of life are questions that often are never faced squarely until we have to. A series of newly discovered wrinkles on a once-fair, smooth skin is shock enough to start the process of examining more than just the facial topography.

The Menopause

One of the major landmark physical changes of middle age for women is the menopause. ("The pause that depresses," as my husband calls it.) This is the name given to that point in life when a woman ceases to produce eggs, is no longer fertile and cannot become pregnant. It is a time when, it is said, women who realize they cannot produce any more children feel an acute sense of loss, become very depressed and feel a drive to use their remaining creative powers in new ways. One hears middle age and menopause spoken about in the same breath. Actually, although, the menopause can begin anywhere from the late thirties to the late fifties, most of the middle-aged women I know who are around fifty, have not experienced the symptoms yet. Furthermore, the menopause is by no means responsible for propelling their energies in other directions; most women's creative needs, at least in the metropolitan areas, don't seem to be totally met by having children, and quite often they go on to find other interests long before there is any sign of the menopause.

It is difficult, at any rate, according to Dr. Ronald H. Gray of the London School of Hygiene and Tropical Medicine, to say exactly when the menopause begins because the onset is not a clearly defined event. There seems to be a gradual cessation of a woman's ovarian function over the years. He points out that variations in the length of her cycle or menstrual period are more common after age forty, and the percentage of women who have short cycles of less than twenty-five days increases. Doctors say that fertility declines markedly in the ten years before the menopause. Some authors have suggested that the age of menopause has increased by about four years over the past century in industrialized societies, and the average age of its appearance has been estimated to be 49.8 years in the United States. There are, interestingly enough, says Dr. Gray, corresponding changes in men. "There is apparently evidence that the testicular androgen secretion declines after age forty due to the deterioration of certain cells, and this may account in part for the reduced sexual activity and potency observed among older men.''

Because the typical woman of today wants few children, a good number of years will have gone by between the time when she last thought of having any more babies and the time when the menopause is obviously upon her. In fact, because she has spent the last twenty years trying not to become pregnant, the shock can't be too great. This loss of the ability to reproduce may bother a few women who, for a short time, shudder at their approaching sterility and think, "My God, I can't ever have any more babies," and who want the machinery working even if they don't plan to use it. And it may disturb women with larger families whose entire lives have revolved around their children and the whole culture of motherhood. But I think the impact of the menopause on most women today has been greatly exaggerated. For most of us, I would guess, the fact that we no longer have to worry about contraception would be a blessed relief.

In either case, the loss of the ability to reproduce at the time of the menopause is one of the definitive signs that a woman is no longer young, that she is well along in middle age. This concrete biological fact of aging, rather than the inability to reproduce, may be the shocker; and for most it also means there will be some physical symptoms of headache, insomnia, irritability, night sweats, excessive perspiration and hot flushes. Most women I've spoken to, though, are not bothered by such symptoms, or not for long. In cases where they do exist, however, there is added stress during this period.

I went to my gynecologist, Dr. David Rose, one day for my annual checkup, and as we were sitting in his office lined with books and diplomas I asked him how his patients were feeling these days about the menopause. He said that many women had read a lot about estrogen therapy, felt there was the risk of cancer in taking hormones and decided they didn't want to. "She may decide she is going to come to grips with the flushes until they pass which, in most women, happens in three months to one year." The hot flushes, he explained to me, are the result of increased pituitary hormones in the blood when the inhibiting presence of estrogen no longer exists. In times ot tension or stress women feel more of these flushes, but the pituitary finally stabilizes its secretions and the whole problem usually disappears in most women without hormone therapy. Dr. Rose said that he also sees many women who are adamant about wanting estrogen. These are career women who tell him, ''I can't afford to get wet, to perspire, to have my hair dripping. Everyone will see me.'' They feel that being unattractively wet or flushed will hurt them at work.

There has long been a rumor that estrogen therapy keeps your skin youthful and therefore makes you look young again. ''Well, Dr. Rose,'' I said, preparing to ask for a trial bottle of pills, ''is it true?'' ''No,'' he replied. ''It is not.'' But he went on to say that estrogen does help arthritis, which hits so many women at this age, and it seems to help the demineralization of the bones, so your disks don't disintegrate. Another thing it definitely does is to counteract the dryness in the vagina which afflicts women as they age and makes intercourse unpleasant. With hormones the lubrication returns.

''Does the menopause really upset women?'' I asked, and he concurred with my own observations that many women don't mind it. ''Some women like to bleed because they consider it feminine,'' he says, ''but more women are happy to end their menstrual periods and know they can't have children. In fact many of them are being sterilized even before the menopause could stop ovarian production of eggs because they don't want any more children.''

The figures bear him out. Though startling, it is apparently true, according to Princeton University's Office of Population Research, that surgical sterilization is the most popular method of birth control among couples married for ten years or more, or those who have all the children they want. Eight million men and women in this country have had themselves sterilized.

The Awful Illnesses

Unfortunately, many people at this time of life begin to realize that there are illnesses that are getting the better of them. The organs that we count on start breaking down in middle age, and many men and women encounter serious illness for the first time. There is arthritis, which is fairly common in women, also stomach ulcers, ovarian cysts and tumors, heart attacks and cancer. This is the age when many women have mastectomies, for example. (One woman in fourteen gets breast cancer today.) Some of these illnesses have taken twenty years to develop, and it is only in middle life that they finally manifest themselves. It is not only personal ill health that is difficult; but the loss of health in a spouse can cause such serious problems as loss of income. Even without a specific illness, the morning groans of wakers getting out of bed and stretching their stiff legs and aching backs and disintegrating spinal disks would cause quite a cacophony across the land if they could all be heard at once. People at this age don't have as much energy, they are not as strong, they have more real pains and perhaps some loss of hearing, they get tired more quickly and need to moderate sports and other activities requiring strenuous exertion. Vision often gets worse and it's hard to focus on a telephone book until one breaks down and gets bifocals. The teeth need root-canal work as the gums recede.

The memory falters. A woman told me that when she can't remember a name she automatically assumes, "Oh God, I'm senile," until she sees that a younger person may have the same trouble remembering things. Wounds that used to flip together again almost overnight take longer to heal, hair thins out and bones stay broken longer. It has also been noted that as men and women come to the point where middle-age transitions are necessary, most cope fairly well. Those who cannot make the necessary changes easily, who become stymied by the problems, are very likely to become physically ill. There are a variety of symptoms felt by men and women in middle age that are real but psychosomatic in the sense that they are caused and aggravated by mental problems. These range anywhere from chest pains to headaches, back pains, arthritis, shortness of breath to stomach cramps.

Unless a person faces the recurring transitions in life and makes the necessary adjustments, the physical and mental stresses that are likely to descend will make it pretty rough going. A person must be prepared to recharge the psychic batteries. If you allow the need for change to depress you, you will stagnate and feel even older and more decrepit than you are. You can push old age upon yourself faster if you open the doors to it. You can hold it off longer if you find something new to keep you busy, keep your mind active, find projects, new jobs, a new career, new sports, whatever. Middle age is usually the time for the integration of all the input from all the years before. A new ability to use and enjoy life will make the physical changes much less noticeable.

4

The Inevitable Tensions

Coupled with the physical problems that arrive with middle age are the psychological effects of realizing that we are this far along in our lives. Though most tensions produce a lot of mental wear and tear, there are stresses that can be beneficial while, at the same time, putting pressure on us. The middle-aged vision of life is, for one thing, far more complex than the one we had when we were young. We can no longer be blindly impetuous. We now see the choices. There has been too thick a layering of experience for us not to have learned many things that come into focus at this time of life. In youth, life is more like a game of checkers. You can jump this way or that way and it doesn't matter. In middle age, it is the far more intricate game of chess we are playing. Because we see multiple possibilities, we are apt to be more cautious, more thoughtful, willing to plan more carefully—tendencies that unfortunately sometimes lead to a generation gap.

This new way of perceiving things is beautifully illustrated on the tennis court by thirty-six-year-old Ilie Nastase. He says,

"Before, I used to play instinctively. I'd see the ball coming towards me and I'd hit it—and it would be the right shot. Now I think of three different ways of playing the shot and by the time I decide which one to choose, the ball has gone past me."

Is There a Mid-Life Crisis?

There has been a lot of talk about something called the "mid-life crisis," which presumably rolls in out of the blue at age forty, give or take a few years. As I approached forty I sat there waiting for my mid-life crisis and it never came. What crisis was I supposed to be having anyway? Was it the awareness of one's own mortality that comes to men in the late thirties according to psychiatrist Elliot Jaques? I have been afraid of death ever since I was ten years old and tied a magic Egyptian amulet around my neck to keep me from ever dying. Was it the approaching menopause and the fact that I knew I would not be able to have any more children? I didn't want any more. Besides, I haven't reached the menopause yet. In fact the crises I was supposed to have at twenty and thirty didn't happen either, nor did they to any of my friends. In reality, it is not the age that is crucial; it is where you are in life, and how well you adapt to any change. The biggest crisis of your life might well be not getting into the college of your choice at age eighteen.

Moreover, the usual transitions themselves are not as predictable as we have been led to believe, or as they once may have been. For example, the woman who used to marry at twenty-one is now living with a man until maybe twenty-nine. And instead of having babies at twenty-two many women are now waiting until thirty-two, and their transitions into different stages are going to come at totally different times than the woman who follows a traditional pattern.

I object to calling the normal reorganization of life, as one moves from stage to stage, a crisis. Obviously there are continual changes in our routine, but to assume that these are crises —or even traumatic, predictable events—is being a bit overdramatic, unless you want to sell a lot of books, as someone joked.

Some experience the pressures of change less than others and move in and out of growth stages smoothly, not feeling any interruptions because they are looking forward to something new. Others cannot cope with problems at any age and break down. It doesn't seem logical that there is one mid-life crisis that comes precisely at a certain age. Women are constantly facing turning points when they leave college, begin to work, have children, when the kids go to kindergarten, become teenagers, become independent or if they go through a divorce.

There are critical moments as they notice that their looks have changed, or they discover that their husbands are having affairs. Problems like these can occur at any age. A few stresses do tend to cluster around certain periods, though. It takes just so many years before the kids are independent, and there you are—somewhere in your middle years. As Dr. George E. Vaillant, the well-known Harvard psychiatrist, points out, the existing "definitions of middle life crisis such as Gail Sheehy's 'Catch 30,' or Daniel Levinson's forty-to-forty-two, are as arbitrary as suggesting that adolescent crises occur at sixteen." He says there are many people who "between thirty-five and fifty get divorced, change jobs and become depressed. However, divorce, disenchantment with job and depression occur with roughly equal frequency throughout the adult life cycle. Progression in the life cycle necessitates growth and change, but crisis is the exception, not the rule."

But there are many things during the period of middle age to be understood, such as physical change, which are less likely to be noticed and are obviously less severe in youth. These may trigger the kind of introspection that causes women to redefine their lives at this point—the last age range when they have time enough to backtrack and begin again in a new direction.

Time and Terms

The idea of having time enough or of not having time enough is something that will be mentioned from chapter to chapter throughout this book. It crops up here and there in our minds.

It is one of the prime psychological concerns of middle age. The shortening of time is something that we live with, a vague awareness we acknowledge, like our mortality, but try to suppress. It is much easier to admit that you don't have time to go to the hairdresser than that you don't have time to become what you always wanted to be. We assume at this age that there is still time enough to do most of what we realistically think we can do. Yet the pressure of time is there, as never before, urging us on in the backs of our minds. It keeps popping up in most conversations about age. For example, I was talking to a woman once about whether she felt middle-aged, and there it was, attached as an imperative afterthought.

She said, "No, I don't feel middle-aged. I feel thirty. But my hands look forty-five. This must change my perceptions. It really brings you up against the ultimate question—there's not much time left."

I knew exactly what she meant. I remember when I was a child, time seemed endless, a series of long, warm, languid summers with days of swimming or chatting with friends or playing games or reading, then eating ice cream in the evening after dinner. There was no rush to do anything or be anybody. Time had little value. As we get older, the summers and years bounce by more quickly. This pressure to hurry, the realization that time is running out, can cause a great deal of initial panic, and a concentrated effort to more tightly organize what years remain.

The anxiety about how much time each of us has left is very often connected in our minds with another of the primary psychological pressures of this age, and that is what people refer to as "coming to terms." They become resigned to what is possible and what is not. It's true that by middle age many of us are expert at what we do, but obviously not all of us can reach the top of every profession, and many of us have secret dreams of doing things later on, when we have the opportunity, that are totally different than what we do every day. Because of our keen awareness of aging during this period, it is an era in our lives when many of us have to realize that if we haven't reached certain goals by now, we aren't going to; we have gone as far as we are going to go in certain directions.

We learn to take pleasure in what we can do and have done and not bemoan too seriously or too long what will be impossible to do. This understanding and accepting of what we are, this stabilization of our goals, is typical of people in the midpoint of their lives, particularly late middle age. For those still in early middle age, the same pressures translate themselves into a "now or never" lunging out to make the remaining goals come true, before it is too late. However, even here the frantic efforts may have to be tempered with reality. "Yes, I will be a lawyer after all, but I'll probably not have the time to do the years of research and specialization that I had originally had in mind." Most of the women in middle age whom I spoke to were measuring the time span and their unused talents and deciding that, though there may not be as much time left as they would have liked, there was plenty of time to do the most remarkable things.

The Adolescent Analogy

The tensions of being middle-aged today have been compared to the stresses experienced by an adolescent. The thought process is equivalent. You sit around and try to imagine what you want to do with yourself. You weigh the options, you think of possible careers. It is an interval of experimentation after living in the more rigid environment imposed by one's parental responsibilities. There is a new opening up of choice, a new freedom that can become quite a heady sensation. You try things you dreamed of but were never able to do before, like Ginny, who went on the archaeological dig. But at the same time, as her horizons are expanding, the middle-aged "adolescent" is likely to feel insecure and scared. Like the young person who needs encouragement from school and family, and direction from both, the mid-life woman may need stimulus from her friends and husband. She needs to be told she can do it.

Athletes are always in the position of making mid-life career switches because they can almost never continue to play past age thirty-five. Some of them, like Bill Bradley, the Knicks basketball star, plan well in advance by using their free time to develop new activities. In Bradley's case it was politics. When age forced him to retire from basketball, he had already been active in New Jersey, campaigning for candidates, speaking at fund-raising events, and could seriously run for the U.S. Senate, win his party's nomination and then the election. He was able to go from star basketball player to U.S. senator in one easy bounce because he had planned for the middle-age period of his life.

Some women, too, know their lives must change at middle age and plan for it. Singers like Beverly Sills, whose voice will last only so long, and athletes like Billie Jean King, whose knees will carry her only so far, know that they have to think of a mid-life switch in careers, and they prepare for it. Sills has just been appointed director of the New York City Opera and Billie Jean has a number of business interests besides her tennis.

It is the average person, whose arrival at middle age is not so dramatic, who has the greater problem. She can ignore it for a while but eventually she will have to create new goals from her own background. It may be tough to give up singing and tennis, but it is even harder to give up nothing and try to create something out of it. Of course the "nothing" has not been really nothing, but it can appear that way on a résumé and in a woman's mind.

The wise housewife-mother who wants some years home with her children will, in the same way as Bradley, Sills and King plan for her mid-life transitions. She will work to develop a career, then have her children, and take courses and part-time jobs that will keep her in training for what she wants to return to full-time, later on. Few people today would ever take a job that has no future. Yet raising children is one of those jobs, and most women take it. There are rich satisfactions but no future. Sooner or later the job ends. So for women who accept the position full-time, there must be a deliberate strategy for the middle years.

To Work or Not to Work

In addition to the physical and mental stress of this time of life there is the pressure from the media, which is enough to unsettle any complacent souls who may be left untouched. If you haven't already asked, "Who am I?" and "What do I want to do?" and reappraised your present and your future, the media will do it for you. There are daily articles written on the unusual things women are doing like working as jockeys, sports reporters, bankers, train engineers and garbage collectors. I recently saw a deodorant ad in which the woman in uniform rushing across town to make her plane turns out to be, not the stewardess, but the copilot.

How can any woman who is at home not ask herself whether she also should be out doing new things? With so many people leading active, fascinating lives, how can she tell people she is a housewife and offer her best chicken Kiev recipe for conversation? She feels she has to explain why she is not going out into the job world, why she continues to do what women have always done. In past generations, it was those who went to work who had to do the apologizing, explaining that, no, you weren't a lesbian (if you didn't marry) and, no, you weren't sterile (if you didn't have children) and, no, you didn't have to go to work to support an incapacitated husband (if you spent your life in a career). The reverse swing of the pendulum has unsettled a lot of women and their husbands who met and married under the delusion that he would provide the family income and she would provide the chocolate chip cookies and oven roasts, do the laundry and keep the children clean.

On the other hand, not all women want to work. They may be enjoying their lives and activities at home. Often, however, their reluctance to leave is because their expectations have been ignored from the beginning, their talents have lain dormant so long that they no longer know what they can do, nor have they developed any interests. The need to develop the mind, explore the self and fulfill one's potential is not felt by everyone, particularly when there is no encouragement to feel it. If these women don't sense it, or if they think they are not good enough and can never hope to succeed or even find a job, they will vigorously defend their right to remain housewives. Or if they enjoy the leisure, the lack of pressure, not having to go to an office and prove themselves every day, they will say quite vehemently that women belong at home.

For whatever reason, the backlash to breaking out is staying in—with a vengeance. Because fewer women are now able economically to stay at home, the stay-at-homers will soon be a minority. Today half the women with young children work and many more of those with older children also work.

Women in the urban centers who have always been involved in a larger network of events and people will certainly find it relatively easy, if they change their minds, to change their lives. Women in small towns will have more trouble. For them, going back to a university or community college with continuing education courses might mean leaving the family, moving two or three hundred miles away and coming home only on weekends. The scarcity of openings for middle-aged women, where there are few employment opportunities of any kind, may make starting a career almost impossible.

For the woman who does work, the stress of running several parallel lives at once—the now-familiar problems of managing home, career and husband-children (the mother, wife and job triumvirate)—is something that she has to learn to handle. The mere fact of having what she wants does not make the situation stress-free; this kind of life can be quite harrowing. But fortunately for the young woman, it is no longer a question of frustration, of not being allowed or encouraged to do what interests her; it is more a matter of becoming proficient at managing a tight schedule. Her hope will be to find a housekeeper or some kind of help and to get her husband to share the home chores.

Today, most young women who plan to have children also plan to have careers. (Several national surveys of first-year college women show that although in 1967 almost half favored a traditional housewife role for women, in 1977 only 20 percent did.) And if the results of a 1978 survey of young Princeton

University alumnae can be generalized to include young people recently graduated from other universities, it would appear that even fewer do today. Almost all plan a career as well as marriage and a family. With enough cooperation from the husband, it is working, though not all husbands cooperate and the first years may not be easy in terms of finances, schedules and child care.

The woman in middle age, however, now has the advantage of doing those things consecutively: first the kids, and then the career. With that sequence the juggling act is easier. It's too early to say, but perhaps with her added experience and wisdom, she may, on the other hand, also advance in a career faster than a woman who is younger. However, it is true that the older woman is starting later and may not have as much time to advance as far as she would like; and her husband is likely to give her more trouble than a younger man would when things are no longer as they were when she was a full-time housewife.

The Children

Regardless of what else may be going on in a woman's life, whether she works or not, children remain one of the primary concerns of this age period. From the moment a woman takes her child to school, from that first day when she leaves him at the gate, she is known as Billy's mother. First, she loses her identity; then, as the kids grow up, she loses her patience. By the time the kids have become teenagers, their bio-rhythms are off somewhere on another planet, their tastes and demands are foreign, their energy is limitless, their time schedule and sense of priorities often appear reversed and the disorganization and vagueness about everything they do would give most orderly parents a nervous breakdown. Yet mothers must live with them, deal with them, not nag them too much, watch what they are doing and attempt to remain cool. Children are, in many instances, more than enough to send a woman racing out into the job market, just to get out of the house.

First of all, they are expensive. Their cars and insurance,

their cameras and film, their tennis racquets and skis, their clothes all cost. Through no fault of their own, their colleges can also cost more than $9,000 a year each. Helping to pay these bills often forces a woman to get a job to contribute to the family income. And second, kids are boisterous and demanding, difficult to live with. They want to play their rock records in the basement all afternoon, give parties all night, drive your car wherever they go, experiment with drugs, expand their hilarity with drink, and are seemingly able to exist without regular food or sleep. The exigencies of teenagers are part of middle age.

Has it been worth it? As anyone who has had them can testify (and those who have not had them can never imagine) having children is one of the most draining of physical and emotional experiences. There is scarcely any other pursuit that a woman would willingly engage in that not only has no future, as I have said before, but that also pays nothing yet demands so much time and energy. The years of feeding, clothing, walking, bathing, nursing and talking to young children are totally absorbing to the mother. But she is not always left with the result she might have hoped for. The disappointments of motherhood can be many. Kids you once thought were geniuses when they built those fantastic bridges of blocks may turn out to be college dropouts. Middle age is a time of being realistic about children and of adjusting to our disappointments with them.

Some women enjoy their families heartily, finding it fascinating to watch young minds develop; and whether the kids succeed or not, they would never have missed the experience of having them. But many others feel that the involvement leaves them too little time for a creative outlet. (A 1975 *McCall's* magazine report said that, given the choice, one woman in ten would decide not to have children if she had it to do over again.) Although most mothers love their children and have willingly given of themselves, some think the job of raising children is not worth the years of devotion to endless menial chores. Some young women today don't plan to have any children at all. They may keep postponing childbirth in favor of a career until they are too old and it is too late. Among those who do want children, few intend to dedicate themselves totally to the maternal experience.

In any case, when the teenagers finally go off at eighteen, the woman's response is complex. She is happy not to have to worry all the time about their constant foibles, but she misses their youthful charm and presence—misses them much more intensely than she lets on. Their sudden absence leaves a great void in the woman's consciousness. They don't need her anymore, and her husband doesn't need her full-time attention. There she is—strong, available, experienced, bright, well educated and useless.

The woman's choice is clear. She becomes stale, bored, grows old, or she breaks out, finds a new role, and does something. She puts it all into herself for a change. For her, or for a mother who has been working, the departure of children is an opportunity to devote more time and thought to what she wants, perhaps take a job that involves more travel, and responsibilities. It is time to throw her entire self into the full flowering of her own achievement.

For the woman who has stayed at home, it can be a very empty and dreary time. So many other women seem to be doing so much; beginning cold in the job world is a frightening prospect. Joining the race when it's half over may seem utterly hopeless, winning impossible, but women are striking out, and they are making it. They are forcing colleges and businesses to accept them and to offer the necessary services. Remarkably, they are succeeding.

The Empty Nest

One hears a lot about the post-children condition known as the "empty nest" syndrome. Women are supposed to feel depressed and lost when their major role of caretaker is at an end. In a recent study of the effect of the "empty nest" transition on women's psychological and physical well-being, Elizabeth Bates Harkins of the Battelle Human Affairs Research Centers in Seattle, Washington, questioned 318 women in North Carolina. She found that the "empty nest" problems are slight, that the period is not particularly stressful in most women's lives and is not a major threat to physical or psychological well-being. What effects there are are reported to be transitory and to have largely disappeared two years following the start of the "empty nest" period.

It's probably true, however, that some psychological problems do exist in this period, one of which must certainly be the question of how to revitalize the now-childless marriage. The Indiana Institute of Sex Research suggests that the ideal sex partners would be a man in his early twenties and a woman in her forties, because they are then both at their "orgasmic peak." Unfortunately that is not the pattern of sexual pairing that we follow. The woman who is at her sexual peak in middle age has to deal with a husband who has passed his peak. Furthermore, it has been found that among couples married for twenty years (which would put them in this same mid-life period) marital satisfaction and presumably sexual satisfaction, because the two are so closely connected, is at its lowest point when their adolescent children are in the process of being launched, discovering sex for themselves and speaking out freely on all subjects. Parents are reported to develop increasing feelings of anxiety and helplessness. Certainly for the woman whose time has been so occupied with children—their comings, goings and doings—the intimacy that she once shared with her husband may have slipped away. But for many rediscovering the mate results in a period of great satisfaction. According to a recent Quality of Life study by Dr. Angus Campbell and his colleagues at the University of Michigan, the time of life when the youngest child is over seventeen years of age, and has probably just left the house, is the happiest time for couples—surpassed only by that period in the lives of young married women when they have no children at all.

What a woman must apparently expect, then, is a transition phase of perhaps a couple of years when the emptiness hurts until she begins to revitalize her old life, to find new goals and to get to know her husband all over again. She and her husband must face living alone for the first time in at least eighteen years. Many couples will no doubt find their new freedom as stimulating as their children find theirs.

Being alone again, though, is not guaranteed to rekindle romance. Sometimes it's just too late, and although some couples may develop better feelings about each other than they've known in a long time, there are a few women who will continue to miss their children terribly, regarding the sudden departure almost like a divorce.

Divorce and Widowhood

The difficulties of bringing up children (which seem to come to a climax just before they leave), their actual departure and the search for a new intimacy are all part of a network of mid-life mental stress. An extraordinarily traumatic change at this time is divorce. Divorce can come at any age and, in fact, people do split up most frequently in the late twenties; but when it occurs in mid-life, the divorce will be particularly stressful for the woman who has never been alone and has never worked, because at this point she will have an especially difficult time earning the extra money she needs to support herself. Since she may find herself in a critical situation without the time to develop added training or schooling, she may have to take a menial job, at least in the beginning. However upsetting that may be, it probably isn't as bad as when divorce leaves a woman with a houseful of young children to raise by herself. The sudden death of a husband poses similar financial and personal problems. Both divorce and widowhood are panic periods that not only give a woman little time to plan and organize her new life, but also force her to cope with the added pain of the loss itself. Handling the problems of finding a job and getting over a divorce or death is the most difficult combination imaginable.

The complications of revising her life, with or without a husband around, can be quite distressing for a woman until she gains more experience. But women are willing to begin to redesign their lives because something inside is pushing them. Somewhere there has to be some goal in all the living they've done, the hundreds of thousands of hours they've gone through. Where is the prize? They've been good contestants, played by the rules and now they want the shrieking, hysterical payoff. There ought to be more.

The Widow Sarah

I have known Sarah for several years, but had not really talked to her until long after that awful day that changed her life. She told me the whole sad story as we sat in her den one night. Sarah herself was neither sad nor lonely. She had adjusted to one of the unfortunate causes of mid-life stress in the best of all possible ways.

Sarah is from a small southern town. She was married at twenty-four after majoring in biology at college and taking a master's degree in statistics. She has three children who no longer live at home. "I always knew I wanted to do something," she told me, "but I never tried to buck the southern formula. You smiled, did flower arrangements, fixed a pretty table, helped with church bazaars and went on house tours. My friends are still doing that. I paid my dues by doing the proper things, but I added to the southern-belle syndrome. I got out of the kitchen, read some books and was on the school board. Before I married I had worked as a secretary for one year, but from the point of my marriage on, I was totally wife and mother. Then after my third child entered school, I got a part-time job as a librarian. I worked till 2:30 and I was home every afternoon when the kids got home. Working part-time was not a career, it was a diversion. I realized that what I was doing, which also included a lot of volunteer work, was trivial. But I never had the idea of having a career other than my family. It never for a moment entered my mind that what I did as a librarian could be a career, or that I might advance myself. I never cared about money or promotion.

"Then my husband died when I was forty-six. He went on a

business trip one day and dropped dead of massive heart failure. Everything changed 360 degrees. That was the total shakeup. My kids were teenagers when he died.''

I asked Sarah what she did when she lost her husband so suddenly. She surprised me by saying she couldn't wait to get back to work after the funeral, to that half-time job as a librarian. That was the only side of her life that her husband hadn't been part of. She could feel natural there. Then she described the aftershock.

''You spend a year not believing it, thinking it isn't true. Then you spend a year telling yourself you've got to get hold of yourself and strike out in a different direction. Your first impulse is you've got to find a man somewhere and marry him. You can't stand being alone and single. You're really pretty crazy for a while. You do a lot of foolish things. You're sort of manic-depressive. It affects the children in a similar way. They have their lumps too. Then you gradually begin to climb out of it. After a few years you become a person instead of a dangling half of something that isn't a couple.

''After two years I was able to deal with reality. At that point I decided to make deliberate changes in my life, after I felt I had my head on. I did a whole list of things. I needed money and to be out with other people. I decided to sell my house and move closer to work; to get loans to help my two kids through college; to rent a house for two years, then buy one; to change jobs from my part-time job to a full-time job. I needed to expand my career. I became assistant dean of the faculty at a nearby university. It paid little, I did menial work, but I had this prestigious title. A full-time job was no longer just a diversion, it was a career-type job.''

She explained that life was different for her in other ways. After her husband died, the most amazing transformation took place. All his business contacts who had been their pseudo-friends, disappeared. He had fifteen complimentary subscriptions to magazines because of his business, and within four months of his death they had all mysteriously been cancelled. She said, ''I was suddenly a nonperson. Then three years afterwards I felt I wanted to go back to the summer place where we had had such good times, where his annual board meetings were held and where we had so often been honored guests. I wrote to my 'dear' friend the general manager and said I needed a job at the resort. He gave me one as a waitress and I worked from 6 A.M. to 3 P.M. six days a week, living in the employees' quarters and looking at that same place from the other side of the counter. They were not quite so nice to me then. And when I backed the waitresses in a strike they held, the general manager never spoke to me again. Then the board arrived for their annual meeting, and there I was a waitress instead of an honored guest. No one knew what to do or say. I worked there for three months and I loved it. It was sort of a liberation. Something I was doing myself. It turned out to be one of the best summers I ever spent. All the other waitresses were college kids and good friends, and we camped and hiked together.

"I continued to work at the university. I had to. My husband's insurance was not enough even with the company contribution to the kids' college costs which his employer had given me. Even now, if I were not working, I would not be sitting in this house." After staying on the job for nine years she was fired in a budget crunch. She was one of the last hired, so the first fired. She was pretty scared, immediately went skiing as therapy and broke her leg so badly she was incapacitated for one year and unemployed. Finally, when her leg healed, a friend who recognized a woman in need when he saw one offered her a job at an aeronautical research engineering firm in one of the divisions called data-base management. This division develops computer programs for businesses. As an account executive, Sarah is the liaison between the customers who use the programs and the systems designers who invent them. Everything she learned about computers she learned on the job. Electronic computers hadn't even been invented when she went to college.

"We produce indexes and booklets from the stored material. I'm involved in that, I also do marketing and write proposals for services we will perform for customers all over the U.S. I have to know how a computer works, what it can do and what our system does. I need some understanding of the theory of pricing and negotiating contracts and how to schedule work. I have to know marketing so I can sell the system and how to respond to inquiries from those using our computer program who might have problems. It's a very difficult and important job. It pays very well, but I don't have a prestigious title."

I was frankly astounded that this gentle southern flower who had never worked in anything this complicated could take hold of herself and plunge, at age fifty-six, into the business of taking on a challenge as difficult as selling computer programs and carrying business needs for new programs to her company. I asked her where she got the confidence.

"It was desperation. I didn't see anything else to do. I really didn't know what I was getting into. If I'd known I'd have been scared. I just went there as green as grass and had an enormous amount of support from the people working there. Everyone showed me what they were doing, how to do things. Also, I discovered to my amazement, having never had a job except in a nonprofit place, that now that I was plunged into a profit-making business, I had a taste for making the buck for my company. All my coworkers are in their thirties or younger, the same age as my children. I'm very aware they are much swifter at comprehending the whole computer world, much faster than I. As far as technical acuity and swiftness are concerned, they run circles around me right now. But some of my confidence may come from the fact that I know more than they about some things. I have a better view of the long-term effects of certain decisions or actions. They are not so good at judging consequences of actions. In these things I'm better than they, enough to keep my self-respect."

According to Sarah, companies she visits are generally astonished to see someone of her age in this field. Most are around thirty. There's a stereotype of the person who works in computers. "I'm so far from it, it pricks their attention. But regardless of age and sex, I can't go in there and be charming and motherly. I've still got to know my subject. You can't fake that."

Sarah had always wanted to be more than a southern housewife. Unfortunately it took the death of her husband to force her to develop her talents. Without her ability to work and learn, she would not have been able to survive, and she would have been faced with a double tragedy rather than the successful new life she has made.

5

Breakdowns and Breakups

Women react in various ways to the many-faceted transition from youth to middle age. Usually moods and events are controllable, but some desperate responses to pressure can be dangerous and create even more misery. Tensions that have been simmering for years often come to the boiling point as a woman experiences the added stress of change. In some cases she feels a conflict between her inner needs and self-esteem, the way she wants to grow, and her husband's preference for the roles of the past that hold her back.

The husband's attitude is critical and often a source of concern. Lucky women will have men who offer them the maximum encouragement and support if they want to go to an office or sculpt or write. Others will have husbands who support them with ambivalence and grumbling, and still others will find their husbands totally disapproving. If her husband is not supportive, she can try to educate him or learn to live with his disapproval, while trying to overlook it. The worst possible situation is probably experienced by the woman who wants desperately to break out while her husband is just as adamant about her continuing to be a wife, mother and hostess—someone who is always there when he returns from work. If the woman insists on doing what she wants despite his wishes, the marriage may be the casualty. If the woman saves her marriage but gives up the idea of doing something of her own, *she* may well be the casualty instead.

The National Institute of Drug Abuse substantiates this point. They say that the stresses suffered by many women are related to "traditional views that women's role is to serve, that they are dependent and weak." These attitudes put many women in an intolerable situation where they feel "torn between their own dreams and ambitions and the expectations of a still-traditional society." Women who cannot resolve these two forces yanking them in opposite directions protect themselves from complete disintegration by hiding behind pressure-proof solutions that are usually unacceptable to society, but that guarantee they will finally get attention and be helped out of their misery, their hopelessness.

It has also been pointed out by Dr. Carol Nadelson of the Harvard Medical School Department of Psychiatry that successful adaptation to mid-life depends on a sense of continuing usefulness and the breadth of outside interests. I know from trying it myself that one of the hardest things in the world to do is nothing. The boredom is mindracking. Never to be in demand, to have no driving purpose, to feel the empty hours press heavily like suffocating pillows, to sense the surrounding silence like mute waves rushing over one is enough to unbalance a woman permanently.

Reacting with Drugs and Drink

Some women who cannot fill their lives with activities that keep them busy, who cannot express themselves creatively, who find there is no one who needs them, no one to communicate with succumb to using drugs as an unhappy alternative. The National Institute of Drug Abuse says the main factors that make some women more vulnerable than others to alcohol and drug abuse are isolation and loneliness. A woman I spoke to, who stayed at home after her children were grown, told me about the incredible solitude she felt. She found nothing to do; the phone didn't ring and she became jealous of friends who said they were so busy they couldn't see her for weeks. "I live in a silent vacuum," she said sadly. "I am the only occupant of a submarine miles under the ocean." If she doesn't wake up and move out, this woman will soon be taking drugs, drinking or cracking up.

Other factors that can lead to using drugs and alcohol include lack of self-confidence and feelings of worthlessness, frustration and inferiority. Many women who take drugs to excess do not seem able to identify or solve their own problems. Some lack the basic skills needed for survival, says the institute, and some find the demands of life too overburdening. For others, life is too easy and for yet others, it is too hard. It has been reported that an estimated one to two million women, mostly between the ages of thirty-four and fifty, have problems because of prescription drugs, and more women than men use them. Thirty-two million women have used tranquilizers compared with nineteen million men; sixteen million women have used sedatives compared with twelve million men; and twelve million women have used stimulants compared with five million men. About 60 percent of all drug-related emergency-room visits involve women. Almost two-thirds of these are the result of suicide attempts, the remaining one-third are the result of drug dependency. Whereas the median age of drug-related deaths among white males is twenty-eight, for white females it is forty-three. Housewives who do not work are the largest users of barbiturates, antidepressants, diet pills, relaxants, minor tranquilizers and other sedative/hypnotic drugs.

A 1978 report issued by the institute examined the extent of abuse among women. Their conclusion was that the statistics they have collected are only "the tip of the iceberg," because they include only those whose abuse has been so great they have been forced to seek treatment, whereas the majority of unknown abusers have not. The study found that 60 percent of psychotropic drugs, 71 percent of antidepressants, and 80 percent of amphetamines are prescribed for women. Half of the presumed ten million Americans who are alcoholics are women. Ten years ago it was only one out of every six. Recent surveys show the highest percentage of heavy drinking for women is in the forty-five to forty-nine age group. Not only has there been an increase in the number of women alcoholics, but deaths from cirrhosis of the liver have risen. Women who live in the cities' ghettos, in the affluent suburbs or in the isolation of rural areas and who feel unneeded when their children leave home or a husband divorces them or dies, who have no vocational training and feel they cannot get jobs, or whose husbands don't want them to have jobs, constitute the group of women who are most likely to turn to drugs and alcohol.

Rural women in Nevada, for example, show one of the highest alcoholism rates in the country. In communities where they live, a woman's major role is that of homemaker. She does not have access to other activities such as local art or literary circles, consciousness-raising groups, cultural endeavors or continuing education. And even if she did, like the suburban woman or the ghetto dweller, if she has no self-confidence or usable ambition, she would be just as paralyzed as they are, surrounded by all their riches of choice.

Telling this group of women who are having difficulty coping with life in general that they now have the freedom—in fact the right, perhaps the obligation—to go out into a business and professional world that doesn't yet completely welcome them and for which they were never trained or psychologically prepared results in a very disturbing situation. A few will try to meet the challenge, want to be useful; others will become petrified and unable even to try.

Among the women I spoke to there were three who had serious problems. There was Carrie who became an alcoholic, Carol who had a nervous breakdown and Agnes who ran away from her husband and children. All these women are as normal as you and I. Some may be more sensitive, more high-strung, more volatile people. I know that these women are perfectly able to handle life and its difficult circumstances in more conventional ways. What happened to them could, I think, happen to most of us.

Carrie and the Bottle

This is the story of Carrie. She is married, has two children and lives in Massachusetts. She is an example of a woman who felt she had been sat on so long by her husband that there was only one way to get him to recognize that she had personal needs of her own. Carrie started drinking when she was forty-one. We sat one day, cross-legged on her couch, as the dogs came around and sniffed. She was wearing a white, loose-fitting outfit which hid her excess weight. White made her look younger and more helpless. I think she was completely sober the day we talked.

"I thought people in middle age had it all made," she said, giving me a bittersweet smile, "but we get it from all sides. My mother is dying, my daughter is in love, my brother's kids are calling me—I get crazy when I keep giving and nothing is coming back to me." There they were, those ubiquitous stresses of middle age. The loss of parents and dealing with teenagers. And there was more.

Carrie married for the first time in college, graduated and was going to study psychology, but her husband got a fellowship. "To have thought of putting my ambitions first was unheard of, so I gave up dreams of a career," she said. "I wanted to do something. You sound like a terrible ass if you say you want to write. 'What do you do?' they ask me. If I say, 'Oh, I write poetry,' their response will be, 'Well, who doesn't.' I thought of anthropology. You see, I didn't know what I wanted to do by then. I knew I wanted to have children and read and write. It was all by the book. It seemed like my life was all right on the surface. But I was fooling myself. Our marriage broke up when I was thirty-three.

"I remarried and my former husband sued for custody of the kids. It lasted two years and nearly killed us. All these unexpected problems made my new husband angry. And he wasn't getting ahead in his career. He'd storm at fate. I was the captive audience with my two children asleep in the next room. He'd spend the evening pacing back and forth in the living room, yelling. I said finally I'd had enough. Women have been sat on for so long, we don't express ourselves. I wanted badly to scream out and talk about my own needs, but he wasn't interested. Since I couldn't lose my temper unless I was drunk, I started drinking. I drank for five years.

"It's funny, you spend half your life learning to do things the right way. By the time you are middle-aged and have learned, you no longer care about doing things the right way anymore, how you dress or what the gossips say. I let myself drink. It was childish anger. 'You're not listening to me,' I was telling him. 'The only time you'll pay attention to me is when I get a bottle and go into my room.' I was sick. I don't know how much I drank. I didn't have it hidden in the bathroom to start the day with. But I might have a drink for lunch and then when he came home in the evening I'd have a martini and wine. Then I'd have a few more drinks and escape into sleep. It was acting out. Childish, angry, helpless. I couldn't do anything about it. I had no hope of anyone understanding.

"I wanted him to stop bullying me, forcing me to listen to him, to stop saying I'm sick, all of those put-down things. He wanted me to stay grateful for what he was doing, taking care of me and the children. At last I began to write. He would write too. He'd want me to listen to his work, but he didn't want to listen to mine. He wanted me to do for him what his mother or nurse failed to do when he was six months old. He hasn't grown up, he's grown older. He could get very angry.

"I'd never seen anyone rant and rave like he did when he was angry. He was capable of acting like a lower-class street bum. He'd push me with the back of his hand and really hurt me. I could have been killed or had a concussion. He doesn't know his own strength. He hated me to leave when he was talking to me. Once I went into our bedroom to get away. I didn't even lock the door, but he broke it down. I always felt I could handle him, though. Many times I thought of going away for my own peace of mind. I deserve a better life than this. But I never left. Not because I was dumb. It would have been damned hard to go. It would have had to have been a question of saving my life or my children's. It wasn't that bad. After the storm he'd always be charming and sweet and I'd forget it all. The next day if I told him about it he'd say, 'I didn't mean any of that stuff.'

"The dumbest thing I did was to drink. I tried every possible drinking pattern, and I'd drink whenever I damned well felt like it. I was the boss of me. At last! After drinking, though, I didn't wake up with guilt and say, 'You stupid ass, you did it again.' If I chose to take in that chemical, it was me, taking responsibility for what I'd do. I was sick and hurt, but I was me. Guilt is wasteful sorriness, self-pity, dodging responsibility. I didn't waste time with that. You're a long way from helping yourself if you do. My drinking was like the child in class when the teacher says 'you were not paying attention,' and the child was, but gets punished anyway. The child thinks, 'I might as well not pay attention.' People believed I was sick and he was innocent, so I decided I might as well drink and be sick. But I told myself, 'You're hurting yourself doing this.' And that is terrible.

"I stopped trying to fight with him. I was not going to let him make me sick. What will that prove? I have to take care of myself. It was like people watching carloads of starving Jews being carted off. They'd say, 'Let's get rid of those diseased, filthy people,' forgetting how they'd gotten that way. I kept hoping some justice would see how this had happened to me.

"Finally I made myself the master of myself. I wasn't addicted and I stopped. I bought out of that whole game. I'm back to having a social drink once in a while, maybe once a week. My husband drinks beer now for his own health. He has more trouble with hangovers now that he's older. Drinking affects him faster. I took a job last year that a friend offered me because I knew my second child was going away and I'd have nothing to do. I had done volunteer work for the church and read a bit of psychiatry, but nothing I could get my teeth into. Now I work in a prison and am paid by the department of corrections for teaching prisoners how to relax.

"Relaxation is the lightest trip you can take. If you relax you are open to thinking about things in new ways. I ask them to think of themselves and their lives and what they want to change. I get them to focus on a tense scene and a calm scene and tell them they have it in their power to choose which way they will react. If a guard has it in for them, instead of getting angry, they learn to take a breath and say, 'That's his trip. I'm not going to respond to that.' I use what I'm learning on my husband. I don't respond to him if I don't want to. I'm learning how to be positively assertive—to turn myself off during one of his scenes and say what I have to say in my husband's terms, in a positive way so I don't hurt him. Then I talk about what I want to say.

"A few days ago I dreamed about drinking, and in the dream I realized I was still angry. When I did all that drinking, I was being too cool to express this anger. If I could have punched a pillow and gotten the anger out, it would have been preferable to buying the bottle. You have this physical adrenaline inside. 'If I could just get my husband and punch him.' But the way I was brought up, we just don't do that, or break the furniture. I suddenly understood what that technique is all about. Releasing pent-up anger! I am going to punch the hell out of a lot of pillows before I go out and buy a bottle again. Who, me? I can't believe I could have a problem like that. A therapist I knew once told me a long time ago about how he could not cry or react after a friend of his had killed himself. One day he was demonstrating the punching technique in his workshop and all of a sudden he heard this tremendous howl and he wondered what this noise was. After a while he realized it was coming out of him. And he could finally break down and cry. When he told me about it, I just didn't understand and I said, 'What else is new?' A lot of things make sense now.

"My marriage hasn't changed. My attitude changed. I had to give up my expectations that we would learn to love each other more and grow. Other circumstances are different too. My husband isn't pushing me; he can't take chances with the relationship. Now that I work, and the children are gone, I can leave if I want. He is more secure in his job. He's reached a time of life when he doesn't blame the rest of the world (which turns out to be me) for what he hasn't accomplished. He has recognized his limitations. He's as far along in his field as he's going to be, and he's relaxed about it. We don't really understand each other, but we have more respect for each other, give each other more space, I choose what I want to do. There is no pressure now. Our age, his career, the kids away, it's changed. I do what I enjoy. I have learned and grown. I must be easier to live with, a nicer person to know. I'm older. I can deal with things more effectively. I'm not doing things for the first time. Life is easier. I've seen a lot. Done lots. I'm good at my job, and as long as I'm learning I'm happy. I'm glad someone wants all this useful talent. It makes you tense not to have an outlet. It needs to be used, this talent.''

Isolation doesn't need to exist in a lonely rural farmhouse. Women can be equally isolated in their big-city apartments, wherever they are ignored, undervalued, put down. Fortunately Carrie was able to pull herself up from the morass into which she had fallen (although it is extremely unusual to be able to accomplish a cure by oneself). With the help of a friend who offered her a job, she suddenly became useful and was able to do something she was good at and win back the self-worth that her husband had annihilated. Many are not so fortunate and need long years of professional help in controlling alcoholism. Carrie said she was never totally out of control. And maybe she was right. The last time I talked to her she told me she is still working but has enrolled in graduate school to become a professional therapist.

Suicide

Though some look to alcohol to alleviate unbearable pressures, others may consider even more drastic measures. In a study of women, *Four Stages of Life* by Marjorie F. Lowenthal and her colleagues, published in 1975, it was found that among women of all ages, ''The middle-aged women were. . . . the least sure of themselves of all groups and their uneasy and often

conflicting characterizations of themselves suggest identity dif-
fusion if not outright 'crisis.' . . .'' The future in general looked
bleak and empty to them, and the majority did not feel in control. They reported themselves to be unhappy; they reported
more psychological symptoms than anyone else; and they were
the most likely to say that they had at some time considered
suicide. There are those middle-aged women who turn to suicide
when problems seem insoluble. In 1963–64 among females aged
thirty-five to forty-four, the suicide rate was 10.7 per 100,000
women. In 1973–74 this had risen to a peak of 12.1. In the
forty-five to fifty-four age group, in 1963–64 the rate was 12.5
and by the most recent available figures this had risen to 13.9.
Actually men have a higher rate of suicide than women, more
than double the female rate at every age group. And among old
men the rate is seven times that of women. But many more
women *attempt* suicide than do men. Men are simply more successful in carrying it to completion. Men use the irreversible
and immediately self-destructive means of shooting or hanging.
Women are more likely to choose relatively slow acting poisons
or barbiturates.

Carol and Her Nervous Breakdown

There are less drastic ways of responding to intolerable pressures than self-destruction. A report from the U.S. Department
of Health, Education and Welfare's National Center for Health
Statistics indicates that far more middle-aged women than men
feel tension and anxiety to the point where they come to a
nervous breakdown or actually have one. Between 1971 and
1975 among women aged thirty-five to fifty-four, 48 percent reported symptoms of nervous breakdown compared with only 22
percent of men. It may be that women allow themselves to fall
to pieces mentally more easily than men. But it certainly is true
that women have more reason to feel frustrated and caught between their internal needs and the demands of others to the
point where, if they don't find a solution, they can go literally
out of their minds.

One day while I was at home keeping so busy that I would not have time to clean or make beds, the doorbell rang and there was Carol, a friend of mine, standing there looking distraught in the chill of the fall morning.

"Come in, come in. What's the matter?"

"I've got to get out. I don't know what to do," Carol blurted out in a high voice. She came in and we sat over a cup of tea. "I can't cope. I can't do anything. I can't do the laundry or clean the house or buy the food or cook or answer the phone. I'm going to pieces. I literally can't cope with anything anymore."

I tried to comfort her, offering pitifully little help, and soon she left. I thought it was probably one of those bad days. But that morning she was in the first stages of a nervous breakdown, which no one by then could have prevented.

"I spent a summer in a psychiatric clinic which was like a medieval prison," she later told me, "and five months in another clinic having shock therapy, art therapy and physical therapy. Finally, that did the trick."

Why did Carol, a presumably happily married mother of three children, end up needing shock treatments? She tried to explain what was going on inside her that caused her complete mental collapse.

"I was so enmeshed in one identity because my husband insisted that I maintain that identity. My entire time was spent in caring for others. My husband said the house had to be a certain way, the kids had to be a certain way. He was too threatened to let me go out in the world. What I wanted to do myself was only valid as long as it was done with the entire family. I had no block of time for me. I wasn't happy with just that. He'd go away for hours playing tennis or whatever he wanted, but I couldn't do that. When I did try to do things, I ended up hurting him. Instead of trying to understand, he used my efforts to make a life for myself as a punitive device. He'd hold it against me and use it in fights we had.

"Finally it became obvious that I could no longer keep the identity that he made up for me. And he couldn't stand it even if I talked to a friend about my problems. I felt like someone was holding my head underwater. I couldn't function. I became totally numb,'' she explained. ''I didn't feel or see anything. I went to a psychiatrist who sent me to a mental hospital in Philadelphia. They kept me in a room by myself. I was considered unsafe, because I tried to take my life.''

During the previous year and a half she had gradually been withdrawing from reality. She finally had become so depressed that one particularly bleak afternoon she went into the garage, closed the doors and turned her car motor on. Her ten-year-old son was responsible for saving her life. He missed her and heard the car motor running. He ran to the door of the garage, opened it, saw her in the car, ran up to her and said, ''You can damage your brain doing this. I've seen this all on television. You better come out.''

On another occasion, she said she swallowed ''tons and tons'' of aspirin until she heard a tremendously loud buzzing in her head. ''I felt so sick and the buzzing was so loud and I didn't die, so I just stopped taking them. That kind of depression is more incredibly painful than anyone can know,'' Carol said quietly as she tried to recall her state of mind. ''You just feel you can't endure any more, and then you turn the gas on or take some pills.''

Alone in her drab hospital room, she was totally isolated from everyone except the nurses who did guard duty twenty-four hours a day and didn't talk to her. The only thing in the room was a Bible. She had to eat by herself at a small table ''like a punished child,'' and once a day she was taken down in an elevator to spend a half hour with a psychiatrist who did absolutely nothing for her. ''You can't be helped by talking when you are that depressed,'' Carol said. She remembered there was a loom for weaving (''but you have to feel good in order to weave'') and some cold, gray clay. There were no instructors. They fed her on pills all the time to keep her from causing any trouble. She remained catatonic and wasn't helped at all.

In the meantime, the children didn't know what was going on, ''so they went along with the existing power, whoever was holding up the ship. My husband told them I was crazy and they believed it.'' Finally she was allowed home for a vacation and went to see another psychiatrist. This doctor ordered her sent to a totally different kind of clinic. She had gotten the idea that perhaps hypnotism might help her. When she suggested this to him, he told her that wasn't what she needed, but electric shock was. It was not much like the screaming agonies of electricity shooting through the body that one has seen in films. Here in the new clinic she received shock therapy but was given sodium pentothal, which sent her into an immediate sleep, and then the electric shock treatments, which she didn't feel at all, were administered. When she awoke, there were gentle, smiling nurses hovering all around her offering her warm donuts and hot coffee. During the days there were group sports like volleyball and basketball, and she spent a lot of time with people. It seemed as though she was a guest at a country club.

Now, the whole regimen of treatment produced a gradual awakening. "It was like coming out of a long sleep," Carol remembered. "I had my own reality back. I felt functional. I could eat and dress myself. I did a lot of sculpture and yoga. It was the first time I felt like talking in three years.'' Friends came to see her and she got a lot of support from them. She was permitted to go out in the evening and teach a jewelry course where a number of bright, friendly women also gave her a sense of importance. There she was, teaching all those people. She found she could do something herself.

When she finally came home from the clinic, her husband continued to tell the children she was crazy and treat her badly. "I think he wished that I had succeeded in killing myself," she said. "Even Hitler had his sweet side too. If I ever spoke up for myself, I had to be out of my mind. He needed to be absolute boss. It took my daughter until she was twenty-one to realize that I'm not out of my mind. He had negated my whole reality, and he tried to poison the kids' minds.''

When she had been home from the clinic for some time and her husband's behavior didn't change, Carol made another desperate, though this time more calmly calculated, decision. She felt strong enough, and had enough confidence, to understand what was happening and what she would have to do to survive.

"I kicked him out. I realized what the game was. He was doing a whole power number. I'd never have a chance of expressing what I wanted. He was like a rebellious adolescent. Even after he left, during our separation, when he came to the house to see the kids, he'd bring me his dirty laundry to do, then get upset about something and break the screen door. Thank God I'm finished with all that. Now I have my own business and I haven't needed to see a psychiatrist since then."

Carol had been pitifully caught in the crunch between an egocentric husband and the new ideas that told her it was all right to express herself. She let go of reality, an obnoxious reality, because she no longer could stand being used selfishly by her husband while her own creative desires and her need to be recognized as an independent human being were ignored.

Why Agnes Ran Away

There are personal solutions to middle-age problems that fall far short of the out-of-control answers that lead to hospital emergency rooms and mental institutions, to rehabilitation clinics and therapy cures. Sometimes a woman who is upset by things in her life or by the direction it is taking figures out for herself some kind of compromise solution. When middle age is upon you and you start asking yourself whether you can go on this way until the end, there are those women whose answer is "no!" They want something more, so desperately, that they leave their husbands and children and run away still trying to express their true selves before it's too late.

Agnes, from Wisconsin, went to college for two years and had four children during a fifteen-year marriage. She had been working as a management consultant, and writing at night; she was very unhappy. The day I saw her she was in the process of chucking her marriage and leaving her children to go off and marry another man. What stresses drove her to this point? In Agnes's case it was her father, rather than her husband, who may have caused her problems. Growing up, Agnes thought she wanted to be a ballet dancer but never imagined actually having a career. Her father was domineering and had no aspirations for her. "He recognized I had a good mind. But occupationally he couldn't figure out that I could be anything more than an executive secretary. Mother wanted me to marry and have kids. It didn't matter to them if I went to college. My father would never have taken out a loan to send me. He sent my brother, but when I went, I had to earn most of the money. He could have sold his Thunderbird and sent me to school, but he didn't. And all my mother was interested in was what I would wear at college. She was always saying, 'Agnes, you can't go around like that.

"I quit college when I became pregnant. I thought I was going to get married but didn't. I had the baby and put him up for adoption, though this continued to upset me. I was ready for a kindly, protective man, the sort my father had never been. He came along and I grabbed him; two months later we were married. Since my father had been dominating and my husband's mother had been dominating, neither of us knew how to argue with the opposite sex. It was two years before we had an argument. He was happy not to have a woman screaming at him. We were happy to depend on each other, and it took me about twelve years to recuperate from the traumas of my life—my father, the pregnancy and the adoption."

In the job she has now, Agnes does a lot of traveling. She began to realize that she was a self-sufficient person. She realized she and her husband disagreed on things but their differences had been paved over by common interests. Her husband was proud of her working and supportive. "But I did not enjoy my job too much," Agnes explained. "I'd find myself in a paper box factory thinking of how they could better manage things on a conveyor belt. I was a roaring success, but I was not cut out for it. The job was not creative enough. It was too much. I was trying to be superwoman, working fifty to sixty hours a week, staying up half the night doing free-lance writing (which is what I really wanted to do), having the responsibility for the kids, being away all week sometimes. My husband didn't oppress me. I oppressed myself. Ask me to do anything, and I'll do it—to get approval. I'm still trying to prove to my father I can do it. My father told me, 'You'll never be good at anything, you'll always be a dilettante.' When I was ten years old he said, 'You were really a nice little kid but you haven't been worth a shit since you were six.' My mother always thought I was too intelligent to have a happy life. She said, when she saw I was bright, 'What did I ever do to deserve this. I finally got a baby and it's like him' (the husband she hated). She wanted me to be like other girls, not a bookworm. There was no approval for being myself.

"My marriage was really a brotherly relationship. We were best friends. Then it happened. I really fell in love with someone much older than I whom I met where I worked. No doubt I was ripe for something like this to happen. If not this man, it would have been someone. I went through a period of feeling I should go off by myself, rather than running to one more protective situation. Then I decided that would not be right. I told my husband that I was finally in love with someone and he said, 'All right. We'll open up the marriage. You can have him and come home too.' But it wouldn't do. I worry, of course, what if it doesn't work out? Then I say, 'Okay, so it doesn't.' If it doesn't I'm not going to kill myself to make it work. I want the chance to live with someone I can love and be very close to.

"As a child I thought this was unthinkable. My father didn't really talk to my mother for ten years although they lived in the same house. Now I know really caring about someone is not an unreasonable thing to expect. I plan to do what I want to do now, which is write full-time. I could have gone on with the marriage, given up the job, cut our salary in half and written. I just want that primary relationship. Once I realized I could have the kind of marriage I wanted, to stay in this marriage, at my stage of life, would have been unbearable. I felt gratitude toward my husband for a long time. My family and everyone felt I was so lucky to have someone to take care of me. I owed him so much for marrying me. It took me years to get over it."

It was not only finding a real love that made Agnes decide to leave her husband, it was time pressing in on her. She said, "If you're a woman between thirty-five and forty you really are going through an appraisal. Whether you have kids or the rat race of a job, you really are thinking, 'Is this the way it's going to be forever until I retire and go to the "Aloha Home" in Miami?' Leaving my husband is not something I would have done at twenty-eight or thirty-two. But at thirty-six—yes. As for the kids, either one of us would have taken all of them. They should be in an environment that is best for them. It's not nice not to have your mother full-time, but it's not essential either. My kids' childhood, even with its faults, is way ahead of the kind of childhood I grew up in with all its strife. I tell them, 'I'm not going to Mars. You can pick up a phone and get to me.'

"A friend of mine told me, 'Most of us live our lives like a rehearsal but the curtain never goes up. Good for you.' Another friend said at first he thought I was suffering from a hormone imbalance. One nice thing about marrying someone older is that it takes the sting out of middle age. I'll be the young one. In business, men perceive the man of fifty or sixty as being powerful. But when they meet his wife who is the same age, she looks old to them. His wife is viewed as being from another planet. She needs to be younger to go with this image of the all-powerful man.

"I feel tired and exhausted now. When I go to the house we've bought in South Carolina it is so much like a fantasy, what I dreamt of having someday, that it's still unreal. I can't believe it's happening. Suddenly, all this total freedom. Everyone has a fantasy. Now I will be free to set my own schedule, sleep and write when I want, put all the pieces together. Everything I've needed—the person and the life—has appeared all together in a package. It's too good to be true." Like most people with a puritanical background who do not feel they are good enough to deserve success, Agnes felt she would have to pay for her happiness. "I'm afraid it carries the seeds of its own destruction," she said. "But I know that I have a strong need to get close to someone where there's a hell a lot of affection."

For Agnes, there were the pressures of time warning her that if she didn't get out of the marriage she was in, this would be her life forever, that if she didn't take advantage of a real love she might never have another opportunity, and that if she wanted to devote herself to writing and didn't do it now, she never would. She also felt a desperate need to exorcise all the negative putdowns her father lavished upon her and prove she was a person of value. Most women have no mentors or role models the way men do as they change and develop. They usually have only critics who expect little from them and repress any unusual interests. There are so few females who have succeeded, so few available women to emulate that they have to break ground pretty much alone.

Shortly after Agnes and I had talked, I told my husband about her case, and his "male" reaction really startled me. "That bitch," he called her. "How awful that that bitch left her husband and children. Just walked out. He hadn't done anything to hurt her. He probably loved her."

I looked at him and then coolly pointed out that men leave their adoring wives and children every day and no one thinks anything about it. If a marriage isn't right for a man, he falls in love with a secretary or friend and then walks out. But if a woman does it, it seems as though she is evil incarnate. She is not. She is simply looking for a way out of the unendurable pain of a marriage without love and a life without doing what she feels is right for her. That's what divorce is all about. Getting a second chance to make things right.

My husband listened to me, then slowly picked up the lapel of the corduroy jacket he was wearing and sheepishly covered his face with it. Touché. He conceded my point.

Whether the psychological pressures come from her family or herself, a woman at this time will become sensitized to the alterations in her life—her own aging, the loss of friends and parents, the departure of children, the increase in serious illness and chronic pains, the more frequent doctor visits, the lessening of energy, the realization that life is moving faster than she thought toward an irrevocable end. Most people live with these facts of life and try to concentrate on the pluses of their age; more leisure time, more money, more power. Those who are going to crack up are likely to do it now.

But how well the middle-aged woman in general responds to this period in her life, how many get depressed and how many are happy with their new freedoms appears uncertain. There is conflicting evidence. Campbell and his colleagues observed a sense of general well-being in women in the empty-nest state, whereas Lowenthal and her co-researchers found middle-aged women to be the most distressed age group of all. The key to the answer probably lies in the kind of women the researchers happen to sample, what questions they ask, how they phrase the questions, and what specific period in the lives of these middle-aged women they observe. Happiness is a very subjective and volatile element. The same person can feel really down one week and up the next. However, if the drug and alcohol statistics for women represent "only the tip of the iceberg," as the National Institute of Drug Abuse believes, there is obviously a strong need for women to consider the alternatives. Somewhere, somehow, every woman has to go out and find the solutions that are there, realize where middle life has led her and what the next steps ought to be.

6

Finding the Skills
and the Self

It takes a lot of support after years of living behind blinders to
know where and how to break out into a new phase of life. The
mind must be exercised carefully. It is stiff from disuse and
suffused with negative self-images. A woman I talked to confessed, "I hesitated to try things because I thought I was stu-
pider than other women. I had always been made to feel that
way. They all seemed so confident, seemed to know what they
wanted and how to get it and what was going on in the world.
Then I listened to those who were said to be so intelligent and
they didn't sound any different than I did. So I decided to try to
do what I wanted to do."

A woman may very well need plenty of help and stimulation
from friends and husbands, or counselors and life-style groups.
These groups, which offer advice and direction, have sprung up
everywhere, like mushrooms after a summer storm, in response
to the booming demand from women who want to get out of the
house. Even women who work and want to change careers or

advance further in their field will find counseling services geared to their needs.

Despite the proliferating availability of classes, workshops, group sessions, lectures and consultants, many women so often seem to sit by and wait for heaven to send them the answer— the opportunity, the job, the neon-lighted direction. They don't know what they're selling, so they don't know how to recognize an opportunity. You have to know your marketable, portable, convertible skills. Even the woman at home with kids needs to know what skills she wants to keep a pilot light under. But most women not only don't know what they want, they have no idea where to find it. They don't think or plan. They are, despite all the busy work they have done all their lives, quite undirected, usually leaving most of what happens to them to fate.

Women need to harden their mental muscles, fill in all the missing areas that society told them they didn't have to bother with. They must acknowledge that they make very good businesspeople, admit that they make super managers and that they are better at getting along with others than a lot of men. They have to fill in with courses in business, logic, economics, politics, mathematics, statistics, accounting, computers, finance or corporation law.

Women today who are breaking into the world of business are not very different from black women breaking into the world of everything. Talking with one recent university graduate who is black, I was impressed by what she had learned about herself. She said, "I'm confident that if I can't do something now, give me the shortest amount of time that it takes, and I'll learn it. The university taught me I can learn anything. Fighting for everything made me stronger." This black student's making it in an elite Ivy League university struck me as being like women trying to make it in the all-male, elite business world. Who wants them? Some of the men do, but the older ones often don't. They have to make themselves wanted because they are so good, even though they are hired because businesses are forced by law and equal-employment practices into hiring them. Middle-aged women are getting positions for which no young woman would ever be hired. They are pretending they know more than they do, keeping their ears open and learning voraciously on the job, studying the books at night. They are asking for help and demanding to be taken seriously.

But women must get out of their chairs and devise a plan, even if it's just visiting a nearby community college to discuss their interests with the deans. A woman I talked to one day said she wanted to do this but hesitated. "I'm afraid to call the school and ask about programs and getting admitted. I haven't been to school in so long, I'm afraid I won't get in, I'll be rejected," she said.

I told her to go ahead and call, just to talk. Besides, she probably would get in. In each woman there must be some pressure-well that has been capped over the years and is on the verge of exploding. Women who used to dream of being Margaret Meads on their way to Samoa can stop dreaming and be Mary Does on their way to the tenth floor of the life insurance company or the publishing house. What lies ahead for them can be just as mysterious, exciting to understand, worthwhile and more attainable.

So often women who are widowed like Sarah or divorced, or former housewives in a new career, are told by their friends who now see them alone for the first time, "I never really knew what you were like. You were always sitting quietly while he did all the talking. You're really interesting. And you look so great now." Coming out of one's shell not only develops the mind, but the looks begin to change. Women whose creative sides are allowed to expand, whose minds think and reason, who express opinions, begin to actually look younger and happier. The empty-headed, worried looks disappear. To have your friends care what *you* think, not only what your husband thinks about something, can be a most gratifying moment. With the mind in shape, the body usually falls into shape because life becomes more disciplined. You eat less and let your need for exercise lead you to some sport, and as your interaction with people increases and your salary checks start coming in, the image of the depressed middle-aged woman who is graying and busy popping pills and drinking too much to alleviate her aches, pains and boredom becomes the image of the fit and useful woman who has negotiated the middle-age transition. She has actually started a whole new life. This creative middle age which lies dormant within each woman is supposed to emerge with a little help somewhere after forty.

Visit with a Career Counselor

I went into New York one day to see a career consultant who is president of her own company, Katherine Nash Associates. As I walked into the lobby of her building on Central Park West and waited for the elevator, along came a middle-aged woman. I should say "ran." She came jogging into the lobby, completely attired in white sweat shirt and pants, smelling of fresh air, gasping for breath. "I'm Katherine Nash," she said, "I just ran down to the store and back." Soon we were in her living room standing and looking through the soot-stained windows out at the reservoir in the park. It was about to be spring. We began to examine what a career consultant does and how she had become one in 1947 when she pioneered the new field.

Katherine had worked in radio and television, married when she was thirty-five and had two children. "Then I had a nervous breakdown, otherwise known as a slipped disk. At home I had always been defined by other people's needs. 'Hey Mom, I need a tube for my bike tire,' or 'Dear, we're having people for dinner, get something good.' I would try to hold on to ME when all these requests came. But if my husband wanted good meals, then I would go to cooking school." At that time in her life she was completely devoted to the job of homemaker and trying to do it in the best possible way. "My dinners were like opening nights at the theater."

She went on, "But wisdom comes out of pain. When I went to bed with that nervous breakdown, I read and thought. I told myself that I know why women are sitting there crying. They don't like who they are. They wake up in the morning and try to decide if they should take uppers or downers, Dexedrine to stimulate them or Valium to calm them. They don't want to face themselves. They need help sorting out their emotional needs.

You can't live your life open on all fronts at all times. That's what most women do.''

So, lying there in bed with her slipped disk that was really a nervous breakdown, she read the paper and waited for the phone to ring. ''I couldn't stand staying home, but I didn't know what to do. I got my résumé and looked at it and thought, that's only one small image of me.'' She took some long, white shelf paper, spread it across the bed and decided she was going to write down what she knew, everything she knew how to do, whether she had been paid for it or not, to find out who she was.

That's how she thought of finally going into counseling. She recognized there were so many women like herself who needed help. After counseling for many years, Katherine has accumulated quite a fund of information and advice which I attempted to benefit from that day. One of the most vital things to do if you are married, she suggested, is to get male support. ''Your first job is to get your husband on your side. Men are action oriented.

''*Don't say: She:* 'Darling, I really feel I'm not getting anywhere. I think maybe I ought to do something, maybe take a course.'

''*He:* 'Dear, do anything that makes you happy.'

''*Do say. She:* 'Darling, I'm taking a photography course on Tuesday. What do we do about a baby sitter?' ''

Men, says Katherine, cannot deal with abstractions. But most men will address themselves to action problems. Men will tell their wives, ''Pull yourself together and look for a job.'' ''But,'' she says, ''men cannot understand what pulling herself together entails for a woman who has been at home and then goes to work. To enter the work world,'' she explained, ''you have to serve, throw up the ball, get the most amount of confidence you can muster. The dilemma of women today is that they need a totally different set of muscles to reenter the work world than they used staying at home.''

Then Katherine turned toward me, put her white sweat-suited legs up on the couch and crossed them. Leaning forward, she raised her arms in the air and addressed me as though I were all the helpless and confused women packed into one. ''Ladies,'' she exhorted, ''for God's sake. You have to have something.

You have to say to yourself, some day what if . . . [Here she, of course, meant divorce or widowhood.] You have to be ready for a contingency day. Find your major skills. Look for a career around them. Women have to be in charge of their own lives, not dependent on someone else for food, shelter and clothing. That is untenable. There is no safety in dependency.'' She said that all a woman had to do was look at the life-table statistics to know that there might be a day when something happens. Or look at the divorce rate.

"But I love my husband," women will say. Katherine says, "Dependency erodes a relationship. You must know you can take care of yourself. You may come to a point in a marriage that isn't doing too well where you either say, 'I'm going to leave,' and you make the decision with some self-esteem. Or you say, 'I'm not going to leave. But I need to know I can.' "

Katherine looks at me again and says, "Work is gorgeous when it fits your skills. Work is forced growth. To set your own goals by yourself requires enormous maturity. It's one of the hardest things to do." A doctor's wife once admitted that she was not self-sufficient enough to stay home. (There's a twist.) She needed the structure and goal of a job. So what Katherine Nash does for her clients is to help discover hidden skills, skills buried since school days. She mines these skills, rediscovers success patterns. Then she does research to find jobs that use the clusters of skills that she has helped dig up. Among those who come to see her are women who want to enter or reenter the work world, women who have just a job and now want a career and those who are stuck in a dead-end position and need to move elsewhere.

Discovering skills is not easy. We perpetually hear so many women say, "Oh well, I've been doing nothing." But it is Katherine's opinion that every human skill has a commercial correlative. "Every single thing you can do," she says pointing at me, "someone else is getting paid for."

Some women say, "Well, what I do at home is private."

Katherine says, "Horseshit." She explained, "What you have to do is refer back to a known, visceral, palpable success feeling. Assess your skills BEFORE the sex role, before cooking, cleaning and mothering. When you were young. You will see the long lines of continuity in life. You must find a tool to scream back at the world. You need tools to deal with life. You must make yourself sensitive, worthy to be loved. We all have abilities. The more skills a woman has, the more options she has.

"You have to think back, tell your story of a success feeling, but slow it down. Find the dynamic at work. Look for the active verbs and use them. You have to reverse the passive role, see life actively.

"Don't say, 'We did it together.'

"My first job is to get women to report their lives as though *they* make things happen."

She gave me an example of what she meant. "A woman looking for a career came to me, and when we looked back at her life and her résumé, we found that she was a student in an exchange program. She told me, 'I was chosen to go to Europe on a student exchange program.'

"I tell her, 'No one came along and pointed at you and made you go.'

"She said, 'Oh, I got to go. . . .'

" 'No,' I say, 'That looks accidental. What did you do actively?'

" 'Well, I won this essay contest.'

"Then say, 'I wrote an essay that earned me this trip.'

"It takes me an hour of mind-boggling effort to draw this out of her. You have to go slowly and be loving or you injure their self-esteem. She had a writing skill, but she said, 'I've never done anything.' I made her retell the story of that success. She told me everyone had to write the essay. I told her, 'When you decide to win, you write with your whole self.' It seems she started thinking of winning in the eleventh grade and saved all the winning essays, year after year. It began then. She said she didn't tell anyone. I asked her what her essay had been about, and she said it was on citizenship."

Katherine: "No. No, what was your subject?"

Woman: "I wrote about my grandmother who came from Italy. I saw everything through her eyes."

Katherine: "By doing that you knocked out seven-eighths of the competition. How many people have grandmothers who came from Italy? Did you just write it and hand it in?"

Woman: "No, I showed it to my favorite English teacher."

Katherine by now was on her feet pacing up and down the room. "What that woman was telling me was that she did research, she was creative and had a competitive judgment. Then she told me she had written the essay, submitted it for criticism (not all of which she agreed with or took) and that she had rewritten it after editing it. She was making crucial judgments that had risk in them. She was leaving in or taking out the right things. So she has competitive skills and creative judgment. One can't just say, 'Oh, I wrote . . .' She had a cluster of skills I call a success pattern. If you think of your whole life, you see this pattern through your life, the pattern that makes us each different. Given a chance we recreate the world so we can apply our success pattern."

We had now migrated out of the living room and into the kitchen for a cup of tea. Over the kitchen table, the dialogue continued. "A woman must do a lot of marketing research and ask herself, 'What can I do?' 'Where can I do it?' 'Where would my skills be most advantageous?' Even someone who is working has to keep this in mind because things change, old businesses die and new ones spring up. Then you have to ask, 'What is it worth in terms of money?' The most natural choices after being a homemaker are: decorating, fund raising, publicity, teaching, nursing, social worker. I steer women away from these because there are a million other women in them. I research out careers that are not in the traditional area."

Katherine gave as an example a writer, of whom there are many and therefore a great deal of competition for the few writer's jobs. If she has such a client, "I see if she's comfortable with science. Then she becomes a science writer for which there is a definite demand. I get a lot of librarians. One was bored. We talked. I found out she had a pilot's license. She could get a job at Boeing's research library. Even without the license she could go to night school and learn aeronautical terms." She tries to look for the unusual pathways. She also tries to discourage women from trying for the glamour fields that are overcrowded, underpaid and have little future, like TV, publishing, broadcasting, show biz, airlines. There is little potential for growth in these fields.

Another thing she sees often is pride, which she considers very bad for women. "They want to see themselves in an attractive setting. A woman will go to a beauty parlor to be a receptionist. The surroundings are pretty. I see her as a dispatcher. She could get much more money dispatching trucks. Women tend to find acceptable environments only where they can be found sexually desirable.

"Before going into career counseling, I once got a job as a sound man for NBC-radio. A fellow on the show would scream, 'All right, Jack, let's break down the door,' and I would crunch a flimsy wooden box which I was holding under my armpit. Cuuuuuuuuruunnch! You have to get in wherever you can get in. Get your foot in the door. In six months I went from sound man to radio producer. Get in at whatever level you can and learn, learn, learn. Look at Mrs. Jones who just got her law degree. She is Mrs. Lawyer Jones. If the first job she can get is a receptionist in an ad agency, she is now Mrs. Receptionist Jones. She has lost status. Women tend to look at their situations as static. Men look at their situations as developmental."

Her very astute point is that you have to begin somewhere and you don't have to stay there. After you have begun, then you think of ways to develop, move on or up. She gives another example of the difference in perspective between men and women. A boy in the mail room sees himself as on his way up to being a vice-president. Most girls in the mail room see themselves as being cheated, exploited and betrayed. Women don't tend to see their work as constantly evolving. The girl in the mail room could say, "Now look. I'm researching, learning the grass-roots operation of a large company from the bottom up."

We look at another aspect of what she means. Take typing. She says, "Typing in this society is almost a necessity for a man or woman. It's a basic tool. There is no reason to feel that if you know how to type, you will get stuck forever in a job as typist. You are in charge of that tool. It doesn't define you. You can deny you know how to type if you're applying for a management job, or say you do just rough copy."

Katherine also advises women on how to interview and write their résumés. "Some women come to me and we rehearse a business interview. If there's a space of four to five years that's blank, she'd better have a damn good answer ready." But it can be referred to as a "time of exploration, examination and experimentation." In her résumé examples she always uses active verbs like "I designed, I instituted, I developed," and she warns women during interviews not to sit there and have a gossipy and pleasant conversation with an employer but to try to convince him she can help him solve his problems.

I ask her whether she thinks middle-aged women are not starting a bit late to be able to develop a career. Can they reach their goals? Is there time? She admits there is less time. "But usually women don't know how to play the game. True, our society is youth oriented, but there are things the older person can win on." We think of what these assets are. First, the older woman is more stable, she's not going to run off and get married. She is more reliable, her absentee rate is lower. She has a sense of loyalty, and she's not looking for someone to appear and "take me away from all this." Katherine points out that many people have two or three careers in a lifetime. "A middle-aged woman ought to think of this job in middle life as a second career, and it won't seem so late to be starting."

On the way home on the train, I pull out a sheet of paper and think of my work as a housewife and how varied a job one can make of it. I jot down all the things that I have done year after year until I have become pretty expert at some of them, and it is quite a long list of accomplishments. I try to visualize my crummy chores in commercial terms. I know I've left things out, but my list looks like this:

> buyer
> teacher
> politician
> seamstress
> fashion designer

receptionist
hostess
secretary
electrician
plumber
bookkeeper
mediator
budget director
nurse
psychotherapist
social worker
gardener
cleaning woman (sanitary engineer)
cook
bartender
waitress
chauffeur
laundress
interior decorator
auto mechanic
social director
consultant
office manager
convention organizer
hotel manager
camp director
baker
typist
photographer
house painter
wallpaper hanger
flower arranger
dog breeder
rug cleaner
carpenter

I am very impressed, indeed. Of course I might need a bit of training to actually operate in any of these fields, but I have had the experience, I know what is needed, what to expect, how to do many things, and if I decided to change careers someday, learning more would be relatively simple for me compared with someone starting out with no experience at all. I realize, for example, if I have sewed and handled patterns all my life I could go into as unexpected a field as sheet-metal work.

Conferring with a career counselor who can help ferret out your skills and suggest where you can use them is one way to go about breaking out. There are other things that can be done, and they are not mutually exclusive. They can all be tried; they all tell something different; they all help make us understand ourselves, and particularly our buried selves, that much more.

A Weekend of Transition Planning

There are an incredible number of ways to find out who you are these days. It has even become fashionable to keep asking. One no longer contemplates one's navel to reach a state of nirvana. One keeps asking 'Who am I?' and goes to one or more of an astounding variety of group sessions for days of intensive psychic exercise and discussion, or of silence, or touching, or meditating or charting one's life on paper. Besides career counselors to give advice about skills and available jobs, there are the more esoteric routes to self-analysis. Among the possibilities are Transition Planning groups to provoke a self-examination; assertiveness training to give you the nerve to say how you feel; family-life seminars; meditation retreats; dream therapy that probes what is surfacing in the subconscious; and a technique using what is called a Lilly tank, where you stay isolated in about a foot of water, in a sound-proof, light-proof tank. With all the usual distractions missing, you are supposed to be able to get closer to your real self. There is yoga which is designed to help you control your body and mind to the point where you can understand yourself better, and T'ai Chi, a form of relaxation and meditation in movement. There are encounter and Gestalt groups to help unravel your fears, get rid of your resentments and get you back in control of your life. If you are serious, work hard and don't use these various encounter and meditation groups as a crutch and a substitute for logical thinking, you may find one or more of them extremely helpful.

A seventy-six-year-old friend of mine, who has just received her doctorate in sociology and still hopes to write a novel, told me about a Transition Planning Workshop. She had tried it and suggested that I would understand my middle years much better if I took it too. The workshop takes place on weekends and is run by the Center for the Study of Adult Development, affiliated with the Department of Psychiatry of the University of Pennsylvania. Dr. Peter L. Brill, a psychiatrist, is the director. The cost is two hundred dollars. The purpose: to find out where you are and how you got there, where you are going and how to get there.

We all arrive one sunny Friday evening at the former Eleanor Widener Dixon estate in Chestnut Hill, a suburb of Philadelphia. Obviously the pain of examining ourselves, perched on the brink of one of life's transitions, suffering as we try to develop from one stage of life to the next, will be done in splendor. The old mansion, supposedly full of secret passages, is secluded behind walls and gates, diagonally across from the mayor's house. It becomes home, laboratory, inner sanctum for the sixteen of us who arrive, clutching everything from tennis racquets to the wild hope of a miracle in our lives.

We have come together for two days and two evenings during which we will try to pick up what the business of being an adult is all about. The first evening we begin to launch ourselves on a series of exercises that will lead to the point where we can understand our problems and our goals and plan for them. We sit in the dark, wood-paneled living room with family portraits looking down at us askance and Peter says, "The single greatest factor that makes change difficult is the need to see yourself as you've always seen yourself. People cling to their identities," he says, "even at the cost of unhappiness. They are afraid they will be someone else. They feel, 'I want to be the same, even if I am miserable.' " He tells us that in the workshop we must give up, temporarily, "some of how you see yourself." If we give up a little piece, we will be opening up the door to change. Not everyone can do this, and not everyone will change by the time the weekend is over.

In one of the exercises, that evening we are assigned a partner and, silly as it seems, we take turns leading each other around the house blindfolded, up and down stairs. The blindfolded person learns to place complete trust in the other person. This will help us share our lives with these strangers and open ourselves to change.

Another time we divide into groups of four and, without speaking a word, we write down what we think of each of the other people, what we imagine their childhood was like what activities and hobbies they enjoy, whether they are indoor or outdoor people, have few or many children, are interested in sex and what their relationships with others are like. Peter tells us that we have all experienced pain and joy which we project, and even without talking, people can know a lot about us. Usually the descriptions run about 80 percent accurate. The point is that if you hide things and pretend they don't exist, you're not kidding anyone. It shows in your face, the way you dress, look and even walk.

One interesting exercise we try the next day is to construct a life chart. On a large piece of paper which we place on the floor we draw a horizontal axis with our age in increments of five or ten, or any number of years. We then draw the other axis, a vertical line which we mark minus ten at the point where the lines meet, zero at the mid point, and plus ten at the top. We have three fat colored pens: red for the measure of our satisfaction or happiness; green for our affiliations or friendships with others; and black for achievement. We pinpoint our lives on this graph marking a dot at whatever age we felt we were achieving something either positive or negative. We do this on the same graph for our other two values. If, for example, as happened to me once, I was achieving something in a job, but had few friends and was lonely, yet managed to be fairly happy, my job line (black) at this point (age twenty-five) was way up in plus eight, my affiliation line (green) was way down in minus four and my satisfaction or happiness line (red) was around plus four. You start the graph at the age of your earliest memories.

When you connect the dots and hold this chart up, it can look like the Swiss Alps or the plains of Kansas, but whichever it is, some interesting patterns that weren't obvious before become quite dramatic. Some people's graphs are continual ups and downs as they go from positive to troubled times. Sometimes through all the chaos, either personal or professional, the other two lines stay way up. Sometimes everything drops like the Dow Jones average on a bad day. A careful analysis of your chart will give you a lot of information.

We now are assigned permanent (for the weekend) triads (groups of three) and choose a spot where we will meet one another during the weekend to discuss our various exercises, say honestly what we think and presumably open up enough to accept change. We will share our feelings and get the others' reactions to our lives.

We huddle on the floral-slipcovered couch in the library filled with leather-bound books. The woman on my left begins, "All my life I did what I thought I *ought* to do. Now I want to do what I *want* to do. I did things because they were expected of me. Years ago I worked, but I don't want to return to doing the same thing. Now I have more time because my children are in school. I want to focus my life, find my identity." She is looking for a new career.

The woman on my right says she thought she was supposed to get married and have kids. "Even though I didn't enjoy kids, I was not supposed to work. My husband would have felt a failure if his wife had to work." When her three children went to school she was worried and plagued by what to do with her life. She finally did go to work but has now stopped. She feels her life is fragmented among her many interests. She feels disorganized and doesn't know what she wants to do. "There is something wrong with my life. I don't know what I like. I don't know where I'm going. I have time for little. As I get older it takes longer to do less and less. I feel overwhelmed. I feel harassed and inadequate. If I'm asked to do something, I never say no, even though others do those things better. I haven't had time to think before. I now have time to examine my life style. I never thought about my feelings before. When do I think about ME? If not now, when?

"The aging process is happening inside of me. There are aches and pains. In my last year of work I could not believe my mind was so dulled. I can't remember things. My mind is blurred. I'm getting senile at fifty-three.

"For me family and home is sometimes more important than a job. Women live more in two worlds. For the man, it is only one world. His career takes precedence. I was submissive. I always did what I was told, like a good wife. Women's lib made me hostile. I felt angry with society because I was forced into this role. And I became angry with my husband. I was angry all the time. I didn't understand my own feelings. He was reading the paper. I was on my feet all day, talking all day. His work is sedentary. My work was more difficult and tiring, yet I was the one setting the table and he was just sitting there waiting to be served. We're still ambivalent about women's roles."

That afternoon we all meet in the large living room again. Peter describes the thirty-year-old female, and as he points out different things, I see that she is the epitome of the woman who is going to have to break out at forty or go berserk. She has lost her identity, first of all. What more serious and abysmal state is there to find oneself in. She is attached to a stronger one, a man to take care of her, she feels like she will drown without a man, all her energy goes toward pleasing the man, she makes the family for him, she envies him for being on the periphery of the adult world, she is a child-mother. She is both a mother to child and husband and a child to her child and husband, and she has sadly turned off her ability to be an adult to her husband.

Saturday evening we get involved in what Peter calls the most valuable exercise of the workshop. He tells us that every major change in our lives on the deepest psychological level involves the issue of death in some way. The ending of one thing, the beginning of another. The exercise is to write the eulogy we each would like read at our funerals if we were to die one year from this day. We do this slowly, painfully, and take it up to a bedroom where we meet the two other members of our triad. Each of us in turn lies down on a bed and designates one of her triad to be a member of her family or a friend and read her eulogy.

It is my turn. I have written that I will be remembered for writing many good books beginning in the middle of my life, for my love for animals, my kindness and generosity to several organizations that I believe in, for having a hair dryer installed in the men's gym so my husband and other men can dry their hair in winter (here we all nearly crack up but the sadness of the occasion prevails), for working to get more equality for women, for being an interesting mother and wife. One of the women reads this over me as I lie on the bed with my eyes closed. Her voice sounds as though it is far away, almost in an echo chamber. I feel dead but able to hear her. I mourn my own passing. I feel affection and liking for this person I am, and sadness that she is gone. I begin to weep. I have left my body and am floating, hearing, watching. Both women stand quietly at the bedside. Voices are hushed. Heads bowed. Then she has finished. I wait a few minutes and open my eyes. Wipe the tears away. I feel proud of what I have accomplished and I awake with an urge to enjoy life and use it well, work harder for my goals. I have a strong feeling that, having symbolically died, I may never be quite as afraid of it again. Having to write what I wanted to be remembered for also made quite clear what my goals ought to be.

The next day is Sunday and we begin our meeting with a Force Analysis. We write what our present situation is concerning one of our problems, what the worst possible outcome might be, and what the ideal would be. Then we figure out the forces that restrain us from reaching the ideal, the forces that motivate us toward the ideal, what would make us change, and what keeps us from changing. There it is all spelled out. Now what are we going to do about it? We make a workable plan, a PERT (Program Evaluation Review Technique) with a time frame. We take another sheet of large paper, scoot down on the floor and write on the left side of the paper where we are now and the date. Then far across the paper on the right side we put our goal and what date we'd like to achieve it. For example, on the left side of the paper I mark April 17, and write "dominate my son," one of the remnants of the problems of my forties. To break this pattern, I go over to the right side of the paper and write down May 17. During the month I would like to forget about vitamins and let him make his own breakfast (begin April 18), forget about safety and let him take a trip by car himself on April 20. On April 23, when he is sure to be back, I will send him out to go look for a summer job so he can earn his own money and be out of the house every day, and so on during the month. By May 17 presumably, if I follow all my self-imposed steps, the tie will be completely broken. Others who want to lose weight, or are looking for a career, plot their goals—"lose three pounds the first week," or "go visit a college to see what programs are available in continuing education."

Last we construct a Social Systems Map of where the resistance to our changing will come from: friends, family, work, and community. We put us in the middle of a circle, and our closest friends in quadrants near us. Others are farther away. Then we decide who will support us. We move people away who can't encourage us and move others closer who can. Someone who is out in the peripheral zone may suddenly loom important in helping us find a new career, and that person we will contact and plan to see often. Some are shocked to see their maps so empty, the space in some of the quadrants such as friends so void.

As we struggle to finish and keep everything in mind that we have unearthed in this crash course in self-examination, Peter says we must prepare for the exit process. He says our sense of understanding has deepened, we have opened up, trusted others, there has been an outpouring and directness. But while all this was happening to us behind the walls and gates, the rest of the world has remained the same, especially our friends and families. We will have to explain slowly to them how we wish to change and how we plan to do it.

We say goodbye to strangers with whom we shared everything during the weekend, people we may never see again, though Peter has arranged a follow-up evening, and we drive in different directions, out of the gate, away from the old house that may or may not have secret passages, but has heard more secrets than most people care to tell.

For many, life doesn't seem so hopeless any more. We don't feel so trapped by the problems of our age and circumstances; it seems easier, now that we have been led down the pathway once with help, to examine future problems and plot how to change them. It is not easy to do alone, but any reader can try some of the exercises and revise goals, work up plans for change with concrete steps of what must be done by certain dates. One learns that no matter how boring or difficult, it is not necessary to allow life to lead us around. We can be in command, we can shape our own lives.

Several days later Peter and I are talking on the phone about the reasons for the exercises we did, and he says, "The weekend tried to give you a model of where you are now and a sense of how to perceive your future. We tried to free you emotionally from the things that were sticking you in one place. The leaders of the seminar were meant to convey a sense of urgency to implement your plans and to make the atmosphere right for you to create your own motivations."

I asked Peter for more information about the life chart we all did, plotting our achievements, our friends, our happiness. He replied, "The life-chart exercise is a framework for people to hang all their experience on. Usually when you look at your life, it's like lighting up one dark corner in a dark room, and then another. It is a disjointed experience. The chart lights it up all at the same time. It's a framework, and it's a catharsis. You go back in your life and talk about things you may never have talked to people about before," he says. "People can also see how experience has impacted on other parts of their lives. You see the connection between one part of your life and another. And lastly, you understand how satisfaction or happiness relates to the rest of your life." Looking at my chart, I could visualize my green, red and black lines and see what I was doing when I was happy.

I wanted another of Peter's interpretations. "What," I asked him, "did that eulogy really mean?"

He said, "If you can build tension over the weekend, and then crack it with an emotional release, you can find a clear spot, you can see past yourself clearly. Death is an avoided issue in this society. It's a national phobia. The eulogy is a chance to address death, face it. If you live in fear of death, you must be afraid of living much of the time for fear you'll die.

Death is uncontrollable," he says, "and as people face death, they have their uncertainty about it erased. Also, it gives you a clear view of what you value in yourself and your life which can be incorporated in your ego. It gives you good feelings about yourself. You deal with death. You let go of things about the past you were afraid to let die. It's also a way for groups to get close to someone they are not sexually involved with. It shows you what this closeness can feel like."

I was interested in a remark Peter had made once about transitions. He said that whichever way you make a transition in your life, however you approach this change, you will always do it the same way. "It's as characteristic as a fingerprint." But a person learns to shorten time spaces involved in the transition and learns to anticipate, so the transitions are not so destructive. He gave me an example using himself. "I know," he explained, "it takes me six months to get my feet on the ground when I go to a new job. I expect this. So if things don't get moving in a new place at first, I'm not upset, since I know it usually takes those six months."

In other words, if we look at how we accept change and what happens to us during periods of transition in our lives, we can shorten the effect and avoid any really disquieting period by simply knowing this is the way we are, and our inner feelings during this period of metamorphosis will always be that way. It would seem to me that, knowing we behave in a certain way at such times, we could do more than merely shorten the effects of transition. We could eventually do away with them completely.

For me the weekend was helpful in several ways. I found my life chart very revealing. It told me as I examined the red, black and green lines that happiness for me came mainly from accomplishment, rather than from friends. Though lovers made me happy, it was brief compared to the joy of accomplishment and success. I think this exercise is one of the two everyone ought to try. It's a fascinating way to get to know yourself. A second excellent exercise is to set a goal for sometime in the future, a month from now, or six months, and figure out, again on a graph with time intervals, what you will do each day or week in order to reach this goal. It's the kind of exercise that enables you to do things that you've been mulling over for years. It moves you forward, at a time when you have to move.

There are several books you can buy that will lead you along in life-work plans. They come replete with exercises that help you use words to describe yourself, the things that make you happy, the things you would like to do fifteen years from now. They help you evaluate yourself. However, although it is fun to play around with lists and exercises, the program, to be most useful, should have a professional leader to point the way. You will do best with a guide through this route of discovery.

Of the many kinds of courses that are offered to awaken the self, not all are concerned with work goals. One woman I know was able to restructure her marriage at this mid-life point by taking an assertiveness class. She had always been terribly dominated by her husband, almost to the point where she lived in terror of displeasing him. When she was forty-five, she heard about the class in her hometown and took it. It resulted in her finding the inner strength and learning the techniques to talk to her husband, tell him what she needed. Now they understand each other better, and they like each other more.

At a Buddhist Retreat with Maggie

One chilly spring morning I knock on the door of a house in the suburbs. I have come to talk to Maggie. She has reached the age of fifty and is looking for new sources of strength in her life. She is also thinking of going back to acting, something she hasn't done in a long time. Maggie went to college for two years, then to acting school. She says she knew she wanted to be an actress from the time she was eleven. She found a reference to it looking back over her diary. As a child, she experienced great loneliness, felt like an outsider, had been misunderstood, particularly, she thought, by her mother. She may have become an actress because, "as people, we feel that living life with our feelings is dangerous, so we choose an occupation where we can discharge our feelings vicariously. You have to discharge your feelings or you go crazy. As an actress you can get through a whole range of emotion, and it's not really happening in your real life.''

Maggie was one of seven children. Her father believed women should do things and support themselves. They could be teachers or in the arts. It never occurred to him that they could be in business. "My father was my major influence. During my formative years my mother was a martyr, having all those children. She was my only role model. But in no way did I want to be like her. She would say things like, 'A man's job is to make it in the world, and they can't do it unless you help them.'

"I had a very successful career for twelve years. In Hollywood I was typecast as a young mother—the tougher kind, not the sensitive vulnerable type. But the high point in my career was when I had my own television series. I did it for two years. It paid for my therapy. Now that I'm fifty I can think back over the decades. I can see that therapy gave me the tools for getting involved in the growth process. That's what my life is about. I feel I've grown a lot.''

Part of the process of growing came about at a Buddhist retreat, one of several kinds of retreats that Maggie has tried. "Growing for me," she said, "implies there's a place to get to. I did a Buddhist meditation retreat for two weeks. There were lots of kids in their twenties. I began to see the difference between them and me. All the release of energy is being used by them to get something, acquire something. They're on that track. But I realized my gears are shifting. I've already become someone. Now I'm in the process of peeling away the layers of all these acquired things I thought were so important, and it's not sad because it's part of the process of living. It's inappropriate for me to want to become something more. I don't mean that I just stay in bed all day. You don't stay in bed. You still do things, but getting ahead is not the motivation any more. There is nothing I want in terms of power, of being approved of. It was a strong desire for approval that made me do everything I did.

"There was really no way of getting all the approval I wanted. It was an insatiable drive. I know *approval* is not where it's at. Now it's just learning to take things as they come. *Acceptance* is where it's at. If I have four or five accepting moments a day, it's great. The rest of the time I'm getting angry. Accepting is what brings me the satisfaction I thought approval would bring. Approval is fleeting; then you have to win it again. If I could accept every hour of the twenty-four-hour day, I'd be a very happy lady. It's something to strive for. But you can't strive for it because once you are struggling, you're not accepting. You have to try to get more and more of that in your life.

"I used to think, if I could become an actress and become successful, then I'll be whole. Or, if I become a wife and mother, then I will be whole. Or if I get close to God. Then I'll be whole. But whatever is going to happen will happen regardless of what I do about it. I'm not being fatalistic. You have to have goals and you have to do things and be accepting when things do happen. I might go back to acting just because it's interesting. I don't need it in order to be somebody. I'm sure this has to do with my age. I see the pattern of my life. Successes and failures contributed to NOW. And it's been an interesting and rewarding life.

"I didn't marry until my thirties because I didn't want to be the kind of footstool my mother was. You are going to get a trip laid on you as a kid and you are going to have to battle and keep trying to open doors. My own kids will have to suffer and find their way through.

"I realized in my thirties I have a terrific head for business. Socially I found I enjoyed talking about business with our friends. One of the reasons I wasn't on a power trip was not because I was virtuous, it was because I was afraid. Had I been trained differently the way women's lib says, 'Goddamn it, train women from the beginning to go for power,' I'd have had that trip. At the age of eleven it never was an option open to me. Later I discovered I'm really goddamned smart."

Her decision to get married was clearly a decision not to be an actress anymore. In her late twenties she was in Paris, knowing few people. She'd sit and read books wishing she was out having fun the way everyone else was. "Suddenly I just threw my book across the room and, God, I realized I didn't have to be an actress anymore in order to be worthwile, to be loved, to count, to matter. But I'd have to find something else so I could be loved.

"I knew everything good and bad about being single. I could support myself and be independent. That day I decided I was going to look for a mate and have some kids. During my thirties and early forties I saw the burden I was putting on, being a wife and mother. That was what was going to make my life count. Women's lib started and people wailed, 'How could you give up your career to be wife and mother.' I could shut them up because I really made the decision. And the interacting with my two children and watching their growth, just living with them and watching me in my supermother role turned out to be as exciting and as valuable and as interesting as those years being an actress. I learned more about myself interacting with them. Sometimes I hated it, but it was as important as my teenage years, or the years I spent going after my career. My career was glamorous. I loved it, I loved signing autographs, but it was also full of misery, constant rejection, constant hustling and empty times between jobs. As a mother you have the duties of nurturing a child. I bought that as a profession.

"In my twenties I had acquired some valuable skills I could use all my life. At first I thought acting was a third-rate profession. If you were really first-rate you'd write. Later I saw it was truly an art. Theater was my whole education.

"Although I never missed acting, I knew I had to do something to keep from making my children my whole life. So when they were younger, I went back to Stella Adler and took lessons from her. When my children were four and five, a friend who is on a college board called me and said they were looking for a Ph.D. who could direct and teach students. My friend had told them she couldn't give them the Ph.D. but she knew someone who has been an actress for fifteen years and can teach.

"I went into teaching drama part-time. I see it as an extension of my growth in dealing with my children. I decided to teach for two reasons. One, I thought I'd be a better mother if I were not hanging around getting annoyed. I wouldn't zero in on them all the time. And two, I didn't want to be like my mother who just lay around all day like an invalid and felt lousy. My father treated her as though she was totally inept and had to be taken care of. I wanted to be a better role model for my daughter. It was a stunning experience. Stuff I'd once done by intuition, I now had to put together and explain. It made me a 100 percent better actress. Now I'm not as uptight. I've been teaching for seven years.

"Recently I was in a play at the college. I tried acting after fifteen years. It was safe. No one would see me. I was rusty, but pleased. I was relaxed and could get into the character. The process interested me. Yes. I'm good at it. It's good to have something you can do that well."

"Becoming fifty has had a gigantic effect on me. You're supposed to become decrepit and end up on a slag heap. But I see myself preparing for the next phase. I've had some pictures taken, and I'm going to see my agent again. I have as much energy. It's uncertainty that wears you out. One must keep moving in some direction.

"What's going to make the next decade fun? For most of my life that I can remember I thought the things of value were the very high moments and the very tragic, despairing low moments. I thought, I'm really living, and all the stuff in between the poles I labeled nothing. Well, you spend most of your life there, between the poles. The big lows are not worth it, and I'm willing to sacrifice the big highs. The middle I've found is terribly rich. I want to explore that middle ground. Of course I experienced the middle ground, but I was unconscious of it. My current thing is a rich and rewarding place. I've discovered there's a new land to explore."

I had the strong feeling that Maggie had gotten very close to what was important to her. She seemed to understand why she had done things in her life, which is more than most people stop to analyze. The retreat must certainly have helped. I wanted to know more about what you did there. Two weeks is a long time. I doubted if total enlightenment could come from any one course or one experience, and I knew Maggie must have thought about her life at many points—certainly she did when she decided to give up acting. But I asked her to describe what a day at a Buddhist retreat is like.

5 A.M. . . . Rise.
5:30–8 . . . Sitting and walking meditation.

("First I was bored and wished I were home. Then I said, 'Okay you're not home, so how do you get the gold stars, be the best meditator? I was afraid I was doing it wrong. After a few days you realize there is no right or wrong. You watch your breathing, your mind slows down. When I asked myself, 'Where am I? What is it I feel?' the boredom left.")

8:00 . . . Breakfast of nuts and fruits.
9:15 . . . Meditate until 1 P.M. Sometimes a lecture, yoga or movement.
1:00 . . . Lunch and time off until 3.
3–6 . . . Meditate.
6:00 . . . Light supper.
7:30–10 . . . Meditation.
10–11 . . . Dancing but not with partners.

"In the course of a day I saw those violent swings—highs, then lows, then anger. We were awake eighteen hours a day. We meditated twelve hours a day. I didn't talk to anyone for ten days. I had the luxury of not having to go through my social act.

"You find you get to know people by observing them, by their vibrations without talking to them. At first I thought the people were creepy, then I saw their other qualities. In the end I thought everyone was terrific. For the last four days we talked. When we did finally talk, shared our feelings, there was little chitchat. We shared our reactions to meditation. We talked about where we're really at. At first I thought I didn't want to talk, I was afraid I'd go back into that claptrap nonsense. But you don't take anything personally. Some people were angry. You know it's nothing you did.

"The result of meditation was that I began to value the middle ground, those middle stages. My emotional middle ground. In group things you realize you're not unique. You're more conscious. At home in sixteen hours of being awake, I daydream, watch TV, do puzzles, read pulp stuff. I'm only conscious for four hours a day. At the retreat I had no choice but to be conscious. I know it's a lie for middle-aged people to say, 'I'm old, I have no energy.' I experienced more energy than I ever had before. Emotional and mental conflict is wearing. Lots of people cop out of living. They say, 'I can't do that because of the kids,' or 'I can't do that because I'm too old.' Those are meaningless excuses you give yourself not to do things you're afraid to do. I don't know what my fifties will be like. Part of me is scared shitless. Part looks forward to it. But each decade has been better than the previous one. One's structure has to change.''

The climate of a retreat, a transition workshop, a visit with a career counselor, any of the many assertiveness or relaxing courses, enable a woman to think about herself and her life in new ways. These sessions guide her, help her see there are others with the same problems, help her locate the source of her problems and motivate her to move outward to new things. With or without these aids, we can certainly do a lot of thinking and looking back.

Finding out what skills you have by adding up all the things you've ever done, finding out what you are interested in by thinking back to when you were single, finding out how to plan your life and set up goals and reach them, finding out how to know yourself and what you are will instill confidence and help you to break out into a new stage of life. But you have to begin, somewhere, even if it is just asking other women or a librarian or an employment agency for advice. You need to be a little pushy.

7

Back to School

Going back to school in mid-life is another way of finding out who you are, what you want to do and what talents and skills you can develop that are up-to-date and marketable. A lot of women with just this in mind are invading the college classrooms in preparation for storming the business and professional world. Most who return to school are scared, have little confidence in themselves and doubt that they will be able to keep up with the younger students. They are afraid they have forgotten how to study and will be unable to memorize all the facts and prepare for exams. Actually their fears almost always turn out to have no basis in reality. As Dr. George E. Vaillant points out in his *Adaptation to Life*, "There is a real possibility that the brain continues to change in structure and complexity until age forty to fifty. Longitudinal studies . . . suggest that human intelligence is stable or even increases until age forty to fifty."

It is heartening to think that our brains continue to mature until perhaps age fifty, and it certainly should encourage a lot of women who stopped using their minds after having finished school to keep at whatever they find interesting. The more they use these brains, the more they will continue to grow. Jogging the mind as well as the body seems to be essential for well-being.

Continuing Education and Matriculation

There are two ways of continuing one's education: either working for a degree or a skill. In the early 1960s, a middle-aged woman could not consider going back to school to expand her education. It wasn't possible. The programs didn't exist, and schools did not have space for older women in their classrooms. There were only twenty continuing-education courses in 1963. The number now is said to include over two thousand courses which are offered in over six hundred schools throughout the country. There has been a phenomenal rise in educational possibilities for the woman in mid-life.

Colleges and universities like Harvard, for example, which opened a Continuing Education Center and offered its first full-year curriculum in 1977–78, do not grant degrees for these special courses. One can study about wine, how to write children's books, or how to write adult plays. They offer practical information on growing and propagating house plants, small-business management, stock market strategies, fundamentals of fund raising, creative problem-solving in business and women in management. Such courses which provide practical knowledge are designed to help the woman either find a new career or advance in the one she has. They can also help her simply find a hobby.

There is, however, another large group of women who want further education. Many are high school graduates who married young and now, twenty years later, need training to get jobs; others are college women who want to complete their college educations which they interrupted to get married and support their student husbands or have a family; and there are college graduates who are looking for a more pragmatic skill after majoring in such economically useless subjects as English litera-

ture or art history. For all these women, the immediate goal is
matriculation for a degree at a college or university where they
must compete for acceptance with all the young people. They
must take the required courses and work to graduate just as the
other students do.

Going back to school for a degree has become a driving ambition for many divorced women of middle age. Law school in
particular seems to attract them as a sure way of guaranteeing a
future with money, power and security. As many as 33,000 of
the country's 118,000 law students (or 30 percent) are women,
and a growing proportion are middle-aged. In 1965, only 5 percent of the total were female. The same sort of increase applies
to women in medicine with smaller but marked gains in veteri-
nary medicine, dentistry and engineering. It is estimated that
the number of adult women in higher education will rise by 60
percent in the next five years.

The influx of women students who are old enough to be, and
usually are, mothers is not at all a problem for colleges that are
used to dealing only with the young. Because of declining birth
rates for the past two decades, there are fewer high school graduates and an increasing amount of space in classrooms for older
students. In fact, although it is a recent phenomenon of the
seventies, society has quickly accepted the idea of having students of all ages on campus, and they are by no means ostra-
cized or made to feel unwanted.

There is so much understanding of the needs of middle-aged
women, in fact, that over three hundred colleges and universities have decided to accept experiential learning (skills learned
outside the classroom, perhaps at home) for course credit. A
source book for these schools appears in the Appendix.

Pressures of Returning to School

Much of whatever tension there is for the woman who hasn't
done homework for fifteen or twenty years or longer comes
from the woman herself and her uncertainty about being in a
scholarly environment. The motives that finally impel her to

return to school are a complex layering of feelings and frustrations that have added up over a long period. Sometimes a woman goes back partly because she resents her husband's success, money and prestige, and is jealous of his belonging to a world of which she knows nothing. Having her own money and a patina of importance may save her withering self-esteem. But there is no one thing that makes her act. It is a mélange of such factors as pride, money, boredom, opportunity, peer pressure, loneliness and self-expression.

Talking to women who have mulled the whole option over and over and then gone back to school makes it very clear that it is no simple decision, either to make or to put into action. Aside from the fact that normal routines collapse in a shambles, the logistics of running a house—the who now does what—have to be reassigned and renegotiated. Sometimes it works and sometimes it doesn't.

Some women feel guilty about being away from their families and try to play both student and homemaker without neglecting either role. It is impossible, and they are certain to suffer from the conflict of being caught between needs pulling in opposite directions.

Some women are helped enormously by their husbands who share chores and give complete support and approval for what they are doing. Others contend with husbands who complain, not always so quietly, but in the end enjoy the extra income and take pride in the accomplishments of their wives. In some cases the woman's going to school breaks up the marriage. That husband cannot take the competition for his wife's time, her neglect and the change in their relationship. One woman who went back to school ended up getting her divorce along with her law degree. Another's marriage broke up as a result of her change in life style.

Though returning to school may exacerbate the problems in an already shaky marriage, it may also be the saving opportunity for a recently divorced woman who needs more income. One very thoughtful man I knew in Michigan realized his marriage was no longer on solid ground but waited for several years to get a divorce, while his wife went to graduate school and earned a degree in social work. Then, when they parted she was prepared to be self-sufficient. Such patience and foresight are rare. In most cases, the woman who hasn't worked during the entire marriage is simply set adrift. Though distraught and emotionally unbalanced at the time of divorce, she has to make immediate life and death decisions about her future.

The need to retrain the two to three million divorced and widowed women (now called displaced homemakers) at once for speedy entry into the work world has prompted a number of state legislatures to consider appropriations for this purpose, and several centers opened solely for this rescue operation have been started. Some examples are the Center for Displaced Homemakers in Oakland, California; Baltimore, Maryland; and Buffalo, New York. In addition to rebuilding their egos and investigating the job market, many of the women at these centers are able to return to school at local colleges either at no charge or at a reduced rate.

Aside from the confusion of roles in the mind of the woman who is married and goes back to school, the reaction of her children if they are still at home can be unsettling. Most children find a student mother quite interesting and don't resent her absence. At times it can even be a convenience. But occasionally a child will be angry at the fact that his or her personal chauffeur-cum-cook-cum-maid is missing in the afternoon, which means he or she will have to arrange alternate ways of getting to lessons and friends' houses.

The back-to-school woman is also affected by the reaction of her professors. Some can be snide, but many end up criticizing their younger, rather than their older students, saying they feel no sense of urgency, or don't push themselves to do better because they have all the time in the world. In contrast, their older students, like the veterans after the war, tend to spend more time on their studies and can compete equally. "You don't lose anything by being older," one teacher said.

Older women bring experience and wisdom to their courses and are thus often able to write better papers and do better work than their younger counterparts. The young students themselves are reported to be helpful and encouraging, generous with their tips on which cram books to buy to help pass tests, often teasing their older classmates to make them feel welcome. At first, though, it's likely to be a very hairy experience.

A woman I know who returned to graduate school to get a degree in sociology said, "I was so scared I couldn't open my mouth. Then I spoke to another student, a young Radcliffe graduate who was half my age. She said she was so scared, if the professor called on her she would throw up. Then I realized even though I was an older woman, I wasn't the only one who was shivering in my boots. The younger ones were too. So I could relax a bit more."

I discussed with six mid-life women their return to school and how it changed their lives: Pat, who went back to finish up the two years she needed for her degree; Annie, who decided to go to graduate school; Kathy, who went to law school and was ridden with guilt; Cora, a black woman who went out for a law degree and wrecked her marriage; and Cindy and Noreen, two very interesting mothers who went to medical school while their children went to grade school. They all had different experiences and observations because their backgrounds, internal pressures and the behavior of their husbands varied.

Back to School with Pat

After thinking about it for some time, Pat decided to return to a nearby university and finish her degree. She had left school to get married after two years, as so many women did, but always thought, in the back of her mind, that she would return. "I wanted a degree. I wanted the pure sense of having had that experience, a sense of completing something I'd started. I thought, too, that the degree was the basis for finding a job. It had become a plan. Do I want to go to school or get a job? The school came first."

She attended college part-time for a period of four and a half years. At the beginning she worried quite a bit about classwork. Writing the first papers was very difficult for her. But eventually when she got good grades, she developed confidence. It took her a half dozen papers, though, before the good grades started coming in. Homework became a family situation.

"My two daughters were in high school. All three of us studied together around the kitchen table. Sometimes we ended up studying the same stuff and quizzing one another for exams. I majored in history and was a help to one daughter. She could come and ask me about the significance of the Fourteenth Amendment, and I could tell her. In some ways going to school brought us all closer. She had exams and papers. She understood what I had to do."

Her husband learned something too. "He used to enjoy hearing about the lectures. We'd get excited about the Civil War." He was proud of her, though sometimes he wished she didn't take it so seriously. At times the demands seemed unreasonable, like when she had to read eight books, write seven papers and take four exams in one course. "And I did it all. I was superconscientious. I have friends, though, whose husbands gave them a hard time. They'd say, 'Why do you have to write your paper when I want to go see my mother this weekend?' Some men are frightened by their wives' going to school or getting a job. They resent the time not devoted to them."

Pat said that in college they had a club of women aged thirty to sixty who were all going back to school. They had their own lounge and counselor. "And we had each other. It was great support!"

The professors' reactions varied. There was a whole range of attitudes. Several made slightly derogatory, age-related comments like, "Well, isn't this going to be a little difficult for you?" The clear implication was that they should be home taking care of the kids. Others were very kind and some even enthusiastic.

But the whole experience of going back to school was very special for Pat. "It was one of life's experiences that meant the most to me. It was totally mine. I didn't have to discuss it with anyone, I didn't have to share it. It belonged to ME. I went up and had *my* classes, and *my* profs and *my* papers that I had to write. It sounds possessive. But I don't mean that. It was *my* work. I'd never had anything like that in my marriage. I had a sense of doing something well, a sense of achievement. I had proved I could do it.''

One of the things that was new for her in school was learning to handle competition. ''You compete against yourself and others. The older women cared intensely about their grades, and in general did very well. They felt handicapped because they were older, so they tried harder.''

Finally after those long but interesting years, it was time for graduation. Pat's elderly parents came for the celebration. ''It was a moving experience. I had a great sense of completion. It was a beautiful graduation. I loved having my whole family around. It was the icing on the cake. But I knew this wasn't really what it's all about. It was all those hours in the library. That's what it really was.''

Some months later Pat had a good job as assistant to the president of a small publishing firm. Her job-hunting experiences begin on page 165.

Graduate School for Annie, the English Major

I fell into conversation with Annie from the Midwest who was describing how she happened to go back to graduate school after years away from the classroom. She had majored in English as an undergraduate simply because she didn't know what else to major in. She married and had two children. I asked her what it was that precipitated her return to school.

''The first years of having kids were like a black cloud. My life lacked the kind of vitality I like to have. I fell into some part-time work. As the second baby grew bigger, I could see the pattern. As women got to be forty they were having trouble getting jobs, and they were losing jobs they had. I saw a woman kicked out when the company had to cut back. She had no credentials. This is what lay ahead of me; to go from one frittering job to another, being able to be kicked out at a moment's notice.

''In contrast, I saw my husband's life—security, importance. I felt envious of him. Because he had a career he traveled, had time away from home, was applauded by the outside world. He had variety in his life. In the morning he could get up, get dressed and know he was going out. He could look forward to what he was going to do that day, versus me taking the kids to the park and sitting on a bench till noon, going out of my skull.

"My husband seemed oblivious of how deeply I felt about certain aspects of life, the tremendous restriction on my days, how dull it was. I often felt discontented. He had accepted the fact that I'd married and had kids. When I became discontent, he didn't know what to do. I didn't fit into any system he knew. There were periods when I felt life was passing me by. I also didn't know what to do. There were no role models, women to emulate.

"I loved my children. All life is a mish-mash of ambivalence. I was ambivalent about my way of life. There were forces pulling me both ways. I loved kids, was proud of my husband, and I had a good, comfortable life. On the other hand, I wanted to be somebody, somebody myself, not just someone's mommy and wife. Some women are content to remain home. They feel inadequate and rationalize their staying home. They say they don't want anything else because they are afraid they can't do anything else. Others chafe and feel 'This is not for me. I want something in the outside world.' "

Annie said she was impressed with the constant clamorous demand that family, kids and husband made on a wife compared with the little she gets back. "My mother led a wretched, anxious, pinched life. But for me kids were not sufficient. This was festering in me a long time." In the fifties women were staying home and were happy to be driving their kids around in station wagons. They at least put on a front that they liked it. Now when I talk to them, I find that, despite the rewards of family, they also felt it a restrictive and narrow life. They would have preferred marriage in the seventies.

Lots of things were gathering force for Annie over a period of five or six years. She kept worrying. "It didn't seem that much of a sweat to go to grad school to get some of the goodies. I had a part-time job that was difficult. My boss was difficult. My kids were young. Life was leading nowhere and was not interesting.

I was marginal—whether I got hired and dropped, or hired and stayed in one dreary job forever. It could go either way.''

About this time several things happened which, for Annie, seemed to point the direction she should take. She was on the board of a volunteer group. One day there was a big discussion that occupied a whole hour on which kind of flower, a carnation or a rose, to send to a sick board member. She fumed. ''How trivial. I made up my mind to move on to something interesting. I decided this was not the way I was going to spend my life.''

Another day she found herself away on a winter vacation, skiing. ''They had piped in music (God forbid) on the slopes. As I came down the hill, close to the lodge, I could hear the Eberle Brothers singing, 'I'm dreaming my life away . . . all I have to do is dream, dream, dream . . .' I realized that was what I was doing. At moments like that one's life crystallizes. I went home, made twenty phone calls and sent for college catalogues. That became my theme song.''

Annie nad to gather courage to go to graduate school. ''I took a course at a nearby university just to try it again and was the world's most eager student. I felt I was proving myself. There were forty or fifty kids. I was acutely aware of how young they were and how quick in such things as note taking. But I worked so hard I came out on top, and that gave me the confidence to go back and get a graduate degree.''

She applied, was accepted and found herself in class again. At first she was the proper matron and dressed as though she were going to the city. She had an elaborate hairstyle, wore elegant shoes and suits. But little by little she started to wear slacks and turtlenecks, then moccasins. Her vocabulary changed. She started using contemporary slang. Annie was slowly being transformed from housewife to student.

''I went full-time the first year with a mixture of feelings. On the one hand I felt happy and eager and reborn as though I were twenty-two like all the other students. I was as caught up as everyone else. The professor went through the class one day looking and talking to the students, and when he came to me he paused and asked if I were a faculty wife. I was shocked. Wife.

Old lady? He saw the difference between me and the others. It was that visible. I thought I looked as young as I felt, and when they spoke of me as an 'older woman' I was stunned. But it was such fun to be back with students, drinking cokes and coffee in the afternoon, it seemed as though youth had been handed back to me on a platter.''

At the same time Annie worried a great deal about how she would do. She actually did well, got A's and a roaring case of the flu. She spent a week in bed. ''It was the most psychosomatic disease I ever had. I almost destroyed myself to do well that first semester. I never had that same zeal again and I wasn't ready for the second semester.''

During this crucial first year she continued to run a household with two children aged nine and fourteen. ''I felt guilty if the kids got sick. Once I had an exam scheduled and a child had 101-degree fever. I didn't go. On certain days I couldn't get home for dinner. I asked my husband to cook one day a week and he took that lightly. I'd have a roast the night before and all he'd have to do was slice the meat and put on the veg, but he'd forget sometimes and I'd get angry and remind him the he didn't have to worry about meals when he was in school. Little by little he did more and more to help. By the last two years he was more concerned than I about my getting a degree. It took me six years to get through school.

''After I got my degree in anthropology, it took a while to sink in, maybe six months, that I really had it. It was a great satisfaction. There's a feeling of ease. I felt at ease with myself. And when I landed a research job afterwards everything seemed so simple to accomplish. If I had a report to write for someone, it was chicken feed compared with grad school and I got paid for it.

''Education even changed my marriage. Lots of unhappy men take their wives for granted, but they are not strong enough to dump them so the marriage just endures—a low-grade chronic unhappiness. But my husband and I have this whole new world which we now share. He's become interested in my work. He oversees my career like a stage manager. We share the same work world. We both teach. It's like two lawyers. We have a lot to talk about, and that's nice. And I'm more interested in what he's interested in. It's brought us much closer in our marriage. Unless the husband relates to his wife on a person-to-person level, unless they can share an interest in each other's careers, there's a gulf between them especially after the kids leave home. I travel more, take trips abroad related to my work, go to meetings. A career is such a big thing in man's life. Now I belong to that world."

I asked Annie if there was any advice she would give other women who are still housewives but feeling, as she did, that life was slipping by too quickly and nothing much was happening. She responded with her usual enthusiasm.

"It's important to get training. Prepare yourself. Go back to school. Not only for specific information but a new vocabulary and a whole new way of looking at the world. New words represent concepts that are not even in the dictionary. Computers and their vocabulary are a whole new thing. There are new sets of mental modes you have to adjust to when you go back to school. What are the current thoughts? All that takes time and energy. But you feel so much more alive in the world. You are totally passé if you don't go back to school and study for either business or a profession. For example, you don't talk to a businessman about bookkeeping, you talk to him about 'problem solving.' You can interact on a more interesting level with people you meet in different situations."

I left Annie thinking that, whatever she decided to do in the future, she was going to get far more satisfaction out of it than she ever had known before.

The Fears

Annie had been so frightened that she had worried herself sick the first semester and ended up in bed. Going back to school can not only be frightening for a lot of reasons that are imaginary, it can also be unsettling for very real reasons. But you can learn to combat it. A woman who returned to school to get a graduate degree told me that the initial experience was embarrassing, but her solution is good advice for others. She said, "I had problems. With the first paper I wrote, neither the professor nor any of her assistants could understand a word I was saying. Everything was confused. I didn't conceptualize things logically. At home I had deteriorated mentally in those eight or nine years spent raising two children. I almost had to start again at grade-nine level. I felt one-down for a while. Though frightened, I caught on fast. I had to cut a lot of corners. Since I had children and a husband, I had to find the kernel quickly. The advantage of being older was I was able to know what corners to cut in school. For example, if I took three courses that all required papers, I'd pick a subject and build the three different papers around the same topic. It was a case of management. Maybe you learn that when you have to sterilize a bottle, get dinner for the kids and prepare something for your husband at the same time."

In another case, a graduate student who was separated from her husband and had two children told me that going back to school had made her sick with anxiety. She said she worried about a particularly difficult course, lost a lot of weight, but passed it. "I didn't mind worrying. It's a much more manageable, tidy kind of worrying in school. It's better than worrying if my kids are going to be delinquent. There's a time limit to school worries. Kids are never ending. Now I have a day-to-day sense of growing competence, being busy all day. As a housewife you're often busy all day, but it's not demanding." In school, you get grades, you move on, you get diplomas, you move on again to something new. It's a constant series of progressions.

Despite her concern, this woman found she could do the work as well as others and could concentrate more easily because of her age. "I was much more efficient, I had more self-confidence. I was not troubled by what I am. I knew by then who I was and that I wanted to be in graduate school. There was no crisis of identity."

Kathy and the Guilt of Law School

Kathy graduated from college, an English major, got married, had three children and lived in Chicago. There she got a job as part-time assistant to Saul Bellow, the novelist, sorting and occasionally answering his mail. Although this was immensely satisfying, the family soon had to move to a small town where the kind of job she liked didn't exist. Kathy found part-time work in a development office where she felt underpaid, exploited and abused, having to write reports that her male boss got credit for. The future looked bleak.

"I knew I had to go back to school to get more training, get out of the bind I was in. I didn't want graduate school in English —there was a shortage of jobs. I didn't like economics. I picked law out of a hat." She really picked it off a shelf after going to the library and looking at law school and medical school catalogues. Medical school had too many science requirements, so she decided on law, although she knew nothing about it and didn't even know a lawyer.

"What I really wanted was respect, independence, autonomy and a job that would pay me a decent wage. I never considered that staying home was a viable option." When she went to law school, she assumed that as a woman she would be doing wills, real estate closings and divorces, rather than bringing litigation on behalf of someone on death row, which she was doing when I spoke to her.

Kathy went to school full-time, hired a Norwegian au pair girl to help with the children and house, but didn't look foward to classes. "I thought three years of law school would be harnessing myself to a treadmill. I thought I'd go do it, close my eyes and get it over with." But she found herself becoming more and more engrossed by the law. Because she had always been bright, she thought she would just "breeze through." What happened was she worked harder than she expected and got bad grades. Although her husband was supportive, Kathy felt guilty.

Family responsibilities and commuting weighed heavily on her. "Dinner had to be made, the kids wanted me to do things for them, the au pair girl couldn't do everything. My husband made a lot of demands. He wanted me to do things for him, to listen to him. There were continuous claims on my time." She made a rule about never working at night. Work got done on the train, in the school library, and on weekends. She needed such self-limiting rules because of the ambivalence she felt about doing things outside the home. She constantly was aware of the pressure of making trains, and if one was late, she worried about making her connection. Travel logistics bothered her all day long, and she never relaxed or spent enough time at school because she felt she had to rush home to her family. As a result, her law school record was less than illustrious. "I resented their dragging me back. I couldn't do as well," she said, although she, herself, perhaps even more than her family, was doing the dragging.

At school Kathy's primary concern was not how well she did, but just getting through. "I didn't realize the fact that not being at the top of my class would keep me from getting certain jobs. I was so naive. I didn't realize that by worrying about my family, I was limiting myself professionally. But for my psychological survival, I had to do it that way. Psychologically I had to tell myself that nothing would interfere with my family. I still feel I'm not willing to go whole hog for a career until the children are all in college. I seek jobs that don't demand more than a certain kind of commitment. I've chosen not to work late at night, for example."

Kathy is a woman whose conscience tormented her so that she could not find peace of mind in either the role of homemaker, or that of professional. She felt guilty about what she was not doing for her family, what she thought society expected her to do and what her husband implied he also would like her to do. Although Kathy felt she had to get out of the house and was delighted by the new opportunities, she could not stray far enough from the learned patterns of childhood to follow those opportunities with complete freedom. Managing both concepts of herself meant she performed both roles imperfectly.

Cora, Her Law Degree and Her Divorce

Cora had always wanted to be a lawyer, unlike Kathy who chose it by chance. A really sharp and exciting middle-aged black woman, she found that when she graduated from college in the 1960s there were no student loans, so she had to go to work. During this period she married and had two children. By the seventies money had become available and she was able to go to the University of Connecticut Law School. They lived in a small Connecticut town, and the women she knew said, "Oh, Cora, you're so ambitious," in a disapproving tone. She would think quietly to herself, "So was Caesar." They never offered to help when the children were sick and would make remarks like, "Why would you take on such a hard discipline? Isn't it harming the children?" They'd pat her husband on the back and say how wonderful he was to let her go. This was before so many women went to law school.

Her interest in law had developed despite her father's negative attitude. He wanted her to study art history and thought it was silly for a woman to try to practice law. He worried that her interest derived from an unresolved complex because he had started law school but never finished. Instead he became a labor mediator. The entire family was very verbal, Cora remembers. "We talked and argued all the time. My parents created daughters like us, and then didn't like it."

I asked Cora how she ever found the confidence, as a middle-aged black woman with two children, to decide to go back to school. She said it must have been because she came from an educated working-class family and grew up in Detroit where people were overtly racist. "You'd have to be 50 percent better than whites in college at that time. So I had no academic doubts once I got through college. Black women are forced to have a certain amount of strength that white women may not develop.

"We had to work. Our values and goals were the same, but our salaries weren't. We grew up knowing we were going to work. The question was not *whether* you'd work but *what* work you'd get. It was hard to be a secretary or a nurse, and the corporations wouldn't take you. A black woman could be a social worker, teach or work for the government. Those were the only options.

"I knew there were a few black women lawyers but none of them practiced law. My parents always told me I should be able to work in case my husband died. We did not have the option to be housewives, we couldn't afford it. When a black woman was liberated, she was liberated into being a housewife. I was the only black woman I knew in Detroit who wasn't working. So I didn't need academic confidence. I needed social confidence. I got that from my family. I was used to being odd."

After moving to Connecticut, she found the women there mainly interested in shiny kitchen floors, having the house not just clean, but aesthetically pleasing, and seeing how soon the kids would learn to read. "I was not like that. I didn't have total acceptance anyway, so I didn't worry about the kids or the kitchen floor. But when I got into law school, I used some of my tuition money to get the kitchen carpeted so I didn't need to worry. I just vacuumed it."

Cora's intention when she went back was to get her degree, put it in the drawer, do volunteer work and take a full-time job sometime later on when her two children were grown. She wanted to complete her education so she would be ready. "I felt if I waited any longer, I wouldn't have the physical energy and things would get worse. If people thought it was ludicrous for me to go to law school in my late thirties, it would certainly be ridiculous in my forties. I didn't have a career in mind. I was doing what society wanted, being a very good wife and mother."

The first year she went to law school at night. During the day, she took one baby to kindergarten, the other to a neighbor, studied two and one half hours, cooked dinner, got the kids back and played with them, had dinner, drove forty-five minutes to school and went to classes and the library until midnight. Then she went home and studied some more. She studied the minimum necessary to pass her courses, wherever she could squeeze it in. She took her law books to the playground. It took her four years instead of three to get her degree, even though she switched to the day after finding night school was too difficult to live with. Intellectually, her husband had accepted her returning to school, but actually it wasn't working so well. The attitude in the house was strained, and he said he couldn't stand it. So even though Cora had signed up for courses, she dropped out of her second year of law school because of him.

"He didn't like my being gone. He'd been used to his own timetable. The kids never interfered with his life. Our schedule was geared to his career. I tried to go to school without interrupting his routines. I used some students to baby-sit. But we didn't have enough money for child care.

"He complained. He said he could never find his socks. I had baskets for clothes. I found time to get them washed, but never ironed or put away, so each person's clothes were in a separate basket. He objected to having to put his hands in his basket and find a pair of matching socks. He said I'd forgotten that he was the most important member of the family."

After dropping out for a year, she began to think she was being silly, that the first year is always the hardest. Law is what she had always wanted, so the following year with a fellowship and borrowed money from her family, she went back. She tried not to let school disrupt anyone, even though she was always tired with dark circles under her eyes. But according to Cora, her husband made her feel overly ambitious and strong willed. His disapproval became obvious to her.

"He'd do things like always getting sick when I had an exam or paper. Then he decided he wanted to take a job far away from where we lived. I asked him, 'Do they have a law school there?' He said, 'I never thought to ask.' I suggested that he find out, and it turned out that they did not have a law school. I think he subconsciously wanted the job just to interrupt my law career. In the end he decided not to take it, but not because of my needs.

"Our marriage broke up because of the dynamics of law school. Even though I was doing everything not to hinder him, in a subtle way I did upset him. When I started having homework and research papers, I didn't have time to talk about *his* work and *his* career. He couldn't take that. But I still loved him. Then something happened. As I was studying for the exams of my third year of law school—he picked that time to tell me—he came in and announced that he was having an affair with my best friend. I felt completely drained, punished for having been so strong willed. I thought, 'I want that degree—well, this is the price.' This friend was very feminist. I called her and said, 'Is this your idea of sisterhood?' There wasn't much she could say.''

Cora knew she was failing as a wife, at least as the kind of wife her husband wanted. She was faced with the kind of choice that no man would accept and that she could not accept either. It's never either career or family. It's got to be both. But as a wife, her career plans didn't count. "I am supposed to aid his genius, watch after him, like, 'Einstein, have you forgotten your rubbers?' It was not supposed to be a hardship to want to serve your husband. The other women were doing it. That was supposed to be my role. Not what I was doing.''

About the time she got her degree, she and her husband were divorced. She now lives alone with her two children and doesn't want to marry again. "I haven't seen a man who really understands that when you're in school, or when you're working, it's the same as when he is working. They think women are trained to be their handmaidens." I talked to her another time about her experiences working as a black lawyer. (See page 186). For her husband's side of the story, see page 317.

Cindy and Her Route to School—Medical School

If medical school is supposed to be the hardest, most totally consuming discipline, difficult for even the young, smartest students, how, I wondered, could a middle-aged woman manage to make it. I had always heard chilling tales about the rigor of staying up nights, studying and living in the hospital, caring for patients around the clock, drinking coffee to stay awake. The whole preparation to receive a medical degree did not seem like anything that a middle-aged women would find possible. I was wrong. Among the back-to-school mid-life women are those who want to, and do, become doctors. Cindy, who is one such woman, told me by way of advice to any others who want to do what she has done, "If a woman came cold turkey from the house directly into medical school, she could easily be wiped out. She should go back to school first and take a few science courses."

When Cindy finished college in her twenties she had wanted to go right on to medical school but decided to teach biology instead. "It was not the time to think of becoming a doctor," she said. "Women just didn't do those things. Medicine was thought to be too demanding for most women. When women did do well in school and went to the pre-med advisor, it was almost always suggested that they go into nursing."

Now she has finished her last year of medical school. Ahead lie a one-year internship and two years of residency at a hospital. Then she'll be ready to start practicing. I asked what made her finally decide to go back at the point when she did. "If I waited much longer, all my neurons would have unraveled. If you write or paint, you can change professions and everything is always there, still inside you. But with medicine you have to internalize so much excess information, you may reach a point where you get too old to begin—you can't do it anymore. You have to take so much from the outside and stick it in your headbox so you can call on it later on. The cutoff age is hard to pinpoint. Some people have their threads coming apart at forty, others are as bright as ever at eighty."

Cindy has one child, a boy who is in school and who likes the idea of his mother also being in school. Cindy told me when she first started, she had a class in anatomy and brought a skeleton home. Her son invited all his friends over to see it. As for her husband, she says, "I could not have done it without him and his constant reinforcement. Unless you have a husband who is self-confident, who has already made it in his own field, he could not take the competition. Not only the competition, but your breaking away from his aegis."

She admitted there were times when they both come home tired and are crabby, and the meals are not elegant. "So we don't nave pâté every night. We'll live. And we eat out. When you're in medical school, you can't have quite as impromptu a life. I can't fly down to Washington with my husband. We have to plan ahead and be very organized. But when we do take a vacation, we pull out all the stops. Our vacations are very exotic to make up for the constraints. One year we went to Egypt, another the Greek Isles. We blow everything. We look forward to it. Grit our teeth during the year.''

According to Cindy she had only one really bad year in medical school, and that was the third. Because her husband travels a lot, they had to get a housekeeper, which was a strain. ''The third year is the hardest. You have a very disrupted home life. You are on duty all night every third day. I go to the hospital at 7 A.M. and was on until the next evening. That makes thirty-six hours. Two days and one night. And if I'm working on a patient and want to make sure my plans for the treatment are carried out, I might stay longer. Part of you is devoted to the patient. You come home that second night and are so tired you feel like dying.'' The reward for Cindy is the beautiful part. ''You get a fantastic high when you see your patient improve. It's a fantastic feeling if you've done a good job.'' As a further reward for getting through this period, the fourth year, she found, was the easiest.

Cindy also found that being older has its advantages. You know how to use your time efficiently and you are used to doing lots of things simultaneously. It means that you are well equipped, having done a little living. You can give more, be more objective, see everything in perspective. On the other hand, she says, ''It's harder to memorize. There's a lot of what appears to be gobbledygook, just rote memorization. Now that I've finished my fourth year, I realize it all means something. But being older sets you apart. There are men and women in class who have kids, who don't go to the beer parties in the evening after exams. We go home to our families, we old fogies. But there is no discrimination because of age or sex. We just feel older.'' One time in one of Cindy's classes the professor asked if anyone knew the name Sir Anthony Eden. He was discussing some disease the former prime minister had had. An older woman was the only one who raised her hand, and later she said, "Oh my God." She felt her age. But Cindy finds that the younger students are getting used to older people on campus. "They are mature, with-it people."

On the brink of beginning to deal constantly with patients, Cindy says this one-on-one aspect of being with people is something she loves. She also enjoys the humanitarian side of medicine, understanding the entire range of the patient's problem. "The catastrophes and successes are your own," she said, "and you don't close the door on it at 5 P.M. You take it all home with you." Her involvement makes her happy. "I see young women moving ahead. I see some older women doing nothing, and it hurts me. It's sad they are not doing their own thing. They have thirty or forty years. All they need is to see other people doing it and get encouraged."

Cindy thinks medicine is a good field for women. "It's fabulous. You have to like people, science, and need personal gratification from doing your own work. You need compassion, to really care about the patient. You are constantly learning. It's not a stagnant field."

But Cindy had it fairly easy. A supportive husband and only one child. Women are so expert at nursing their families, taking care of sick people, that medicine seems a natural thing for them to want to go into at some point, especially after all that experience, and the intuition about illness that seems second nature to them. Perhaps this is why, in a country like Russia where medicine has not been an all-male profession so many women have become doctors.

Noreen and the Mother's Residency

Medical school wasn't quite as simple for Noreen as it was for Cindy. Noreen is forty, has four children and a husband who was not as supportive. Originally she had majored in zoology in college and then taught biology. She hated it, applied to medical school and was accepted. At that point she discovered she was pregnant. This meant that Noreen stayed home and had her baby. She did not think of school again because they could not have afforded a housekeeper, her mother and mother-in-law lived too far away to help and her husband "wasn't crazy about the idea." In those days, she told me, women didn't work. "My husband felt that when you have a small child you stay home with it. So I stayed home.

"A big part of me has always been resentful that my husband was successful in what he did. If I had not had the opportunity to do something I would have become bitter and made things difficult for him. In a way this will make our marriage stronger. When he was made a vice-president of his firm and people started to call me Mrs. Vice-President at company functions, I got angry. But I tried not to show it to him."

She finally went to graduate school and took only one course at a time. Then she had a second baby and didn't take any classes for two and a half years. "I rethought what it was I wanted to do." Noreen knew she wanted a job involving contact with people. So she returned to graduate school part-time and got a master's in psychology. More reassessment, and some unhappiness with psychology, led her back to medicine. "My aunt was a physician. I was close to her. She seemed like the happiest woman I knew. I decided to take the gamble and apply to medical school again." Her youngest child was going to be in kindergarten the next year, and by this time they could afford full-time housekeeping help.

Her husband was mildly enthusiastic by then. "He had seen I was unhappy staying home, searching for something. I was chafing at the bit." He told her, "Look, if there's nothing else you want to do, and this is really what you want, go ahead." She did, and she doesn't regret it for a minute.

"There were times during medical school when my husband got angry. It's true and real. He was unhappy during the third year when I was out every third night. I'd get home after being up for thirty-six hours and I was tired. Your spouse is alone and it doesn't make it easy. My husband had had it up to his ears. You have to be determined. Most husbands reach the point where they say, 'Oh God, why couldn't you be a school-teacher.' You have to live with someone who's pretty under-standing. My husband tried hard.

"I went to school from nine to five. I never went back to the lab to study, and I learned to work sitting surrounded by noisy family. I'd come home from school and each one wanted me for something. At times I thought, 'My God, I just can't handle this.' Nevertheless, you manage to get through it.

"I remember the first year. After the first three weeks I had three big exams. My housekeeper didn't show up. I was getting up at five in the morning to get the wash in the machine, taking kids to kindergarten, taking exams I was ill prepared for. All week long I said, 'I think I ought to quit.' And my husband said 'No, everything will be okay. We'll get through this.' But my husband did zero. He never cooked. He'd say, 'I can't cook, but I'll hire someone to do it for us.' We ate a lot of spicy Jamaican cooking that the housekeeper made.

"In the beginning it's fear more than anything else that keeps you from studying effectively. You think everyone is smarter than you are. But I didn't have more trouble than anyone else. The younger students would tease me about my age. The fellows would say, 'You're going to be the first person who retires to Florida and graduates the same year.' Or another would say, 'You're going to graduate and get Social Security the same year.' They kidded me but they were always very nice.

"You feel older. But I just acted like myself. There was no reason to try to act the way they do. I would have felt like a fool, if you want to know the truth. I had a friend in medical school who was also older. We had each other. Someone to talk to who knew your problems. We were partners in lab work."

Noreen found it hard in the beginning to see sick people all day. As a second-year student, the first patient she saw was an old lady. She asked why they wouldn't let her die. She was on a respirator, and she suddenly pulled all the tubes out. I found that difficult. The first time you stitch a live, awake human being, that's difficult, too, but you get used to that.

"I never think about getting old myself. If you start to think about those things, you never do anything. I hear women say, 'I'm too old to do this, I'm too old to do that.' That's when middle age begins. Regardless of how old you are, you've got to do what you want." Like Cindy, Noreen found age helps in lots of ways. "The professors are not so awesome, you can talk to them, laugh with them. You think they're not any older than you are. And you're not afraid of a patient's knowing that you are capable of making a mistake, showing them you're human. When you're young you think you have to be perfect. Later on you're not afraid of making mistakes because you know by then that everyone knows you're not perfect.

"In classes, because I was older, I was sure everyone thought I was an idiot, so I didn't lose face asking as many questions as I wanted. I wasn't afraid to ask. The others were afraid.

"Having something of my own now is really terrific. It made me feel better about myself. When you stay at home all the time, after a while you begin to feel you can't compete in the real world. It's a tremendous satisfaction to know you can. And it's a big extra having kids. I remember when we'd deliver babies, I'd deliver twenty and then just help others cut the umbilical cord or sew the incision. I'd feel very good."

Medical school certainly created a change in Noreen's life. For her it was welcome, even though she admits there were times when it hurt her marriage, though it was always a temporary thing. And sometimes she, too, felt twinges of guilt. "I felt guiltiest the night I stayed at the hospital, which was also the night before school started for my kids. I felt bad about not being home. But I kept my concern to a minimum. You could be paralyzed by guilt, and you'd never do anything.

"And my husband complained at times that my work came before he did. He felt he came second. He often said I was preoccupied, and he resented that. You don't think about family when you're so busy. Now it's a whole different thing. This year has been a salve. The first year I would have said medical school is awful."

Her children complained too. They resented having a housekeeper. They offered to help more, and now that they are older they can be independent. They didn't like a surrogate mother. "I probably didn't give my kids as much as they wanted. My oldest child was the most demanding. She was entering seventh grade when I began school, and she was used to my being at home the longest time. She'd say things like, 'How come you don't spend more time talking to me?' But now, after being home for three weeks recently, this same girl said, 'I never appreciated your working before. Would you go back to work and get off my back? My God, you've hit the pits, staying home and baking cookies.' "

Now Noreen has the three years of residency in a hospital ahead of her. Unlike Cindy, she has been given what is called a mother's residency. It's a program designed so she will not have to go to the hospital as many nights and weekends. There are so many mothers in medical schools and hospitals now that there was pressure to devise a special program for them. Noreen may have to stretch her residency out over a longer period of time, though.

She told me she would like to see more women of her age out doing more, finding a way to fit in all the things they want instead of accepting only a fraction of what they imagine life can offer them. She scoffs at those who say it's too difficult, too scary, or too anything else. "Women erect barriers. They worry about 'How am I going to get kids to ballet lessons.' 'How will they play musical instruments if I don't get them to their lessons.' But you can arrange things if you want to. You have to want it badly to put up with all the stuff. If you want it badly, you can do it later too. It can work out equally well. The older women in my class did as well as anyone else. And that should be encouraging."

Despite the guilt, the inconvenience, the sometimes insuperable odds, an overload of responsibility, the effort of doing two jobs at once, these middle-aged women returned to school and, no matter how many years it took, prepared themselves for a productive future. School was a high cost for them to pay in terms of money, guilt, time and personal relationships. They knew life could never be the same, but they took the risk and, because they would be better for the experience, assumed it would benefit their families too. They are different people now, ready for jobs and for a future filled with opportunity. They need only to pick the plum and enjoy the feast.

8

How to Find a Job

A forty-five-year-old woman came rushing home with great excitement after landing her first job and showed her husband her new purchase.

"Look! At last I've bought an attaché case. I've wanted one for so many years, but I never had anything to put in it. Now at last I will have some papers. I'm a success."

Having a job may be something a woman has secretly wanted for some time but not known what she could do or how she could find work, especially because her résumé is likely to have large empty spaces in it which she has not yet learned to fill with colorful and impressive accounts of her "exploration" and volunteering. Preparing for a business interview, writing a résumé and finding a job are not nearly as hard as they used to be.

Where The Jobs Are

Not only are employers more receptive and many companies even looking for women, but there is an avalanche of books on job-hunting techniques and how to write a good résumé. There are guidance books by career counselors on how to find or change a career, guides to part-time jobs, or full-time jobs, job ideas, how to handle money and a slew of pamphlets published by the Women's Bureau of the U.S. Department of Labor on careers for women. One of the most useful books is the *Occupational Outlook Handbook* published every two years by the Bureau of Labor Statistics in Washington, which provides job descriptions and information on more than 850 occupations and 30 major industries. The descriptions include explanations of what kind of work is required, salary, what kind of person would best fit into the job, the conditions and training necessary and the advancement and employment outlook. They will tell you if the field you are interested in is overcrowded, or in desperate need of people with your skills and interests. In addition to checking particular jobs that you think you might find attractive, try just browsing through the book to find occupations you might never have thought of, with qualifications you can meet.

For example, while leafing through the book one day, I came across bartending, a growing occupation for women. The description cautions that preparing drinks at home does not qualify you to be a bartender. You need to know a variety of cocktail recipes, learn how to stock a bar and know the state and local liquor laws about the sale of alcohol. They suggest you can get practice by becoming a busgirl, waitress or bartender's helper. You will have to like people and working with the public, and you need a lot of stamina to be on your feet for many hours. They describe the types of places where you could find bartending jobs, including private clubs and restaurants. There are over 800 pages in this handbook. The cost is around $8, or reprints of sections on specific occupations can be ordered at a small fee. It probably can be found in a good library, too.

There are also a growing number of organizations that have been formed to help women locate jobs and give them information on how to enter the business world. An organization called WOW (Washington Opportunities for Women) operates a free advisory service and information center for women in that area who need job information, career-planning help or information on further education. This group, with Labor Department assistance, has been aiding other self-help centers in sixteen different cities. (For names and addresses of some of these organizations and departments, see the Appendix.) A letter to the Women's Bureau, Department of Labor in Washington, should help locate a pamphlet, a book or an organization to fill any woman's need. A librarian should also be able to make suggestions. In addition, when searching for jobs, women should talk to local businesspeople, contact someone at a state employment agency, confer with local women's groups and professional organizations or just discuss the possibilities with personnel advisors at several companies.

A woman vice president told me the best way to get a job is through connections from someone you know. She said, "Just ask a friend to get you an appointment with some executive. Ask to see him for advice. Tell him about yourself and ask what he would advise you to do. He will respond, whereas he would never see you if you asked for a job. But while getting advice, you may also get the names of other possible executives to see, or he may suddenly say, 'Well I don't . . . wait a minute, I heard the other day that . . .' and you have a lead. The best jobs are never advertised.''

I spoke to Erna Trubee at a volunteer women's job agency who pointed out that women have a rougher time than men because they don't have access to information as men do. They don't hear of jobs. They don't have contacts, like the powerful "old boy" networks that pass the word on about who is leaving what job and when. Their networks have only begun.

Women are also more reticent than men. Erna told me a story about a man who opened an employment agency thinking himself very clever to be cashing in on this increasing demand for jobs for women. But he soon became mystified that many women turned down the jobs he was able to get for them. He finally began to question them and found that they were just too scared to follow through. They lacked the confidence that they could do the job, and they backed down at the last minute.

Erna advises that one of the ways to get confidence is to take a workshop in assertiveness. This kind of workshop offers exercises that force you to be assertive. She gave as an example a situation similar to one described by a woman in my transition workshop. "A woman feels that her husband walks all over her in the home," says Erna. "Both have worked hard all day. She comes home and gets dinner and does the dishes, while her husband sits there and reads the paper. Finally she sits down with a sigh of relief, and five minutes later he asks her to get the television guide for him. What should she do? Get it? Or make him see that she's tired too and he can get it just as easily.

"A woman has to make her wishes known," Erna points out, "without getting angry. In the job market, you must be assertive about yourself." She says that going out to find a job is selling your skills to some employer. "If you feel you have nothing to offer, you'll have an awful time. There are women who have something to offer, but they don't like to approach people and sell themselves. Women are too timid because they have been taught their role is to be sweet, passive and ladylike. No one taught us that if you're going to get ahead you have to be a little aggressive. Sometimes this is hard to overcome until you get mad enough."

She reiterated what I've heard everywhere, that women lack knowledge of themselves, their skills and information about jobs. A woman needs the motivation and time to spend looking for a job. "The job won't fall in your lap unless you are extremely lucky," she said, "and most jobs come through personal contact rather than through ads. Once you take a job, one thing leads to another and the doors open up. If you sit at home and stay scared, nothing will happen."

Some women think only of want ads and employment agencies as places to look for jobs. She suggested that you can also go to college placement offices, look in women's magazines and, of course, use the library. "There are so many books of advice for women trying to enter the job market these days," she said, "that personnel directors must be seeing a lot of carbon copies of this or that approach, from graduates of this or that course, rather than individuals with their own personal style." One obviously can get a lot of good advice on how to write a résumé from a course or a book, but it would obviously have to be larded with plenty of idiosyncratic touches. A course can explain the rudiments but the results have to sound like you and not a thousand other people. One thing you need when job hunting, she told me, is a thick skin. Women are not prepared for the no's they sometimes get. It can be very demoralizing until someone says yes.

What Salary to Ask For

Then there is the awkward subject of money. It's not only embarrassing for women to sell themselves, but to set the price seems downright gauche. Many women simply haven't thought through the salary question. They compare it with what their husbands are making, not with what they are likely to get. They also forget to add the costs of clothes and child care when figuring out what they need.

Erna's advice to women looking for jobs is, first, to be realistic about salaries, what you can get in the competitive job market. Find out what people in the field are getting paid and decide what you will work for. You might stort low if there's chance for advancement. Try to get information from the company in advance. Some will tell you their salary schedules. Second, realize if you take a job that the job is the first priority—not redecorating the house or the kids. There are things you have to give up when you go to work, such as morning tennis or a French conversation group. When you are hired, you can't say, "Oh, I can't start till next month. I'm going on vacation with my husband."

Third, she points out, the feminist movement has glamorized working for money. "But there are no ideal jobs. There's lots of drudgery in every job. You have to decide if you want a career or just any job. In a job the work may be mundane, the salary not too good. In the career, you require training, extra hours, the ability to travel, extra effort to get ahead."

Wanting just a job for the money and the interaction with others and wanting a career with the idea of advancing in salary, prestige and responsibility are two different kinds of working. A woman has to think about what she is really after and decide which jobs will get her there.

How the Personnel Interviewer Sees You

No matter what job you want you will have to go for that interview with someone, a personnel representative of the organization or the boss. I dropped in on such an interviewer one day to get her version of the women's job scramble. Dorothy Schoch is an attractive, businesslike woman who manages to combine an efficient manner with warmth and charm. She and her three colleagues are responsible for keeping a staff of 2,800 jobs filled. "When I interview someone, I'm trying to see what they've got in terms of jobs that I have open. The common image of the interviewer as some species of dragon is not really correct. The interviewer needs you as much as you need him. It's only your own fear that makes him seem so threatening."

What she does, she said, is to try to help people move back and think about themselves, do some inward thinking and get some confidence. "With the woman who has never worked before," says Dorothy, "I try to get a sense of her talents and find a supervisor who will accept such a person."

Interviewing middle-aged women getting back into the work world has led to a surprising revelation. According to Dorothy, "More women than I had expected stand up after our interview and say, 'I don't really want to work. I don't know why I'm here.' She may have been pressured by her husband who says, 'Why don't you do more than you're doing?' She also feels the pressure from her peers, the other women in her same position who are working. I see one woman a week like this."

Not only do some women really *not* want to work, but some others who do don't necessarily want to get ahead. Dorothy told me of a secretary in the organization. She kept pushing herself to do something more important, kept wondering where she should be going. She even went back to school to learn some new skills. Then one night she sat down at the kitchen table with her two kids. They were doing homework and she was doing homework, and she said to herself, 'What am I doing? Who am I kidding? I'm a good secretary and I enjoy it, and that's where I am going to stay.' Upward mobility isn't for everyone.

As another example of a woman who just wants a job, any job, Dorothy told me of a forty-year-old woman who had worked on and off as a waitress. "When she came to see me I was dealing with nothing on a piece of paper. She didn't want to continue as a waitress because she wanted her weekends free, she wanted more normal work and a sense of security from a group that could give her health and life insurance, the fringe benefits. I found a filing job for her which fit her perfectly. She had limited aspirations, a great deal of intelligence and, unlike a young person who would want to get ahead, she was happy to stay where she was." If you know yourself, you are more likely to find the right job.

Among those who come to Dorothy's office looking for jobs, besides the armies of women whose children are in school, are divorcées, widows and women who have recently moved. She sees the divorced woman as "someone who wants a job because she usually needs the money and wants to prove herself, discover her own worth, get back some of the confidence that was stripped from her during the marital breakup when she was probably told by an angry husband that, despite all she had done, she couldn't do anything properly and she was useless besides being a bore and no good in bed."

A widow needs, like the widow Sarah, something to do. One widow who had never worked came to Dorothy shortly after her husband had died and said in tears, "All I want is a desk to sit behind, a territory of my own." She needed a place to go every morning. She needed, "my job" and "my desk."

"Then there are the women who are often uprooted from good jobs," Dorothy added, "because of their husbands' moving, and they often find themselves trying to find a place in a strange job market that may not have exactly what they need."

There are days when Dorothy gets two hundred to three hundred résumés, and they are all quite different. Once a woman came in with a résumé and asked what Dorothy thought about it. "I said I found it difficult to read. It turned out to be the end result of a course she had taken. If her résumé says I have this skill and that skill, I have to figure out where she got it. I want to know how she thinks, how she sees herself, where she thinks her strengths lie, how well she communicates. If all I have is what she thinks of herself, I have to plow through and find out what's genuine."

One woman who wanted a job as a typist sent in a three-by-five index card and wrote what she wanted to do, and that she would take the company typing test. That was all that was necessary, and she got a job. "No résumés," says Dorothy, "should be longer than two pages. I've seen them nine or ten pages, much too long. There is no right way to do a résumé, but the intelligence behind it, that's what is important. You have to try to figure out what you can say to get my attention. If your paper comes across my desk," she went on, "as having been written by a human being, I'll remember it. No two people present themselves the same way."

Her comment is documented in work done at the Institute for Social Research at the University of Michigan. A time-use study showed that the average employed man spends 11 percent of each working day not working, but on coffee breaks, extra-long lunches, or talking and relaxing. The average working woman spends only 8 percent of the day in this manner. In addition the researchers found that the effort given to the job by the woman is 12 percent higher than that expended by a man in office work.

I asked if there are any advantages that she as an employer sees in hiring middle-aged women? Dorothy quickly pointed out that older women have an edge over younger ones in many ways. Their attendance is likely to be better, their motivation higher, they spend less time on the telephone, at the water cooler, on coffee breaks and put more time into actually working. They take the job seriously and put extra effort into it; they are concerned about where the job will lead them.

But she also sees disadvantages. Some women have emotional problems around the forties and fifties, she finds, and wanting a job can become a substitute for a marriage relationship. As the woman gets older her self-doubts grow. She wonders if she is still effective, still has the energy, or whether younger women are a threat. "Such women," says Dorothy, "can become sensitive, easily hurt, quarrelsome. They need assurance that they are wanted where they are."

The advice to all middle-aged women from Dorothy's personnel point of view is this: She says, first, the most important thing is that you try to know as much about yourself as possible— what you can do, what you would like to be doing. Generalities are no help. "If a woman comes in, as many do, and says, 'Well, I like people,' I'll have to answer, 'Well, who doesn't?' It's too general," says Dorothy. "I want to know where to begin." She suggests that a woman try to think of work fantasies, what she pictures herself doing, then try to look at her work, volunteer or whatever. Look at her talent in terms of her fantasies and see where they might fit in.

Second (in what sounds like a bit of Force Field Analysis from my Transition Weekend), she advises a woman to examine what would keep her from realizing the fantasy. "I try to get an individual to lock herself into the 'givens' she can't change, things that might keep her from realizing this fantasy. For example, she might have to say, 'I have to live in this area, I have kids, I must be home when the kids come home from school.' Look at the REALITY," she emphasizes. Among the things a woman must bring into her vision of reality is ambition. "She might want to be the director of personnel, but maybe the work is too hard and too long. She has to look at her priorities and choose between working full-time and overtime, and being home with the kids. If you want $20,000, then it must be your number-one priority versus entertaining a lot at home and spending more time with your husband. You have to look at the reality and see what you really want and can do. A woman's fantasy may tell her that if she works full-time she'd have more money. But the reality is that working full-time means to five and overtime."

One woman whom Dorothy had employed on an hourly basis called one day to say her kids were growing up and "I have all this time." When she faced the reality of a full-time job and all it demanded, she found she didn't want it. "I don't know where

I was,'' she told Dorothy, ''but I don't want to be there.'' The fantasy didn't square with the reality. Another woman came to see Dorothy for a part-time job. Everything that interested her was full-time. Since she had teenage children, she decided on the full-time commitment. In this case reality expanded her fantasy.

The point, it seems to me, is to try to know as much about what you want as possible, then to be as honest as possible with the interviewer. These interviewers see so many résumés and so many people that they are quick to pick out the straightforward, genuine person who has capabilities and wants to use them. Dorothy ended our talk on as positive a note as one could hope for. She assured me that ''Anyone who wants a job will find it one way or another.''

Job Hunting with Pat

After listening to Pat's experiences in the previous chapter, (Page 136) of going back to finish the college she had interrupted a long time ago, I was very anxious to hear what happened next as she set out, a middle-aged woman with her just-earned B.A., looking for work. After graduating in June, and taking some time off in the summer, she started job hunting along with all the hordes of twenty-two-year-old girls. First she went to a volunteer women's counseling group in her hometown and found it disappointing, totally disorganized. ''I went in and looked at the file of available jobs. Nothing interested me. I signed up for a session with a volunteer counselor. My daughter could have done as well. She was encouraging but deficient in terms of really focusing on the sorts of jobs I might realistically try for with my skills, areas I hadn't thought of, or what to expect in an interview. Women need a great deal of help with interviews. A couple of books helped me. Someone needs to be very hard on you and put you through a tough interview. My husband used to practice giving me questions I would answer. Women have never had this experience before. You have to sell yourself in a positive way. You have to interview the employer to find out what he needs and what you can do for him. Job hunting is emotionally draining,'' she remembered. "You go up and down like a yo-yo."

She learned that you have to find out what credentials you need in each field. "For women to get out there and do their stuff, they need expert counseling, someone to help them see where they can fit in. But in a way women have it over men. It's not crucial for me to get a job. I imagine the tensions for men must be even harder." Yet even without the expert counseling she wished she'd had, Pat began looking. Some interviews went well, and some didn't. "If I didn't do well in an interview, I'd feel less than terrific. It's unsettling." But books and her husband's practice interviews at night were not the only aid she sought.

At the same time that she was knocking on doors, she would show her résumé to friends and get more advice. "I'd show it to people in different fields, and they'd suggest changes. A résumé just gets you in the door. If someone has twenty or thirty résumés on his desk, he can't take time to read the fine print."

In order to look businesslike when she went for her interviews, she bought a brown tweed suit. "I wore that suit because secretaries wear sweaters and I wanted to differentiate myself from them. I got awfully tired of putting it on a couple of times a week. It's not enough to look nice and neat in an interview. You do have to present yourself. But you really have to do your homework. You should learn about the company before you go for the interview." Companies often put out pamphlets or brochures and annual reports describing their products or their activities, and an anonymous visit to them should net a lot of such information from the first receptionist one meets. "I was quite nervous during the first interview. But you get better and better at it. You get confidence. You learn to handle yourself and be specific about the things you can do. And you learn what skills employers are looking for. You may end up discovering you can be good at something you'd never thought of."

At times Pat was disheartened when she went around seeing personnel people and nothing came through. "You can't rush it," she said. "You have to expect to spend three or four months looking. I went on two different kinds of interviews. One is where there's a specific job in question, and the second comes about, for example, when a friend sends my name to the head of an organization saying, 'You should talk to her. She's very good.' We meet for the interview, check each other out and he keeps my name in mind."

Pat went out on fifteen interviews. "People were always nice. I was usually interviewed by men. I talked to one man who cracked jokes for two hours. He was very jolly. I didn't know how to behave. He disarmed me. I didn't get the job."

Pat realized that women in general have a problem that men don't have in an interview. "It's the attitude of women," she found. "If you ask a woman if she can do such and such, she usually says that she can't. Whereas a man will answer, 'I think I can,' and he'll be saying to himself, 'I can learn to.' A woman I know did that and it paid off." Pat said a friend of hers was asked to set up a program using computers to analyze the effectiveness of state agencies. When she was asked if she could handle it, she said "yes." Actually she had never done that kind of job before. But she was thrown the ball and she caught it. "Yes, I can do that. No problem."

She knew what computers could do, though she had never worked with them. And she knew she would have programmers working for her. "She had a feeling for what needed to be done," Pat said, "and how she could organize it. She had to be certain she could do it. You can't promise the moon and then not deliver." Pat seemed to feel that women need to take chances and risks more often, to stretch further and try harder for what they would like, make efforts beyond what is easy for them. They have to push harder than they thought they could, until they try and succeed.

The weeks went by, Pat visited many offices and though she was learning a lot about herself and the business opportunities, becoming more professional, no job offers were coming in. People said, "Be patient. Things come up. Seeds you plant later bear fruit." They were right. At last one day she answered a newspaper ad. "The man who was interviewing me and I both had a positive feeling. I could see he was impressed. During the interview, if money is mentioned, they are serious about you. It was mentioned. I was excited when he finally offered me the job." She is assistant to the president of a publishing firm. She does marketing and public relations. She characterized it as "an entry-level administrative position."

Her life is totally different, and she is amazed at the rapid change. "It's a feeling of being in transition. Now I'm moving into an unknown area. I feel terrific. I feel great anticipation and concern as to how it will work out. I have an enormous amount to learn. In a way the job is like going to school again. But actually what will help me even more than the college I finished is a volunteer job I had in a political campaign where I ran an office, answered the phone, told people what to do. My organizational skills were called into play. I juggled priorities." From the beginning, she was pretty confident about the importance of her first job. She told me, "If it doesn't work out, I can try something else. I need this experience. I have to try."

I called Pat a couple of months after she had started working, and she was breathless with things to tell me. "I was timid at first, then I got things better organized. I'm so incredibly busy, I had to get some household help. My job is enormously demanding, there are production schedules, deadlines, my day goes by in a second. It's funny, almost nothing I did in school prepared me. I have to figure everything out myself. I have to plan each day. I'm given eighty-two things to do, and I have to organize them. It's like having ten children all under the age of six. I interview and hire secretaries. The president often needs things to be done instantly."

I asked her if she didn't miss being able to stay in bed all day if she wanted to. "I never did that when I was home all the time. I like getting up in the morning to go to work. I have so much to do I've even brought work home tonight. So much of it is how you organize your time. You can be a slob if you stay home all day. But at work you have to shape up. One problem is dinners. Lots of working women eat out but we don't like to. I keep looking for easy meals. My husband and daughter and I take turns in the kitchen. We do casseroles on weekends and freeze them. It's a big adjustment, but if you enjoy it, it's worth it.

"At the office I see them doing things differently than I would do them. But you can't come in and start being supercritical and try to change things. You have to learn their way first, then gradually suggest changes. I found that once you have that first job you start asking more questions. Is this me? Is this what I really want? Where can I go in five years? It's a self-education. It will help me focus on what I really want to do forever. You have to be out there to see what people are actually doing. You can't get that at home."

In one quick summer, from graduation, to reading books on job hunting, to going out and doing the real thing after the books had been returned to the library, to finally getting her first job, Pat had slipped from one stage of her life into the next with little trauma and a lot of belief that what she is doing is great for her. "My feeling had been as my kids got older and finished high school, I was going to need an occupation or a job. I wanted it both to help financially, especially with kids in college, but also something full-time that used my talents and abilities, something I could commit myself to. Something ongoing for the next part of my life." She wanted it, she tried for it, and she got it. A new job and a new life, a monthly paycheck, new responsibilities, a new sense of importance—and a couple of new suits.

PART TWO

The Women
Who Work

9

Women Who Need to Work

Middle-aged women today have found themselves shedding an outgrown image of what they are supposed to look and act like and conforming to a totally new concept of what women are supposed to be doing. Yet during this major transformation in society's attitude toward mid-life, the women who go back to school or go out looking for jobs don't feel totally liberated or completely confident. They do it. But many do it on tiptoes, trying not to make waves, trying to keep everything the way it always was, giving up study time and taking vacations when they should be learning, coming home early when they should be working overtime. They try to keep their husbands unruffled, avoiding the real demands of study or work, in a way that few men would have done for them.

They often feel guilty to have had any ambitions. Most men and even women still think of the man's career as number one. Women still behave as though they are being *allowed* to do what they want to do with their lives, rather than that they have a basic right to do what interests them. In time this timidity will disappear as men's and women's life styles become more alike. Because of the way society is structured people seem to need to work, not only for money, but to satisfy their imaginations, or their need for sheer activity, to achieve status, to produce, create, answer questions about the unknown. There are very few people, I would guess, who, if given the choice, and unlimited money, would do nothing but broil on a beach. Sooner or later, they would think of writing a book about their thoughts, painting a picture of the beach or making a business out of lying on the sand and calling it Club Méditerranée. Middle-aged women prove the point. Some of them have the choice of being supported and cared for with a minimum contribution of work around the house, yet growing numbers give up this do-less luxury to develop and satisfy a need they feel within them.

A woman told me, "On a Sunday afternoon walk I sometimes wonder why I'm working so hard when there are not that many years left to produce things. Maybe I should just play. But I can't. It's like I've been hungry for a meal for a long, long time, and I've got to eat it."

Women's Job Status

Today, when a woman works, she not only is satisfying her own needs to activate her mind, there are crucial financial advantages. In fact, this is the main reason why most women work. The women's Bureau of the Department of Labor estimates that 60 to 65 percent of women who work do so for purely economic reasons. Many of them have no choice, because they support themselves. A 1976 bureau study pointed to the fact that over 23 percent of these working women have never been married. Another 19 percent were widowed, divorced or separated.

There have been so many divorces that female-headed families with children now comprise 15 percent of all families with children, according to a study by Dr. Saul Hoffman of the Institute for Social Research, University of Michigan. A major finding of his study is that the economic status of divorced or separated men improves, while that of women declines. These women suffer such a large decline in their financial situations that in 1973 their average household income was about half that of married women in the study. Alimony and child-care payments don't nearly make up for the actual costs of child care. The choice for these women was to go on welfare in some cases, move in with family or friends, or go out and get a job.

But more than half of all working women are married. And often this family needs a second income as well. The money a woman contributes enables many families today to keep their heads above the poverty line, and above the swells of inflation. The wife's working is also a form of insurance which guarantees they will have some income if a husband loses his job. And the second salary often pays for a child's college education or for the purchase of a house. The National Association of Home Builders reports that almost half of all couples buying houses have two incomes. There are forty-one million women working today, comprising over 40 percent of the U.S. labor force. Around fifteen million of them are between the ages of thirty-five and fifty-four, according to the Bureau of Labor Statistics. By 1990 this figure is expected to be almost twenty million. There has been an accelerating rush of all women into the job market in the last few years, but some groups are entering at a faster rate than others.

One might expect that women with young children still at home would be among the slowest to sign up for jobs. They are obviously the ones most heavily involved in the several roles of wife, housekeeper and mother. One would be wrong. The most rapid change, according to the Population Institute in Washington, has been among women who have children under six at home. Only 18 percent of this group worked in 1960; now as many as 40 percent are working.

The well-known irony is that, despite this fantastic effort to prepare for work, then find it, arrange things at home and perform the impossible juggling acts that so many women do, a woman earns less than a man. One of the goals of women's lib, equal pay for equal work, is far from being a reality. Rather than not accepting jobs for less money, women take them anyway and meekly accept whatever they earn. Because they have been taught to think they aren't as good as men, they have little self-confidence. And because they are not used to getting any money for work they do as volunteers or at home, monetary rewards are utterly new to many of them.

The monstrous truth is that the average woman worker earns only 59 percent of what a man earns, and most are employed in two major categories in which there is very little inherent glamour—clerical jobs and service workers. Many jobs, says the Population Institute, are little more than female ghettos populated by what has come to be known as "pink collar" workers. The occupations they list that are more than 90 percent female include bank tellers, bookkeepers, keypunch operators, secretaries, telephone operators, registered nurses and typists. At the other end of the spectrum, the many jobs that have fewer than 1 percent female workers include carpenters, electricians, top corporate managers, airline pilots and mechanical engineers. Big business, they point out, continues to be a male stronghold with only 2 percent representation by women on the top corporate boards. Their rule of thumb is as follows: "In general, as the status and salary of an occupation increase, the proportion of women decreases." One example is the field of education. Although 85 percent of elementary school teachers are women, only 51 percent of high school teachers are women and only 11 percent of university full professors are women. The same applies to school administration where 23 percent of elementary school principals are women but only 1 percent of college presidents are women. And school boards that direct policy, and that one thinks of as being loaded with women, have, in reality, about 20 percent women members, and in 1975–76 one-fourth of school boards had no women members at all.

In another example of occupational sex roles, the Population Institute points to the health profession, where 87 percent of the physicians are men whereas 97 percent of the nurses are women. In the Soviet Union, being a doctor is defined as women's work with far less prestige (let alone income!) than we accord our doctors, and in that country 70 percent of the doctors are women. So, it appears not to be the character of the work itself, in many cases, that draws either a man or a woman, but the way society defines that job. The men have always gone for the status and the money, and they have kept those professions to themselves, while recruiting women to fill the services that they needed done.

A whole profession of dental hygienists, for example, has sprung up to relieve the dentist of chores he dislikes, and it seems to be entirely composed of women. However, less than 5 percent of dentists are women. Eventually women will hold a greater portion of prestigious jobs, but they have a long way to go. Although they are moving more rapidly than ever in history —a quarter of the medical students, for example, are now women, compared with 8 percent 10 years ago—it is the present situation that middle-aged women must confront.

The New Jobs

It is exciting to see so many women entering medicine and law, and to know that more and more of them are older women, but it is also interesting to look at some of the other jobs where one now sees women. For example, have you noticed that the person pumping your gas lately is occasionally a woman, and not a man? Female garage and gas station attendants were one in seventy in 1962. In 1976 they were one in every twenty. Women spend all day walking around, up and down stairs. Why not get paid for it? Women mail carriers increased from one in thirty-five to one in every eleven in the same period. And if there is one thing a suburban woman can do, it is to be a chauffeur. She spends a good portion of her life taxiing children around. This is also a talent she can be paid for. Female taxi drivers (the kind with grown-up passengers) are up from one in twenty-seven to one in eleven. My United Parcel Service (UPS) truck driver is a beautiful woman who has no trouble carting boxes around. (There's a fifty-pound limit.)

Stereotypes get stamped into our minds very easily. We assume that situations we see around us as we grow up are unalterable laws. When we stop to think, of course, we know better.

For example, if every doctor you have ever seen is a man, and every nurse is a woman, if every boss is a man, and every secretary is a woman, that is what you assume you will always find. If you have grown up being used to female telephone operators, and suddenly you hear male voices, at first it won't seem right. Then, when you get used to it, you will find it very natural. Conversely, there is no reason why a woman, and that includes a middle-aged woman, should not be a candidate for any job a man does, as long as it doesn't involve lifting unusually heavy weights. Women obviously do not have the physical strength of men.

Despite the notions we grew up with, there has been a great mixing of sex roles in various occupations in the last few years. Women are moving into jobs that have traditionally been reserved for men. For women looking for work, this trend simply expands the possibilities of employment. The area with the most dramatic increase in the number of women has been the skilled trades, where women's jobs are growing faster than men's. Between 1960 and 1970, for example, the Department of Labor says that the number of women electricians has tripled, women plumbers quadrupled, women auto mechanics almost quintupled, and women painters and machinists doubled. Women are also moving into predominantly male professions such as accounting and law where their ranks have more than doubled in the decade between 1960 and 1970.

Women are also edging into traditionally male sales occupations such as insurance, and real estate, where the number of women agents nearly doubled. Women are going into managerial occupations. The number of women sales managers (except in the retail trade) grew dramatically, almost ninety times in the decade. In certain male service occupations, women began to be seen more often. Female guards have tripled in number and women police doubled. There are twice as many women bartenders now than in the sixties, while the number of males has decreased. This encroachment into male territory has not been without its counterpart among the men. Men have also made inroads into traditional women's occupations. There are now more male librarians, elementary school teachers, typists and telephone operators.

For the first time in history, in 1978, the percentage of American women who work reached 50 percent. In the last decade, of the fourteen million new jobs filled, women filled ten million of them. Whether women work because they must have more income, or they simply enjoy having the extra money and something purposeful to do, the two-career couple has become the new American family. Recently the Urban Institute examined the statistics and came up with the surprising information that only 19 percent of all Americans are members of families in which the father works and the mother stays home with one or more children. When middle-aged women were growing up, one small rose-covered cottage and two cars in the garage was the ultimate dream of the average family. Today, it is quickly becoming a second house and two jobs for every couple.

Does a Working Mother Damage Her Kids?

As soon as older women with children began pouring out of their homes and into jobs, there were great cries of doom and despair about the effect of maternal employment on children. It was commonly assumed that not having a mother readily available was going to cause lasting problems for children, who would collect all kinds of horrid complexes on the way to adulthood. Women have been told that being with their children, at least for the first year or two, is crucial.

As more and more women have to work, and some of these have their first children as late as age thirty-five, the debate continues. On an individual basis, it is often quite hard to say whether a problem child is that way because his mother works, or whether he would have, in fact, developed problems even with her at home. One might just as legitimately ask if a child's problems are the result of having a mother, perhaps a domineering, possessive or overanxious one, around all the time.

In 1970 B. M. Caldwell did a study comparing lower-class

black and white children receiving stimulating day care with a group of children staying at home with their mothers. The home-reared children showed a decline in cognitive development (between the ages of twelve and thirty months) while the day-care group showed a slight increase.

In a study done in 1972 of three thousand employed men comparing those whose mothers had worked before they were sixteen with those whose mothers had not, no relationship was found between having a working mother and a sense of psychological well-being. The only effect of being the son of a working mother seems to be that there was "a greater receptivity to innovation."

According to Dr. Claire Etaugh of Bradley University in Illinois who did a review of this and other recent research, "Two conclusions appear warranted from the data: Young children can form as strong an attachment to a working parent as to a nonworking one, provided that the parent interacts frequently with the child during the times they are together; and stable, stimulating substitute care arrangements are important for the normal personality and cognitive development of preschool children whose mothers work." One indisputable finding has emerged from studies of both black and white elementary school children: "Satisfied mothers—working or not—have the best-adjusted children."

In her review Dr. Etaugh points out that "studies of career aspirations among females have yielded one of the few consistent findings in the maternal employment literature; namely, that working women's daughters have higher aspirations than do daughters of nonworking women."

There have been numerous studies, and many more are still being done. In a new inquiry reported on in 1977 by researchers at Tulane University, children of two hundred low-income families were studied for possible deleterious effects of maternal employment on the children during the first three years of life. In an eight-year follow-up, children of working mothers and nonworking mothers were compared as to weight, IQ, reading, arithmetic and spelling achievement and linguistic ability. It was found that children of workers performed as well as those of nonworkers. When such variables were examined as maternal age, education, per capita income, crowding, number of children in family, many differences were found between working and nonworking mothers, the vast majority of which favored children of working mothers.

It is not only in professional journals that the questions are asked. According to a *New York Times*–CBS News poll conducted in 1977, 60 percent of those interviewed (55 percent of the men and 64 percent of the women) believe working women make as good or better mothers than those who don't work. This figure is up from 52 percent in a 1970 poll done by CBS News.

Many children, in fact, have urged their mothers to go ahead and take jobs when the women were hesitating on their behalf. Said one girl who got fed up with all the vacillation, "I'm embarrassed to have a mother who is just a housewife. All my friends' mothers have careers."

A woman laughingly recalled, "My daughter was at the age when she thought I was nothing but pure shit. When I went out to work, she had second thoughts about me. The best thing I could do for my kids was not to be home after school. They needed supervision, but not from their mother."

It is pretty understandable that many kids will react much more maturely and honestly to someone not in the family than they do to their own mother whom, by now, they have learned to twist around their little fingers.

What a woman with children who goes to work today is bucking are the long-ingrained values society placed on home, family and motherhood, in order to insure its survival at an earlier and more precarious point in history. She also has to contend with the effect of the initial badly planned research which erroneously compared institutionalized children, or those living the communal life in kibbutzim, with children in their own normal home environment, and concluded that the mother's presence in the home was necessary. Recent research has been placing the emphasis not so much on whether the mother is home all day or working, but on her own personality and emotional status, and on the attitude of her husband to her working. If she enjoys her work, is happy and her husband approves and helps, if there are stable child-care arrangements, if everyone in the home cooperates so she is not placed under an impossible strain carrying out two roles, she is reported to be as successful or more so in bringing up her children as her nonworking counterpart. Otherwise, the 70 or 80 percent of child-care and household duties that most working women continue to bear in addition to their jobs is simply too much and will threaten the whole atmosphere of the home.

As a friend of mine who works says, "It's not the amount of time you spend with your children that's important, it's the quality of what you do when you are with them that really counts. My children and I spend less time together than if I were always home, but we enjoy it more, it's more intense, more exciting."

But for me, perhaps the most convincing argument against condemnation of working mothers comes from studies done on how much time working versus nonworking mothers spend with their children. A national study done in 1965 showed that the average nonworking mother spent 1.4 hours per day on child care. One must presume that even if she is home, the child is at times asleep or playing by himself or with friends or watching television. She might just as well be working.

Another study done in Syracuse of 1,300 families in 1968 showed that the average nonworking mother spent 1.1 hours a day in the physical care of all her family members and 48 minutes a day on other care during an average school weekday. Obviously the working mother can spend an equal portion of her time with her children. And for the woman who prefers to work, there is less damage likely to her children than if she stayed at home, an unhappy, frustrated person.

Divorcées Who Have to Work

One of the largest groups of mid-life women who must enter the labor market are women who are divorced. Because they usually don't get as much money as they need from former husbands—some do not get any at all—it becomes essential for many of them to work. A divorcée who is working because she has to may have a different perspective on her job than other women do. She must be serious about it, concerned with where it will lead, what kind of fringe benefits there are, such as life insurance and health plans. She needs to move forward in a career, not just have a job, so that she will be able to count on retirement income and enough money when she no longer can work.

Divorce is an ego-destroying, wrenching, destructive experience for the person who gets left behind. People who once loved each other, who shared a number of good years and experiences together, can become cruel and mortal enemies, full of hatred and deception. Most women who are divorced today are left by their husbands, although a growing number of women are the ones who do the walking out. If the woman is left, the shock can be very traumatic, and finding a job right away may be almost impossible. One woman who was left by her husband had been so put down by him for so long that she was in a daze. "I went to a psychiatrist for two years before he was able to help me realize that I was and could be strong. I had assumed my husband was the brilliant one and people came to our house to see him."

A woman from Iowa who was provoked into finally getting the divorce herself and still was extremely disturbed by it said, "I took a long time to work it out after the divorce. I was on tranquilizers for six or seven months. I tried to cover up my insecurities. When I took a train to the city to see my lawyer I felt I was going to pass out from nervous tension. But I had to get a divorce. I knew if I was going to be sane for the rest of my life I couldn't live under that stress. I found myself alone. But after a while I knew I had to prove things. I had to prove I could manage money, drive long distances myself, sell our house, get a job."

The finality of divorce can make a woman panicky. The hard anxieties about money don't help. A woman told me, "Being without a job scares you. I was advised once to always keep six months' salary in a personal savings account. Even with a job I am conscious of having to watch my money. But there are often ways to save. If I have a healthy business lunch, I can eat a sandwich at dinner. I get all my medical bills paid for by insurance and I buy my clothes at a secondhand shop. I recently got a Courrèges secondhand coat for $10 instead of a new one for $250. There are all kinds of ways to save. It's an interesting game for someone who always had enough money.''

Virginia, Who Got Dumped at Forty-seven

Virginia is a mid-life divorcée who now runs an oriental antique shop. I went in one day and we sat surrounded by the ancient art of the Far East. It was a wealth of brocades, scrolls, jade, exquisite hand design. As the centuries-old bearded men eyed us from their porcelain worlds, Virginia described what led up to her becoming a working woman.

"I thought of myself as a good Catholic mother. I stayed home and took care of all the little chickens. My concept of myself was something the church and family taught me I was supposed to be like.

"I had six children in eight years. That's definitely connected with the Catholic concept of not planning your family. No person in her right mind would do that. But I really liked being at home and being a mother. I didn't want to be anywhere from nine to five. My husband would have slit my throat if I'd put my career first. When I was younger I was conscious of trying too much to please him. Approval is an insidious need that people grow up with.

"But in the last few years, I was getting so much flak from my husband for being such a boring person that I looked for a job. I had never heard of the concept of displacement. Here's this person. Everything is going wrong in his life. Instead of looking at his own problems, he looks at his kids and finds them a pain, tells his wife to shape up. He was pushing his problems over on the other person, me. It was such a dumb thing, and I bit. I wasn't perfect but I wasn't boring. He was always saying, 'What did you do all day? Where's my coat from the cleaners?

What did you do?' So I said to myself, 'Okay, if I'm boring, I'll work.' I was disgracefully obliging. It was a good thing I did. That was a lifeline for me later on.

"I knew there were things the matter with our relationship, but because of my background I idealized everything. After seventeen years of marriage and six kids you are terribly embroiled in the situation. It became pretty apparent, but I couldn't admit it, that something was terribly wrong."

Virginia told me she would have anxiety attacks. She'd be in the market picking out the lettuce and all of a sudden she couldn't breathe. Her heart would start tearing around like a racehorse.

"I went to the doctor. He said, 'There's nothing wrong in your body, but what's wrong with your mind?' I was afraid to go anywhere, even to the city. I was afraid I'd die and people would step all over my body. I began seeing a psychiatrist. I think he spoke to my husband and told him to level with me." She found out that he had had an affair for a long time and had recently moved his girl to town. "I wanted to hold things together. But I got so tired of waking up and thinking, 'This is the day he won't come home,' so I said finally, 'Okay, if you want to go, get out.' I had been so closely knit to him. If the person with all the strength leaves, what will I do?

"I felt a horrible anger at having what I had built knocked down. I had a murderous anger inside, but I couldn't allow myself to admit it. My whole career—all I'd built, he came along and knocked it down like a building of blocks."

Virginia has been divorced for three years now. She enjoys being alone and does not want to remarry. Her husband sends her money but, as the kids get older, it's not a dependable source. One day the woman who owns the gallery called and asked her to take the job. "It was lucky for me. I find job hunting a rather daunting procedure. I didn't get into the nitty-gritty of trying to sell myself. I had simply been telling people I must write a résumé and get a job, but I hadn't done it. My talking did it for me."

Virginia manages the antiques gallery. Because she has always been interested in antiques and had them at home, it was easy. "I don't have to buy them for the shop or be an expert. I arrange them well and meet the public. It pulls my abilities together. I like to meet strangers, I have good interior-decorating abilities and am well organized.

"The reason I went back to work now is not only because of money. Life would be too lonely otherwise. My youngest is in high school. They no longer need me except as a friend to hold the roof on the house. I couldn't stand being alone at home all day and not having a husband come home at night. I need interesting things to think about. I love being alone, but there is such a thing as being too alone.

"Now at middle age I have more of a concept of being myself. I feel consolidated. I am more willing to say, 'This is the way I am,' and not to try to adapt myself to others' notions of what I'm supposed to be like."

More of Cora, the Black Lawyer

In Chapter VII, I talked to Cora the black woman from Detroit who doggedly kept at law school while her marriage fell in splinters around her. With her diploma in one hand and her divorce papers in the other, two children at home and little money, her only desire, in fact her only option, was to find work as a lawyer as soon as she could. She found a job with the Department of the Public Advocate in her state. We talked about what it means to be a woman, a black and a lawyer all alone.

She looks at me and says earnestly, "Don't make law glamorous. It isn't. It's so hard. You have to change and grow. It's physically and emotionally hard. Women in our age group are not used to being alone. How many women are used to being alone in a motel, or at conventions, or in a restaurant when they are traveling on business? We haven't been trained for that.

"Out in the working world we're competitors. We must realize we're taking on a whole new experience. We're not used to the aggression that's necessary. We're not used to making the distinction between social behavior and work. We're too kind, caring and empathetic—that's a disadvantage on the job.''

Cora found that being older sometimes helped in her work. ''People's concept of a lawyer or doctor is middle-aged security. It is an automatic advantage. People think you will have a serious commitment, you will deal with people well, allocate your time better.''

On the other hand she finds problems because of age. ''The senior people in status are junior to you in age. They have difficulty relating to you. They don't know how to teach someone older, because the expectation is that someone senior in age is senior also in experience and knowledge. It's up to you to remind them, in my case, that I'm only two years out of law school. They tend to think you're a little dumb when you don't know things.''

They say color is an advantage for a woman looking for work. But Cora finds that as a black woman, she would have more difficulty getting a job in a law firm. If forced to hire a black, she says, they'd hire just one. ''Even now, there still are signs of closet racism. It comes out when they relax. They make remarks. For example, one day someone brought a beautiful black dog into the office and it was running around and someone said, 'Oh, that's our new affirmative action program.' Then they looked at me and their faces fell.

''And in the courtroom, from the time I walk into the building, the expectation is that I'm a court reporter or secretary. I have to assert myself. I have on my lawyer's suit and briefcase but I have been asked to leave the lawyers' seats in court. The court reporter always stops when I get up and asks, 'Are you an attorney?' There are black women lawyers, but in the totality, we're insignificant.''

I asked Cora to give me some advice for middle-aged black women who have even fewer role models than whites have. What has she learned? Her wisdom is this.

''Go ahead. Try whatever you think you'd like to do. We can't control what's going to happen to us. We're not going to harm them—our husbands and kids. It does make things better.

The work is more interesting, the pay better, you feel better about yourself. Go back to school. Of course the degree won't change everything. We are still socially and economically at the bottom of the totem pole. It just makes problems more bearable. But the problems are exactly the same. And you take on a new problem. The problem of being the only black. I'm the only one in my office of fifteen. No one understands you. You still ought to do it. You might as well be doing work you enjoy. You're so proud of yourself. You feel a greater self-esteem.''

Cora has the residual disadvantages of being a woman, a black, older, kept busy by two kids, divorced by her husband and dependent on herself for income and security in the future. Aside from that, she has everything.

Martha, Divorced Housewife, Makes Good

It's not easy after sixteen years of marriage and children and an opulent life replete with servants to find yourself alone with three children, living in suburbia. Martha, who lives near San Francisco, told me it was her husband's idea to get the divorce. "He went through a forty-two-year-old menopause. He felt his life was over, he needed a new wife, the whole shot. We had been living in Europe for fifteen years. He was in the import-export business. I'd had servants and never kept house. Five years ago he brought us all back to California, rented a house and left me with three children aged eight, twelve and thirteen. Then he went back to Europe. He sent me some money to live on but pretty soon I could see I'd have to go out and do something.

"At first we didn't talk of divorce or separation. I didn't really know what was going on." What her husband did when he returned to Europe was to move in with a Swedish girl, sixteen years younger than he, without explaining anything to his wife. "If he had just told me, 'We are unhappy, and I've met the girl of my life.' I'd have understood. But he didn't say anything, he just left me in California. I didn't go out of the house for a year.

I was a zombie." Two years later they were divorced and he had married his new roommate.

"I could see I'd better get it together," Martha said. "I was forty-two, and the last time I worked was sixteen years before. I didn't want to go back to school and waste time. I'd had only two years of college. I decided the fastest way to get a job without training was to be a secretary. I looked in the paper to see what was in demand. And that was it. Secretaries. So I went to adult education school, learned to type and do shorthand."

Martha had no office experience, so she decided to do something temporary. She became a Kelly Girl at $2.50 an hour, which was as little pay as one can earn. But the more she went around to different offices, the more she learned and the more confidence she developed. Soon she was managing the Kelly Girl office.

Thinking about improving her potential, Martha took advantage of a new development in secretarial technology and became a word-processing specialist. For example, she puts a manuscript on tape and can correct a word, move an entire paragraph or produce copies by practically pushing a button. It's like a word computer, an automatic typewriter, obviously for the office of the future. And the future is on this woman's mind.

"Every day I learn this new typing process the more valuable I become. Few people know anything about it. I'll have the ability to parlay it into more money in a few months," says Martha who is quite concerned about her income and security. "My alimony ends in three years. Then I'm absolutely on my own. I get alimony till the kids are eighteen. Then, baby, that's it. Goodbye. All my friends live on alimony till the last minute then try to get married.

"I'm comfortable with myself. But I'm having trouble dating men. After work I'm too tired and where I live my area is full of divorced women. A man of forty-two can date a woman as young as twenty-nine. I want someone in his forties. I'm not so sure being married is the only way to be, though. You subordinate yourself to husband, his work, then the kids. You're the bottom. When my husband left me, it was pure self-preservation. I had to come first, to start doing lots of things. Divorce showed me all kinds of new strengths I never knew I had. I learned to organize my time, my money, my job. I'm becoming more professional and that's a good feeling. I speak and act like a professional—that feels good. I'm really interested in a career. Before I was just 'somebody's wife,' now I'm me, and I love it.''

Another one of the obvious possibilities for a woman like Martha who must earn money immediately is to become a real estate agent. No one is more familiar with houses and their charms or with the need to be near the best schools, in good neighborhoods, in the right part of the city or in a clean, safe, apartment building than a woman. Driving clients around and talking to them about houses can be second nature to her.

To be able to sell real estate, one must attend a licensed real estate school, then take a state test. There are two-week accelerated courses, which meet for five hours a day; or the student may space out the program over a longer period and go for a few hours in the evening after work.

One of the advantages of going into real estate is the fact that the woman is not bolted down to a chair from nine to five. After years of planning her own life, she may find she fits more easily into a job where she can still arrange her own time, decide pretty much when she can meet clients and when she can't. There is also the instant gratification of knowing that if you sell a $100,000 house, you have the income right away. The firm gets 6 percent, or $6,000, and you get half of that, or $3,000. The motivation to work hard is there, easily understandable and immediately rewarding. Furthermore, although a woman will have to go to school to prepare for this career, the course is brief, and she can quickly satisfy her need to earn money as soon as possible.

The Widows—Another Form of Having to Work

In Chapter IV on psychological stresses of midlife, I talked at length to a widow who was left desolated by her husband's death and in need of funds. Her husband had worked for a company, and his death was the end of her connection with that firm. Her only choice was to go out and find work, and she did make a wonderful life for herself as an account executive in a computer research firm. This is one kind of situation.

It is sometimes the case, however, that when a husband dies he leaves a family business behind. Whether it is a small neighborhood vegetable and grocery store or a large city newspaper, the situation presents a similar problem. Even before the tears have dried, the shock muted, a woman has to face the future, her own and that of the business. She might sell out, relieving herself of problems, but she would then be cutting off a source of continued income as well as an occupation. Many women take on the challenge and do fantastically well. One might even suspect that some of them do better than their husbands were doing.

Here are a few examples of what I mean. There is Helen Boehm, whose artist husband was one of the world's leading ceramists. His studio produced fantastic ceramic reproductions of birds and animals. When he died in 1969, after twenty-five years of marriage, he seemed irreplaceable. His heartbroken wife bought a boat and stayed near the ocean for two years. She gave the 1,500 birds from her husband's aviary to five zoos.

Helen had, from the beginning when she left her own job as an optician, worked as his sales representative and publicity seeker. She kept pushing his porcelain figures until she finally sold two pieces for $60 to the assistant curator of decorative arts at New York's Metropolitan Museum of Art. When her husband died she was forty-seven years old. She limped along feeling that she should continue his work, crying in front of audiences whenever she was invited to speak about him, and fearing that the artists her husband had trained in their Trenton, New Jersey, studio would leave.

Finally one day she decided to go on, to continue, to convince people the studio was going to keep producing fine works of porcelain. She did such a good job that she and her porcelain birds have been received by Prince Philip and Pope Paul. A bald eagle was presented to President Ford on the nation's two hundredth anniversary, President Nixon gave a pair of swans symbolizing peace to Chairman Mao on his visit to China, and Egypt allowed her artists to replicate in porcelain the treasures of Tutankhamun. Her studio now grosses $10 million a year. To give an example of the skill involved in making these porcelain artworks, a single bird is made of hundreds of separate pieces put together so delicately that the heat of a craftsman's finger is a factor in the result.

Helen Boehm decided to pick up the business where her husband left off because it was the thing she knew most about, because she has extraordinary energy, because she wanted to continue the work her husband had started, and because she had nothing else to do and desperately needed to throw herself into something. She says, when asked what sustained her through this rocky period in her life, "I was myself, no matter what."

Another widow I heard of is running her husband's shopping malls, another took over her husband's wholesale wine and liquor company. A third, whose husband died six years ago leaving a factory that produced machinery to imprint dates and codes on food containers stayed home and cried, went to a psychiatrist at $50 a half hour and showed her husband's plant to prospective buyers. The employees had petitioned this widow not to sell, and one day when she showed the plant to a particularly nasty and critical man who wanted to buy the place and change all her husband's good ideas, she decided she wasn't going to let his work end like this. She would stay and take his place. The company now has a gross income of $4 million a year. Her advice, quoted in a *New York Times* interview, is, "You can do it. You've learned it all by osmosis even if you've never set foot in your husband's office. Look at me. My only job before I married was sitting on the ninth floor of Altman's okaying all purchases under $200. Everything over that I wasn't permitted to handle. If they could see me now!"

And there is a fruit, vegetable and grocery store in my own town where I sometimes shop. The widow who runs it had worked with her husband who became ill with a kidney ailment

and died leaving her alone to manage all those fruits and grocer-
ies and order produce from the big city markets. She too could
have sold the store but she needed it for income. So she did it.
She took up the job and doubled her work efforts, arranging
vegetables in colorful baskets, putting her individual touch on
what was now *her* business.

Katharine Graham, the Most Powerful Widow

Perhaps the most powerful widow is Katharine Graham, former Publisher of the *Washington Post,* Chairman of the Board
and Chief Executive Officer of the Washington Post Company,
a terrific role model if anyone is looking for one. Besides the
influential newspaper, her company owns several other newspapers, *Newsweek* magazine, four television stations in Florida,
Michigan and Connecticut, two radio stations, half a paper company in Nova Scotia, half interest with the *Los Angeles Times*
in a news service and a third interest in the *International Herald
Tribune*. She cringes when she hears it, and she finds the char-
acterization offensive. But people say she has more power than
any woman in the United States. They have called her, "Katharine the Great," and "Krusty Kate." Although her son recently took over as publisher at the *Post*, her influence no doubt
continues as she goes about her other company duties. For example, she recently fired the editor of *Newsweek* and replaced
him with someone she thought would do a better job.

She worked because she had to. She had to keep everything
going and improve what her father began and her husband continued. It's a compulsion, a responsibility such widows feel.
They mourn and then pick up the fallen torch and carry on.
They care about the business and the product, and don't want
to see it fall into the wrong hands. They sense an obligation
pressing through the shock, sorrow and insecurity that widows
are inundated with at the time of death. The organization depends on them, other people depend on them, and they grit their
teeth and do it.

Kay Graham's father was a multimillionaire who bought the

bankrupt *Washington Post* in 1933 when it was unable to survive on its 50,000 circulation. Kay had been brought up in a family that included, besides her illustrious father, an equally illustrious mother who wrote books and prided herself on being a superintellectual. Kay naturally grew up with an inferiority complex and felt like a "peasant" in the glittering gatherings of family and guests that filled their house.

But she had an interest in newspaper work and as a teenager spent a summer doing menial tasks around the *Post*. After graduating from college she worked as a reporter in San Francisco, then returned to the *Post*. In Washington, she met and married Phil Graham, a young lawyer who eventually became publisher of her father's paper.

Kay worked for five years, then left the newspaper and submerged herself in her husband's life, volunteer work, and the role of mother of four children. At the time, a management career on the *Post* never occurred to her. In those pre-women's-lib days, she was "honestly convinced that women were inferior to men." After some years, she became ill with tuberculosis, and her husband later developed a manic-depressive psychosis, which finally resulted in his shooting himself in 1963. At this time, Kay was in her mid-forties.

Shy of publicity and uncomfortable with strangers, she cannot have found becoming head of a publishing empire an easy task. Kay was timid. And newspaper people are aggressive. But underneath the feeling that others were smarter and knew more, there was undoubtedly a tough core—a knowledge of what she wanted and really believed in—that projected her forward into the kind of decisions timid people don't make. She says, "It never occurred to me that I could do a serious job," but she did.

What she did was take over her husband's job, apologizing to her staff for her lack of qualifications. She felt "paralyzed with fear," as insecure as "the new girl at school," and absolutely "congealed" at the thought of running the paper. She remained "totally silent for a year" during the editorial lunches, and she said it took great courage for her to ask her first question. But she learned everything she needed to know on the job, "a lousy way to learn," she says.

What Kay has done is sit in on all board meetings, on some *Newsweek* story conferences and on all meetings involving major *Post* and corporate decisions. She has found time to meet with fellow business people and editors. She understands such things as labor relations, high printing costs, problems of automation and what they talk about at advertising sales conferences. She has often been the only woman present at business meetings among scores of men.

She has pushed for more women at *Newsweek,* and she has shown great journalistic and business acumen in hiring Ben Bradlee, now executive editor at the *Post*, because he knew how to get the best out of the best reporters. The uncovering of the Watergate scandal and the fall of Nixon was one result of that auspicious move. It was also her decision to risk her paper's reputation and publish the Pentagon Papers against her lawyer's advice, a move that brought her national recognition and took an enormous amount of courage, determination and understanding of what a free press is all about.

Until passing the job of publisher on to her son, Kay followed a rigorous schedule. She rose at seven every morning, read the *Washington Post,* the *New York Times* and *The Wall Street Journal.* Then she drove to work at her modern office on the eighth floor of the Post building. There she reigned as chief executive of a corporation with a net income of around $26 million. Her own annual salary was $300,000. Her newspaper, Washington's only morning paper, has a circulation of more than a half million, and that includes a subscription for the President of the United States, who doesn't start his day without reading it either.

Working and Single

Some women do not marry. They spend their lives working as men have. They enjoy and guard their life style as does any bachelor. I met one such woman while flying home from Rome. Valerie sat across the aisle from me, resplendent in a dramatic coat and hat. She was traveling with a small dog, a Lhasa Apso.

Because she sat so close, it was not long before I was petting the dog and we were talking about what she does and how she got into it. She told me she works for the foreign service in our embassy in Rome.

Originally she grew up in Boston, went to college and decided on a foreign service career because "it wasn't acceptable to live in the same city as your parents then and be alone. I could be independent if I went abroad." She had wanted to be an architect, but her father said she could be a schoolteacher, a nurse or a dietician. "The emphasis was on the boys. My brothers went to Harvard. I went to Boston University. Most women of my generation (she is fifty-two) married because they wanted someone to take care of them, pick up the tab, not have to work."

She has delighted in her jobs in the different embassies around the world. "There is no difference between a man and woman who works except he usually has more responsibility," she says. And she is reacting to middle age the way a man might. Having worked all her life, unlike most middle-aged women who are anxious to go to work now and get ahead, she is looking forward to slowing up. "I achieved the goals I established for myself," she says, "and I'm on the countdown. I'm getting ready to do my thing, paint, write, garden when I retire."

Also, like many men who are said to think of helping the younger generation or doing something to benefit humanity at this point in their lives, the single working woman is very likely to be sensitive to the same goals. In Valerie's case, what she did was to adopt her fifteen-year-old niece, the daughter of one of those Harvard-trained brothers, who became an alcoholic. "I'm the oldest in the family, I decided I should make a contribution.

"I'm at peace with myself. When I was young I was full of ambitions I've now attained. I have lots of young friends, but I wouldn't be young for anything. I'm glad I've lived through all of that. I've had all the emotional encounters, the highs and lows. When you get older you don't have that any more. It's rather nice. I've had a wonderful life. I'm leaning back and enjoying everything. I'm not struggling anymore."

She had a few comments to make about married women who are in mid-life today. "I think married women use children as a cop-out, an excuse for not doing other things as well." Or the menopause. "Why go to bed with the menopause? I take calcium tablets and go to work." And family. "Children should play a certain role in your life. But a wife becomes dull and boring if she only cares for the house and kids. I think marriage is a job, and if you don't do it well, you get fired. Women should do something else so they're interesting and attractive and not go around moaning because the children are growing up and leaving."

Valerie says that because she has worked with men all her life, she doesn't feel the same traumas about getting old.

"I have the added advantage of working with men all day and it keeps me on my toes and looking attractive. I like working with men, I like being a woman, and I don't mind being fifty-two."

Being single, spending her life working with no one else to support her, and enjoying the exotic surroundings of whatever post she was sent to has given Valerie an interesting, though unconventional, existence. She has worked because she had to. But she chose to do it that way. Despite the fact that she has remained single, she feels the married career woman has the best of both worlds—the job and constant male companionship.

10

The Vanishing Volunteers

At one time in our social history, it was considered demeaning for a woman to work for money, and only the poor went out looking for jobs. Yet countless women worked. But they did it in a way that was socially acceptable, in fact fashionable. They contributed their time free of charge. Middle- and upper-class women who were beset by boredom, who also felt the urge to help humanity, would offer their services as volunteers. They often worked long hours and they worked hard. Many still do, and they are, without doubt, invaluable to organizations that cannot afford to hire the equivalent help. They have recorded for the blind, read to the sick, brought library books and warm meals to the old, helped with school and church functions, raised money for symphony orchestras and art museums. The list of hospitals, conservation groups and community organizations they have aided is endless.

There were so many women giving their time in the past they made up a vast source of work power, a virtual "army of volunteers." This army has gradually been vanquished, eroded away as its recruits realized that the time and talent they were giving away so freely other women were selling and employers were eagerly buying.

Because there is so much more opportunity now, because it is the accepted thing to do and because more families need a second income, enormous numbers of former volunteers have decided they would rather work for the pay and prestige that a regular job gives them.

There have also been increasing signs of discontent among volunteers who feel they are being treated badly. Some say their ideas are ignored, and they frequently are exploited, even condescended to by the paid staff or the men who have other positions that give them added importance. One woman I spoke to left her volunteer job because she felt humiliated by the way the men treated her. She explained that she had volunteered to work for a group that was offering college scholarships to needy and talented high school students.

"I was supposed to do the publicity. Most of the board was composed of businessmen from the community and a few women teachers. I wrote the publicity reports, took photographs, had them printed at my expense, took them by hand to the various newspapers in town and when they were printed, clipped them from the papers. Despite all this work, no mention was ever made of the publicity I got for the group which was, at the time, raising funds. But when the businessmen on the board did anything, suggested anything, there was a great to-do over them and they were warmly praised. The other women said nothing.

"I didn't mind doing all the work, taking the time and spending the money, but I did object to never getting any recognition from the men that I existed, or that I did anything valuable for them. I finally resigned in frustration."

Enough Volunteering for Betty

Betty lives in a midwestern city where she has done volunteer work with the League of Women Voters. When I spoke to her, she was in her mid-forties and had just finished an important volunteer job as president of a nonprofit housing corporation for low- and moderate-income families.

"There were pluses to volunteer work. It was more rewarding than lots of paid jobs. It was probably as important as anything I'll ever do. But there were minuses. It was frustrating. As a volunteer," Betty explained, "you lack prestige. You have to work harder. You have to get the support of the others with prestige, the professional experts. When you have a paid job, you have authority, and when you say something is supposed to happen, it happens. As a volunteer, no one assumes your direction has to be followed. I had to get approval from the board for everything.

"Being a volunteer is like coming up continuously against a roadblock. No one knows how to treat you. You are not given recognition. Volunteer jobs are usually short-term, there is no long-term benefit."

What finally disillusioned Betty and turned her sour on any future volunteering was her experience in applying for a $100,000 government grant for the housing project. She got the idea from the township, wrote the application and showed it to the staff. The assistant administrator of the township thought that, because he was the assistant administrator, a paid employee, and superior to Betty in rank and position, he should rewrite everything. She says he "ruined" her application and she had to struggle to get it restored to its former state. "If I had been paid, it never would have occurred to him to redo my work," she said. "The general idea is that if you are doing something for nothing, it can't be very good."

She feels that no one wants to give praise to volunteers today because they must keep up the morale of the paid management. "If you are paid, the credit flows without asking. It's there. Without the status of a title and pay, your position is in limbo no matter how hard you work. I never was thanked for all that I did on the grant. No one thought we had a chance. No one encouraged me. I know I worked hard, learned something, changed the outcome. That's very rewarding. It's a very private thing. I affected something in this world positively. But people need acknowledgment that they are doing the job."

Betty finally decided to go back to school and get a master's in urban planning. She had become interested in it through her volunteer work and had learned a lot when she gave her time. It wasn't the need for money in her case that was driving her into new directions. It was simply the crushing lack of recognition. "Call it insurance. I want to keep my options open so I will not be faced with some dreadful future. So I don't feel locked in when it's too late. I want to be sure I am marketable in my fifties."

The point of her feelings as she explained them were simple. "If society looked on volunteering differently, it would be important to volunteer. As long as you are not paid, the way things are now, you are never a professional, you don't have the prestige of working for a living. Society is based on the money ethic, being rewarded for your efforts by money."

Nevertheless she feels that doing volunteer work gave her excellent experience, both in getting along with people and getting others to do things for her. She said she learned how to be both political and supportive, and is glad she did it.

The End of Volunteering for Connie

Connie lives near Seattle, Washington. Tall, willowy, attractive in her long skirt and leather boots, she told me a now familiar story. She went to college and married the quarterback and captain of the football team in her junior year. But she did stay on and finish school. Later, she had three children and remained at home caring for them, full of resentment, while her husband played professional football and got his master's degree.

"I sat at home feeling very angry and blaming him. I went through a period of intense anger. As an individual I had the choice of doing something else, but it didn't occur to me. I was at home with tiny babies in a small apartment in a strange city and it didn't occur to me that I could do anything. It was a self-imposed trap.

"It wasn't that I didn't like the mother role," Connie said. "There was just no stimulation, and I'm afraid I wasn't very creative with that role. I did typical middle-class volunteer work, the art museum, the symphony, the alumni group. Once I was chairperson for a successful lunch and I figured out that if we had all given our baby-sitting money, we'd have had more money than we raised. I decided, 'This has got to be the height of bloody absurdity.'

"Those women needed to fill their time for the benefit of society. I was doing it because it was the thing to do. Then we moved. I began working with a group of low-income women and started a Planned Parenthood clinic. I was doing something that had never been tried in that community. Five or six of us did a study and found a tremendous need. That was the first time I'd worked with a group of people, and I had a tremendous sense of achievement. It was an exciting time."

But Connie found that in another sense volunteering wasn't enough. She wanted to earn money. "Society values your contribution by paying you for it. Volunteers are denigrated when they don't get paid but provide services which society is not yet willing to pay for. But I knew I couldn't get a paying job without a graduate degree in the health field. There's a limit to the amount a volunteer can do, and as a volunteer, it seemed to me I was being a dilettante. I wanted to be a professional. Why should I work for free if others are being paid for it?"

Connie agreed with Betty that the staff treated volunteers differently from those who were there for an eight-hour day. "Then, we wrote some books on women with physical disabilities. We were paid by a government grant. Suddenly they treated us differently, with more respect. It was as if they said, 'What she's doing must be worthwhile. Someone's willing to pay for it.' "

Connie also decided to go back to school and get her master's. There were too many things she needed to learn. Although volunteering taught her many things, it also showed her what she didn't know. She found, when it came to budgeting and finance, she was a blank. She couldn't read a financial report at a meeting and ask an intelligent question. She needed economics and communication. She also wanted to prepare for a professional career because she felt a need for security. "Men start dying in their forties of heart attacks, marriages break up with the best love and care, and I'd seen so many women who couldn't take care of themselves. Do men ever have enough life insurance?"

Despite her decision not to do any more volunteer work, she recognizes the value it had for her. "I just had my fortieth birthday. I'm feeling the same as I did on my seventeenth birthday—that my life is just beginning. It was the whole process of volunteering that got me back to school, got me to know myself better, gave me the idea of having a future—things going up and not downhill, things opening up for me."

Other Volunteers

Neither of these volunteers had to give up contributing because they were in a financial squeeze. Both simply felt unappreciated, and that their jobs were getting them nowhere. They were also concerned about having a secure future. In some cases, however, finances do become the main reason for giving up volunteer work. When any family crisis occurs and the income situation is altered, or when school bills need to be paid, there simply is no choice. The need to work for pay is immediate.

A woman demographer I was talking to recently warned that women who don't work for money are taking a large risk. "All you have to do is look at the life insurance tables," she said, "to know that most women outlive their husbands, and although it's no fun being old and alone, being old, *poor,* and alone is intolerable."

Anticipating this possibility made one woman I spoke to give up her community work. She had started a volunteer tennis program and built it into an institution. If you had a child, and lived in that town, he or she automatically took the community tennis lessons. But one day her husband became ill, and this shocked her. She realized she couldn't count on his earning capacity anymore and decided she had to work for money. She turned her tennis knowledge into a job for the United States Tennis Association, wrote tennis books for teachers and held tennis clinics.

Another woman I talked to told me she decided she was going to take ten years and devote them to bringing up her two children. But because she is a woman with a lot of energy and imagination, she also wanted to get involved in the life around her. She decided volunteer work was perfect because she could fit it into her children's schedule. She has become president of the parents association of one son's private school and a volunteer on the recruitment committee that seeks new students. She organizes book week for another child's public school and, finally, she reads and tapes books for blind university students, everything from French grammar to novels and philosophy. She has found her volunteer jobs very interesting, is "learning an awful lot" and feels it will open up future career possibilities for her.

In the meantime, she gets a lot of satisfaction from her activites. "I do a good job, and people are delightful to me. I'm doing things I believe in." For example, she and her fellow volunteers have persuaded a reluctant art teacher to arrange a special program for book week on English heraldry. "He was not enthusiastic, but we succeeded in firing him up, getting him going, and in the end my child will have a better education."

Even though it has been an extremely beneficial experience for her, she too sees her volunteer experiences coming to an end. She needs more money for the kids' schools. But she says, "I enjoyed it and considered whatever I did a job, even though I wasn't paid."

Volunteering can be gratifying because you have the altruistic sense of contributing, without a mercenary reward, and enabling worthwhile organizations to continue when, without the free help, they might have to cut back their services. But when a woman finds herself giving a great deal of her time and energy, then comparisons with her friends who are working for pay become inevitable.

Women who move on to school and/or a job, find that volunteering has been a good beginning experience to sharpen their skills and ease their way into the work world. Interacting with others teaches one a great deal about what working is, and these women say they have learned many things that helped them both in school and later on when they worked. Employers are just beginning to count volunteering as a legitimate job, despite the fact that there was no payment.

Many women who do not wish to work will continue to volunteer and enjoy it, while others who have jobs will also sometimes contribute to their communities. But its place is no longer on the avenues where men and other women are winning money and prestige for what they do. The trend among mid-life women is away from a lifetime of volunteering.

11

Well, I'll Be Damned—
I'm Good at Business

This is a world in which the supermarket and department store, the corporation, the conglomerate and the multinational corporation really run things. Their volume of sales often makes it possible for them to cut prices, and the small business has to struggle barely to compete and survive. Given this situation, anyone starting a small business now might well be risking more than his shirt. Surely, only a crafty and experienced businessman could make it.

How, then, can a woman moving out of the housewife's sheltered and genteel world, as inexperienced in the intricacies of merchandising, finance, profits and losses as a guileless child, find the fortitude, in the middle of her life, to begin a business of her own?

Many such women have taken a small portion of all the varied talents they have ever used around the house, thought about them and decided to convert them into an independent business where they work for themselves and keep a large part of what they earn. Because their years of domestic activity have made them expert in the "care" field, there are several obvious routes they can take if they want to formalize what they do and turn it into a profitable enterprise. They know more than most people about the care of houses, dogs, children, plants and the appetite for clothes and food. Many women are becoming entrepreneurs and opening real estate, antique, dog-sitting, child-care, plant-care, boutique and decorating businesses. And their culinary skills have taken them in a number of food-service directions. Often they work out of their houses, which cuts expenses.

Other women begin ventures that are far more sophisticated and removed from matters of the home. Their businesses go from the most elementary to the most sophisticated. But no matter how small the enterprise, these independent business-women begin by having to do many of the same things. They think up a name, have business cards printed, write brochures, seek publicity, advertise, sell their product or service, keep their books, have gross income and net profit and pay taxes.

Some who start small stay that way; others grow. The business is usually tailored to fit the ambition and resources of the woman. Again, as in most of what she does, her husband's tacit, and in some cases active, support is essential to making it work well.

Most of the women I spoke to said they never realized they could possibly be good at business, no matter how modest. They assumed that because business had always been the province of men, because they had never even tried to understand the basic forces of economics, or even the language—the key to simplifying it all—that it was far too difficult for an average woman to master. Now they know that intelligence in business is not an inheritable male trait.

They find they enjoy this personal challenge, they enjoy selling something they do well, they love making money and find it absorbing to think up ways of cutting expenses and increasing profits. They are usually utterly amazed at how astute about the entire process they are, how hard fisted they can be when required. In some fields, where they compete with established male-run businesses, they have had to fight unfair criticism that comes close to slander. In some cases it is assumed they know nothing, are soft and can easily have their brains picked and ideas stolen without so much as a whimper. Some have not only whimpered, they have gone to court and won.

Decorating

Several women I talked to have become interior decorators, working out of their own houses, offering advice on what to buy that's new and what to do to pump vigor into old furniture. One of them, from Chicago, had recently been divorced and needed to make some money. She decided to take advantage of her talent for understanding colors, fabrics and the placement of furniture to advise budget-conscious customers. Presto, she was in business. She called friends, advertised and slowly began to get a response. She depends mainly on word of mouth to spread her fame. She charges $250 to go into an average house and devise a whole outline of what should be done in the future to that house. She makes sketches to show her clients what each room could look like. Then she sets up a program of buying to take place over the years, so they don't impulse-shop when they see something they just have to have, and later find it's all wrong. She doesn't sell furniture the way other decorators in more complex businesses do, acting as the middle man between the wholesaler and the client. She merely sells her time and advice. For her, this means that no special training, degrees or investment of money are necessary.

Of course, for the average woman who may want to try the same kind of business, a few courses in design would probably polish her natural talent.

Food

Many women I found are involved with some form of the food business, which they run from their houses. One of them operates a "supper service" and will make and deliver suppers anywhere in town. Another has a more complex catering service and manages to do two or three dinners or cocktail parties a month. She prefers large affairs and has a $400 minimum guarantee before she even picks up her measuring cup. This woman chose catering because she wanted something she could do without working for others, and she wanted it to be flexible enough so she could take vacations with her husband. Deciding to use her cooking talents, she thought up a snappy name and advertised in the local paper. Her investment included buying a station wagon instead of a compact car, two upright freezers, two other refrigerators with freezers now in the basement, garage and kitchen. She bought lots of pots and fabric for tablecloths, which she rents at $4 each. Then she added a collection of Lucite bowls, platters, cake stands and baskets. When the reception is really large she hires other women in town to help, and they do some of the cooking months beforehand and freeze it all. Her biggest worry is that storms will cause power failures and defrost the food before the right time.

To have a business, you have to register the name of it in the state licensing department. (There can be only one business with any particular name.) And she advises any woman who wants to try a catering service like hers to carry lots of damage insurance in case someone gets sick after eating the food, or someone carrying a large chocolate mousse trips over an electric wire and ruins an antique rug. You also have to have your kitchen pass a department of health inspection.

She accomplished all this and was in business. But she has had her share of catastrophes: ovens that didn't work during a wedding dinner for ninety people, or finding herself short of quiches and conscripting her doctor husband, who had never cooked anything, into helping her make more of them. But she gets an enormous satisfaction out of the work. Cooking for large groups has made her an expert in planning, assembly lines, logistics, finances, management and employing others.

Having her own business makes her feel "I'm of some use, and I'm doing this thing better than anyone else can."

How Vicki Started a Lunch Restaurant with $1,000

One brilliantly sunny day in spring, a friend and I had lunch in a small, one-room restaurant which was filled with hanging plants and served the most exquisite food. Not long afterward I learned how this haven had come about.

Vicki, the owner, told me she has been married for twenty-five years and is the mother of four children, one still in high school. She started her business six years ago. This is why and how it came about—and what occasionally went wrong.

Vicki never went to college. She thought only of getting married and having children. "Years and years ago, none of us had any money. Everyone was just having babies. I used to fight anyone who wanted to go to work. Sitting in the park with our babies, I thought it was outrageous that people would leave their kids. I simply thought it was ridiculous that some women could not enjoy taking care of their kids, the laundry and kitchen —that they wanted anything else."

Finally the babies grew up and Vicki and her husband needed more money to be able to pay for all the necessary education. Middle age had arrived and Vicki got scared. She had no skills and couldn't even type. In fact, she became desperate. "I felt I had to do something to help contribute to the income. Maybe I could be a waitress (my husband didn't like that idea) or drive a school bus."

One day she went shopping in an area that has a cluster of shops used by several surrounding small towns and met a friend who remarked, "What we really need here is a place to have lunch. Why don't you open a sandwich bar? You like to cook."

"Then I thought, 'Gosh, that would be fun. Why don't I do a restaurant?' My husband thought it sounded exciting." She found a friend to go in with her. They each borrowed $500 and with their combined $1,000, they rented a glass-enclosed porch which could seat fifteen people at eight tables. That was the beginning.

Because there was no water in the place, they had to take the dirty dishes home to wash, and they cooked at home and carried the food to the restaurant.

"We started small, so it wasn't scary. I went to the library and got books on soup. We decided on soup for lunch instead of sandwiches because it was something we could make in advance in large quantities. The arrangement was terribly primitive."

After eight months they rented a larger place, a shop that they still have. It is large enough for twelve tables. They borrowed bentwood chairs, got pedestal bases and bought three-quarter-inch plywood, which they cut into tabletops and covered with cloths. These in turn they covered with plastic so there was no laundry.

For lunch they pass a tray of fresh vegetables for people to nibble on. Then comes a communal bowl of soup for the entire table to help themselves. Vicki and her partner do fifteen different kinds, such as spinach and leek, pumpkin, Caribbean fish chowder, three-bean soup, turkey gumbo. They try to have a soup that's a whole meal. They put sherry on the table in atomizers, and people can add it to their soup if they wish. There is homemade bread and, because they didn't want to be bothered with perishable butter, it comes with cheese. Dessert is a long stick with fruit on it like shish kebob. Lastly they pass a tray of little square cakes, lemon, chocolate, toffee nut. There is coffee and tea, and the entire lunch, including seconds, is $3.75. They freeze and sell leftover soups and cakes.

On an average day they serve fifty to sixty lunches. "I was overwhelmed," said Vicki, "by the number of people who come in. But we need that many to make a profit. We get so busy we once actually had to turn away the governor. Another day Julie Christie, the English actress, was there. She kept asking for 'buttaah.' There always are so many interesting people."

Naturally, they have had their crisis moments. One day Vicki tripped over a chicken that ran across her path as she was leaving the house and spilled all the soup she had made for that day's lunch. Fortunately there was more in the freezer.

About children, Vicki says, "I'd never have four again. I'd have two. I used to get so exhausted. It's too expensive and draining emotionally."

About her business, she says, "It's overwhelming that I've made money. I can't quite believe it. My partner and I each make about $10,000 a year. My whole image of myself has changed. I feel good. I've done something. Made people happy. Our little place is like a theater. And my husband is proud of me. At parties they used to say, 'Meet Hal who does this and that, and this is his wife.' Now they say, 'Meet Vicki, and this is Vicki's husband, Hal.' My husband is really happy that I have a profession. If something happened to him, I could survive.

"The thing I like best is that I'm not like everyone else. I used to be like everyone else. Now I'm different, and men and women really respect me now. If I were just a waitress, I wouldn't get the respect. People would say, 'Isn't it too bad that poor Vicki has to work.' Now, they admire me."

How Angie Became the Plant Lady

A woman in her forties found herself divorced with three children and a husband who didn't send her enough money. She decided to go into some business where she could earn what she needed, $15,000 to $25,000 a year to keep things going.

What Angie did was to take her love of gardening, which so many women share, and market it. She started alone by enclosing the back porch on her house and buying a gas heater to turn it into a greenhouse. She went to the library, got books on horticulture and found out the names of all the plants and what diseases they were likely to get. She used poison sprays at first but then turned to organic recipes like soap, garlic and pepper or boiled tobacco juice to kill the pests. She got help from the county agricultural agent who will analyze soil to see if it is properly balanced.

Her bookkeeping the first two years was done in a Triscuit box. She worked by herself for fifteen months and had no expenditures, aside from buying the plants, which she quickly sold. She took her old car and painted it green and put ads in the local paper. She learned where to get wholesale plants and baskets by poking around in nurseries and asking. In addition to just selling, once a week she visited the houses of the people who had bought her plants and, for a fee, watered, pruned, fed, cleaned and sprayed them for bug control. Two years later she bought a Volkswagen bus because she needed more space for larger and larger plants. She now designs indoor gardens and gives lectures.

I visited Angie in her home-cum-shop one day. Her house and greenhouse are filled with hundreds of specimens of greenery. Ferns hang from the ceiling, vines climb around the windows. There are violets, hibiscus, giant begonias, palms, orange trees and gardenia trees. Most are for sale. Some are for rent to television, theaters or department stores. Others are there on a plant-sitting basis until their traveling owners return home.

Angie saw me looking at them and said, "Taking care of people's plants is a responsibility, like worrying over little children. People are so concerned about their plants. Our mortality rate has to be nonexistent. We have to be careful."

This is Angie's sixth year of business, and her fame has spread. She travels as much as fifty miles to another state to decorate, among other places, the office of the president of a large department store. She now has six people working for her, a part-time bookkeeper who does the bills and taxes, two people in the nearby state who maintain the plants on a weekly basis and three others who buy and maintain plants in her state.

Despite the fact that divorce was the prelude to her business and success, Angie's memory of the broken marriage is quite bitter. "My husband never liked me to have any confidence. Every individual should have the opportunity of developing anything she wants to the maximum, her fullest potential, even if it's cooking or whatever it is. For me, my plant work was the final challenge. I'd been pushed that far. My life almost ended in madness. You know," she went on, "if you've always had the drive and someone diverts it, he makes you feel you have no right to have it. You feel fear first. Then anger. I had to lose my anger creatively. It was a real primal drive for survival."

To go from inhibited, put-down, frustrated housewife to divorcée with her own business, without any background in business, without having learned any of the tricks, methods, the procedures and the pitfalls was not very easy. First there is the consideration of being a female in business. Says Angie, "You have to be asexual. You get looks and offers, but you don't get the jobs because you are a woman. You have to have initiative and competitive prices."

She learned about business the hard way. Several things happened to make her realize that you have to be shrewd, protect yourself and play the game your opponent plays by outwitting him.

The research center of one of the country's major corporations was redoing an area of their offices and asked her for her charges. She said it would be $50 for a visit and a design plan. They asked for the plan and led her to believe she was going to get the job, $800 worth of indoor planting. She told them not only what would look good, but also what would grow in that area. Instead of letting her go ahead, they called four or five other people asking for their prices on the plants that Angie had recommended.

"Hey," she told them, "I gave you a design plan." They negotiated for six or seven months. The purchasing man became ugly and rude to her. She explained to him, "I'm a small-business person. I negotiated in good faith while you picked my brains. You are shabby and cheap."

They finally agreed to pay her $150 for her time. Then they bought the plants elsewhere themselves. "It was hard to believe," says Angie. "It was one of my lessons. Each time someone takes advantage of me I learn. You have to learn to trust your judgment and follow through on it. You can make mistakes and be wrong, but you also have the fun of doing it right."

This was not the only such incident. Now she is in the process of taking a nearby bank to small claims court. The bank president asked her to design a cactus garden. She did research on cactuses for most of a week and sent him a floor plan with the name of each cactus, its location and price. "He refused to pay me for it. He said the board hadn't decided yet. Then when I spoke to him a second time, he said I had done nothing. Later I heard that he went out and bought the same cactus plants from a florist.''

Working on speculation is a risk, and Angie has to learn how to judge this risk, and each client, to decide whether she ought to do the job, or whether there is likely to be a problem. "The world is not what they teach you,'' Angie says philosophically, "that if you're right, you'll get your payment. It's tricky. You have to be thrifty, creative, inventive and have a good psychological rapport, so they don't play games.''

Most people are honest, which her gross income of $60,000 last year proves. But when there is a problem, Angie has learned to stand up and fight. It's part of being in business.

The Lady and the Camera

Janet has been married for twenty-five years and has five children. She went to a junior college near Wilmington, Delaware. She always enjoyed photography as a hobby, took many pictures of her children and now and then went to night classes. "I knew the time would come eventually when all the children would go off, and I'd have nothing to do.''

She was entering her middle years, her youngest son was five, and she decided the time had come. With her husband's encouragement, she set up a studio at home and advertised. The bathroom became a darkroom. "My family didn't mind. Once in a while the little one would ask me to get my prints out of the tub so he could take a bath.''

Because she had a camera, her investment consisted of no more than what some privileged teenagers have for a hobby—an enlarger, a dryer, trays and chemicals. "I was scared to death at the beginning. I was so thrilled if anyone came, and I had my own private client.'' She had about two people a week, just enough for a very small beginning.

But she was also nervous about making a fool of herself by doing a bad job. "If you say,'' Janet explained, "here I am, I'm going to be a professional, it's a little frightening. I felt an overall insecurity. I'd never worked like this. I'd done nothing in twenty years, except take pictures for my own pleasure. If people are going to pay me to take their picture, that's something else. I owe it to them to give them something professional."

How to survive when you are beginning even in the most simple business setup is not easy. The awkward situations that lead to learning abound. Janet didn't spill the soup as Vicki did, nor have to go to small claims court to be paid, as Angie did, but she had her own brush with disaster.

"When I was beginning," Janet recalled, "I had a shattering experience. I had just started taking pictures, and I took one of a family. After they left the studio, which was on the third floor, and were walking to their car, I realized I had put a filter over the lens by accident, and nothing was going to come out. Too much light had been cut out. I stood there and debated. Should I let them go and call a week later to say there had been a defect in the film? Or should I make myself look like a jerk and run after them? I decided, since they were all dressed and thinking of pictures, I'd go after them. I hollered out of the window and asked them to come back. I confessed and they were gracious, although they must have thought I was the biggest fruitcake to come down the road. I was mortified. I never used that filter again. I suppose every photographer lives in fear that something will happen to the camera or film, and there will be no pictures when they are doing a wedding. To have to tell a bride that kind of thing must be heartbreaking. She's not going to get married again."

Having had so many children helps her understand and photograph them well. But whether it's children or adults, Janet says, "I love to go to work. I'm not doing it just to fill time, or there are a thousand other things I could do. I want to do what I do well."

Her words to women of her age are quite direct. "Prepare yourself to do something in addition to housewife and mother. Do it over the years while you raise your children. Trying it after the children are grown is harder. So many women are looking around for jobs who have had no training. That was our generation. We were not expected to do anything. Suddenly now we're being told something else.

"What do you do after the kids are grown up? How many times can you clean a house in a week? It's important for a woman to have something she can do well, something that's her own. Now I feel very independent. Just to sit around with nothing could be awful. I've done volunteer work. I guess I like being paid. It sounds crass, but if I work hard, I enjoy pay.

"I think we all like feeling independent. I don't know if my husband will live forever. And secondly, I'm more interesting if he comes home and we can both talk about our work and what we've done. Otherwise what can I say? Well, what did I do today? I cleaned the house and I went to the A&P. After a while you'd become a very dull person. I get very tired when I don't have anything. It's boredom, not fatigue."

One Woman and Her Advertising Business

Some businesses are more demanding and complicated than others and require more expertise in several different kinds of functions. Advertising is one that is known for its cutthroat qualities. It's a tough, mean business, and competition is the main motivation.

Peggy, a middle-aged woman with one child, was married at the age of eighteen after managing to eke out two years of college. She grew up in a home where her parents were separated and the family was poor. In high school she sold hosiery every Saturday and knew what earning money meant. Perhaps for that reason, or maybe because she has independently developed that philosophy, she believes that people should work. "I am happier and healthier. If you work there is a reason for being. I can't imagine *not* working."

She says she was the typical suburban mother. She stayed home until her son went off to college. While at home, she worked part-time doing public relations for a department store and eventually became fashion and publicity director. She was forty-two when she went to work full-time. In one year, she had become a vice-president of the store. "I stayed one year and then left."

Why would a woman in her forties give up such an excellent job? And for what? Peggy said, "I left because it was time to do what I wanted to do the way I wanted to do it. I enjoyed working with other people, but it was time. I felt I had gone as far as I could in that job. It would be more of the same. There were no more mountains to climb. I wanted to put on my hiking shoes. So I decided to start my own advertising and public relations business. People had always said to me, 'You work so hard, why don't you do it for yourself instead of for others?' I guess subliminally it worked."

Peggy had her business registered with the county clerk, rented a one-room office in a hotel and hired an art director. She was the secretary, and she was on her own. Her business was launched.

She began with a portable typewriter and a slightly wobbly art table. That was two years ago. She now has an office with her own computerized typesetting equipment, her own cameras, processors and an expensive IBM typewriter. The business is hectic. There is a standard of quality to live up to, there are deadlines.

Today she has over fifty accounts. She interviews her clients, finds out what product they want to advertise, decides how it should be done, sketched or photographed, what should be said about it, and what the design of the whole ad should look like. She employs five full-time artists and layout people. But she does the writing and bookkeeping.

"I enjoy it. Bookkeeping is something I can do at home, and I know what's happening. It's not to keep track of the money. It's being in control of things. I have that marvelous feeling of seeing it all on paper. It's real when I see it. I tell myself, 'I did it!' I can't believe it when I see what I'm doing!"

She also wants to see where the money has come from and how she has spent it. "A lot of people can make money. It's what you do with the money you make that determines whether you stay in business. Advertising is hard. There are all kinds of pressures. Most women are happy to work for someone else, make $15,000 and let them have the ulcers. In advertising you have to make decisions all the time and stand by them. Hopefully you have a good batting average. A lot of money is involved. Sure, women are used to making decisions at home. But if you screw up at home, the only person you have to account to is your husband. At work you can lose an account, or respect, with a bad decision.''

Like many other businesswomen, Peggy sees work in terms of problems. ''The way I look at things is, 'How do you attack the problem? How do you solve it?' '' That is what provides the fascination for her, makes for new challenges every day, keeps her from sleeping very much at night. ''I'm convinced the reason I sleep so little,'' she said, ''is because I want to continue working and thinking and solving. I can't wait to get started each day.''

Going into business for herself, particularly this kind of competitive business, has not been smooth all the way. As a female owner of a business in a field that is essentially male dominated she is conscious of the fact that she is not always welcome, and dealing with men is sometimes difficult. ''If they can't regard you as a sex object, wife, mother or teacher,'' says Peggy, ''they are not comfortable with you. Men have a camaraderie they find difficult to share with women.'' In several instances, she was the victim of some dirty play. Men from other advertising firms have been known to tell her clients that they had better change firms because she was ''on the ropes.''

In another instance, an ad salesman from a newspaper actually told one of her clients that she was unethical and unqualified and gave this client names of other agencies which he said were better. When she heard about this she went to the horrified newspaper publisher with the information. He asked her not to take any action, and it would never happen again. Says Peggy, ''When things like this happen, you don't whine or cry. You just take an appropriate action. I did, and the harassment stopped. You have to be very sure of yourself when taking such measures. You can't deal with a difficult situation emotionally or irrationally.''

But there are also advantages to a woman's agency. Because she is a consumer, she is able to judge, perhaps better than a man, what people are looking for. Because women are the ones buying, making those decisions, she has an edge. "Also, I care," she says. "I want to succeed at what I'm doing. I try hard, maybe harder. If there's something I don't know, I find out. I do my homework. I'm still trying to prove I can do it as well or better than a man."

And she finds advantages to being middle-aged. "I have many young clients who look to me for guidance. I'm not a threat to the wives of any of my clients. I think I'm at the right age. The only regret I have is that I didn't start my business ten years ago. It's so fantastically wonderful. I'd have had twelve years by now instead of only two at this age. I'm benefiting from a combination of experience that I've had and timing. People can accept a woman's ad agency now. I'm sure being a woman helped me get some accounts. I had to prove myself first, of course."

The proof was cemented recently when Peggy took on her first national industrial account. Her secrets? One is to listen, so you know what the client wants. Another is to concentrate. Shut everything else out at a given moment.

"I'm fulfilled," says Peggy, "but I don't call myself successful. There are too many things I don't know how to do, too many campaigns I haven't laid out, too many places I haven't been. I'm on the right track, though."

Real Estate

I briefly encountered a real estate woman from the state of Washington. She had left college after one semester to marry and support her husband while he finished school. "I thought being a private secretary was the ultimate goal in life." When she went to work she was surprised to find how competitive she was, but it was a game and she had no goals. Years later after working for others, she decided at age thirty-eight to open her own real estate business. She started with a secretary and two other people. Now, only two years later, she has fifteen people working for her plus a calculator with ten storage banks to add up their $300,000 a year income! The business is two-thirds residential and one-third commercial.

Most of what she has learned she crammed for by herself. She bought the books and studied. The thing she enjoys the most, like Peggy, is the problem solving, taking something that everyone has given up on solving it. She also feels a need to improve, to keep learning, and is taking a forty-hour course in real estate, which includes things like marketing, investment, taxation and multiple-apartment houses.

Being female with your own business is not always easy, especially if you live in a more "traditional" state like Washington, where you might be even less readily accepted than elsewhere.

"I joined the Economic Development Council in town, which does things like giving money to stimulate new business. I wanted to be in a key position to know what was going on in my city. Once we had a golf tournament. They *gave* each lady a present just for playing whereas the men had to win their prizes. It was as though they thought the women were mentally and physically handicapped.

"When I joined the chamber of commerce I said I wanted to do whatever was necessary to help. One of the men there said, 'Boy are we happy to have you. When the time comes we could use some help typing envelopes.' I glared back. 'If I find someone who can do that, I'll let you know.'

"Or men I meet in business will ask, 'Is your husband also in the real estate business?' They assume he's the person, the power, behind me. Or people will come in and see me, a woman, and ask, 'Is the broker around?' "

But she finds real estate a good business for women who are mothers because it doesn't take as much training as other things and has a great financial potential. Furthermore, mothers are used to planning their own time. She says, "The main effort is not selling but finding what's available that people can afford. You don't take people out and tell them how nice the house is. They can see that for themselves. The main thing in real estate, I think, is to get people to overcome their fear of making the investment. The property usually sells itself."

I asked this woman where she got the courage to begin a business of her own. She said she started it after she had taken a lot of management classes, which gave her confidence. "I asked myself, 'What's the worst thing that can happen?' If I can figure out the worst thing and accept it, live with it, I can go ahead and try."

I was wondering why there aren't even more women opening their own businesses, although an increasing number are, and she answered my thoughts. "You don't find more women in business because, it's not that they are afraid, they simply don't know they have the talent. They've been playing second fiddle for too many years. I have a woman agent who has enormous talent and doesn't know it. She chooses to work around her husband's schedule even though he's a big poop. She is unaware of what she's doing, and she's frustrated because she feels torn in several directions—between job and husband. She is trying to take care of her business demands without letting her husband have to do anything for himself. At home I have a housekeeper. Neither my husband nor I do the vacuuming, so we stay equal.

"Why do I work? I have to reassure myself of my worth constantly, try to prove my ability and test it. My mother always said she would do things she wanted to do. 'When my ship comes in, I'll do all sorts of wonderful things.' Well, it didn't come in for her. She upped and died. I decided I wasn't going to wait. I was going to go out in my boat and meet the ship. Though there really isn't one out there waiting. You have to make it."

Consultant in Human Relations

As we expand our ideas of how people can relate to others, a lot of businesses have sprung up to guide the way. This innovative one was started by the wives of two corporation executives who were "dragged screaming to conferences," and said they'd never go back. The business is owned by two partners. One lives in New Jersey, the other in Massachusetts. I spoke with Carla, who is forty-three. She finished college, had two children, did volunteer work and took courses now and then to continue her education. Because of some volunteer work she was doing, she happened to take a course in human relations. "That changed my whole life and thinking. Since then I've taken many courses and studied the subject."

According to Carla, age was a factor in starting her business. Her children were teenagers and didn't need her in the same way they had at a younger age. Her volunteer time had ended. ("I always chose a different kind of volunteer work to add to my background.") She saw a larger segment of her time opening up, and she wanted to be paid. "It's a ripe time for women to get into the field of human relations. It used to be mainly for men, but now women are starting businesses all over the place."

Carla feels that by choosing the kind of business she did, she has the best of all possible situations. She can select what she wants to do, and when she wants to do it, and have time to be a wife and mother as well as a professional.

Carla gives community workshops for women in transitional stages—women thirty-five, forty, fifty, divorced. "We talk about personal planning, life planning, returning to a career. Women in general don't do enough planning for themselves. They wait until the situation is upon them, then start wringing their hands, wondering how it happened and what to do. We give them structured ways to think of the past, present and future.

"It's a new kind of learning," says Carla. "Most people grew up learning with a teacher standing in front of them while they took notes. They didn't talk. I think the greatest learning situation is when you take part, experience things yourself, share experience with others without being threatened." She has found that the greatest problem for women is their concern with their many roles, trying to balance them all, identifying them, sharing their feelings about what they do as mother, wife, volunteer, professional person. "An awful lot of women feel alone. They need reinforcement, support, an association among women. We help people with this, help them feel good about themselves."

In addition to community work, they also do a lot of work for corporations. This is the one area in which their business has grown the most. There's a huge market for programs for spouses (still usually women) of employees attending company conventions. Recently they presented such a program for spouses at the American College of Physicians and Surgeons convention. Usually at these meetings, the women "sit around and wait for their husbands like baggage. We give them an educational diversion."

In another instance, a large paper company had eight women executives who never met or talked to one another. "They asked us to do the management-development skills with these women. We set up a network among them. More companies realize that they have some obligations to women in their organizations. Also, because corporation men feel threatened by women's acceptance and movement up, as more women enter business, there are many new human-relations problems. How men can relate to these women they work with, or even under, is one important one."

More recently, they were asked by a large insurance company to provide a program for spouses at their conference. It worked so well that this fall they will give a weekend session for the insurance agents as well as their wives. "It's almost like a marriage encounter. We find out how the agents and their wives can be more supportive to each other. The company realizes that women are the ones who hold things together."

Carla and her partner work out of their houses and have had their business for three years. They have two full-time associates and four others. Because one of the women is moving to Toronto, they plan to open an office there. They have a brochure, which they constantly send around to companies, and Carla's supportive husband even carries her business cards around with him and hands them out. "None of us females could do it without husbands who were interested and encouraged us. That's really crucial."

When I spoke with Carla she and her partner were earning $12,000 a year, which she expected would double the following year. In her business of human relations, "it takes a while to get established. You don't make money overnight." One advantage of their type of endeavor, though, is that they can do it any-where. If their husbands move or are transferred, the business easily moves with them.

Her age seems to fit the demands of her work. "Having reached middle age you know you are middle-aged, you're not twenty-five. I'm glad to be the age I am. I can do what I'm doing. I have opportunities and time. I couldn't have done it at twenty-five. I find age an advantage because we are most often hired by men who like the fact that we represent maturity and experience. We are the steady, dependable, knowledgeable way. Women respond to us too. In middle age," says Carla, "you have to keep changing and learning. Staying home and cleaning the house? Oh, yipes. I can't imagine it."

Urban Planning

My husband was director of a population commission in Washington once. And one of the women who was on the commission, representing "housewives," was Marilyn Brant Chandler, wife of the publisher of the *Los Angeles Times*. Missy, who lives in California, commuted to Washington faithfully over a two-year period and read every piece of paper the commission was given to study. Somehow the experience changed her. Missy has been married for twenty-seven years and has five children. She went to college for two years, got married at nine-teen and immediately became pregnant. "In those days we didn't think of working, we knew our career was going to be wife and mother."

She stayed home, busily producing babies and doing volunteer jobs. "I thought it was marvelous."

Obviously Missy didn't have to work for financial reasons. Both she and her husband come from wealthy California families. If you watch the movie industry's Oscar presentations every year, you will notice that they are presented in the Dorothy Chandler Pavilion, one of the many contributions from the family.

Missy had been on a lot of boards and in the Junior League, but it wasn't until she served on the population commission that internal needs began to surface. "I got very turned on by the commission. I felt there was a true lack of planning in everything we do in the U.S. There is a lack of effort in our national policy. All our actions seem to be a reaction to crisis. First we were told to have bomb shelters, then we went through the environmental crisis, then the Vietnam crisis.

"I began to worry about the demise of our cities. I became interested in how we would create new cities, move population away from the dense places. I think what we really need is to shore up our cities, make them the lovely places they once were. I decided I wanted to be an urban planner. I wanted to be well known and help this crisis of the city."

When she was forty, she went to UCLA graduate school without ever having finished college. They accepted her on the basis of the two years completed at nineteen, a variety of courses taken over twenty years, a half year of college and two years in Claremont College's continuing education program.

While she was working on the graduate degree in urban planning she took a part-time job with an architectural planning firm, "to get my feet wet. I was really green and they didn't know what to do with me. They wanted me for my business contacts." She worked in the planning department and did business development for two years. "I colored a lot of maps, planned studies, did research. And I worked on my thesis at the same time."

Two years ago several things happened. She was busy on a project, helping to plan the federal capital of Nigeria. There was a budget cut and she was pulled off. Four others on the project met the same fate. That work had been interesting. After that she got very bored. She redid the firm's filing system and finally left. "I knew in the back of my mind I wanted my own business."

Then former football player Rosey Grier came to her and asked her help in doing a budget study to present to President Carter on aiding senior citizens and juvenile delinquents. "I got this team together to plan a nonprofit organization that would help. We tried to figure out how much money it would take."

Both these experiences made her think more about what she wanted to do. "I decided I liked running things, being a manager. I resolved to try my own architecture and urban planning business. At first I worked out of my house, using my kids' bedrooms. I hired several typists, a lawyer and an accountant. I sent out five hundred personal letters to people and corporations. Then we moved to nearby office space. But this is not the way to do it. It usually takes three to five years to put an architectural firm in the black. And it takes $500,000 to get started. What I should have done was have $100,000 of contracts at the beginning to keep me going; or have three sure jobs.

"I made mistakes. My secretary spent all her time on the phone talking to her sick mother. I began with only $55,000. And I didn't realize that it takes from five to ten months after the initial contact with a client to sign a contract, and that architects and planners are the last to be paid."

Missy survived, nevertheless, on determination, ambition and remodeling houses. "I decided to go after every client that comes my way. I'm a predator. I pass my card out at dinner parties."

What her services consist of now are such things as designing commercial office buildings, houses and condominiums, drawing up economic feasibility studies on what to do with land, on the need for office space near airports and redesigning a portion of Wilshire Boulevard in Los Angeles.

One project she worked on was how to develop 280 acres on the ocean in Santa Barbara and stay within the stringent new environmental protection laws. She took the clients through the whole planning process with twenty consultants, including two geologists, a marine biologist and two ornithologists. "There's a bird there, the white-tailed kite, that everyone likes," Missy laughs.

Her youngest daughter, who is fourteen, complains when she is not home in the afternoon. "But I'm close to home and she can stop by if she needs help with her homework." Missy sighs, "I've been mothering for twenty-two years. I'm tired of having the phone calls at 1 A.M. asking me to pick them up at a friend's house and drive them home. It's nice to have some peace now."

Why would a woman like Missy, blond, attractive and wealthy, with five children to occupy her thoughts, decide she wanted to go to work and do something of her own? She was probably reacting to the pressure to become an individual in a family of achievers. Perhaps the aura of Chandler accomplishment and prestige gave Missy the urge to make her own mark.

"Why did you bother, Missy?" I asked her one day. Her answer sounds so idealistic, one tends not to believe she can mean it all. But she does.

"I really worry about the future of the world. I worry about this country's gradual decline. I worry about the environment. I think we'll have to redo our pattern of living." She thinks her business will help lead the way. "People will come to me and I can add my own voice." Success does seem imminent. Her company made a small profit this year, and Missy, like so many achieving women, is out there plugging away at improving herself. She's studying accounting at night and reading books on business, learning about presentations, business development and how to sell. She is also talking of getting a master's in business administration.

What does it all do for her? The woman who could stay home and enjoy her money, her position, travel and parties? "It gives me an independence that I like. It differentiates my two roles. That's why I use my maiden name in my work. It gives me an anonymity, separates Mrs. Chandler of the *Los Angeles Times,* and Ms. Brant, the urban planner. It makes me much more comfortable."

Many people care about the environment and the cities. Some of us pick up our dog-do's when we are told to, keep our cars from polluting the air, write our congressmen to go after industries that pollute the waters. But if the cities go bad, we move out to the suburbs. Here is one middle-aged woman who wants to do something about the problems she senses around her that could lead to further decay and decline. She cares enough to turn it into a business and her new life's work. "I'm really two people," she says, "Marilyn Brant, and Marilyn Chandler."

Most mid-life women today have probably been two people all along. The public personality who was mother-wife with prescribed roles and the private person whose secret personality wanted to paint, become a doctor, or save the world. They lived in a schizophrenic state that surely limited and hurt them. For a lot of women now, the hidden, split, submerged self is free to surface and join the public self to create an integrated whole— someone who has to become a more forceful, useful and happier person.

12

Women Who Move Up

As middle-aged women break into business, the driving desire of many of them is to do the job as well as it can be done, efficiently, even brilliantly, and then move up to new challenges. If they have their own business they are, in a sense, beginning at the top of whatever hierarchy they create. If they have worked for others most of their lives, particularly for corporations, middle age is the time when they have amassed enough experience to try to penetrate the top management and win a coveted senior executive position.

However, as most people are aware, breaking into management is usually not very easy, and the majority of women are too timid even to try. The trip up the corporate ladder may not only be difficult, but it is usually unappreciated. Women are welcomed with almost the same fervor as blacks applying to an exclusive, all-white suburban country club. Many men, through force of habit, because of a number of erroneous presumptions about women's capabilities, and a devotion to a comfortable status quo, would prefer keeping the club exclusive. They do not look upon this feminine ascent with great pleasure.

There are real problems for the woman who wants to move up, many of which have been documented in books like Margaret Hennig and Anne Jardim's *The Managerial Woman.* Women will find that at times men are openly hostile to their ambitions. In other instances it is covert. In either case, they and the woman both know that she is there because of outside pressure. If the company did not open its doors to both sexes equally, it could be sued for discrimination, as some have, and would cease to benefit from any federal funds.

So the doors to the stratospheric levels of management are opening—but only grudgingly. Women are moving into high-level corporate jobs, but not many of them. Those who do make it are sometimes seen as the company's token woman. Often a woman in this position will be excluded from the most important meetings and, in general, viewed as a threat, as someone who is going to edge a man out of a promotion because the firm needs a woman in a visible spot.

There have been innumerable instances of a qualified woman's being passed over in favor of a man, but now, ironically, there are times when a company desperately wants a woman and there simply aren't any qualified women in a given field. The prevailing opinion is that as soon as the many young females who are getting their master's degrees in business administration (MBA's), or their law degrees, move through the pipeline of entry jobs up to the middle rungs of the ladder, there will be many more women who meet the criteria of what corporations and government are seeking.

Women today are estimated to hold fewer than 1 percent of the top management positions, and about 6 percent of middle management jobs. Of all those people earning more than $25,000 in business and industry in 1975, only 2.4 percent were women. One of the best chances they have in playing the upward-mobility game is to work for a small private company or for a corporation that employs many women in low-level positions. Here, according to those who proffer advice, is where the most pressure will be exerted by government to move women up from the lowly regions into management.

Companies that hire women executives often want them with

corporate experience and proven records. Women executives have told me that whereas companies will usually give a man the chance to show what he can do, when they look for a woman, they want someone who has already made it somewhere else. Obviously someone has to give her her first chance. But few want to risk it. It also seems to be the opinion of many perverse male executives, that once they allow a woman to have her first important job, her first taste of previously forbidden candy, she will be satisfied to stay there.

On the contrary, the women I spoke with feel the same nagging need for continual challenge and self-improvement that men have. They also get bored and want new and harder assignments to tackle. But whether a woman can move upward in any particular company probably depends a great deal on the immediate supervisors and vice-presidents. If they are old style and still think of business as a man's province, she won't get anywhere, and if she's smart, she will move out and simply find a job in a different company where she can continue her upward climb.

The power connections that men have constructed to help one another on this route to the top are just beginning to exist for women. Aware that men get ahead through their "old-boy network," women who have become successful are beginning to organize a similar support system for women dubbed the "new-girl network." For example, there is the River Oaks Business Women's Exchange Club in Houston, San Francisco's Women's Forum West, Los Angeles's Women in Business, Chicago's Professional Women's Association, Atlanta's The Network, Washington's the Washington Women's Network, and, in New York, The Woman's Media Group.

Some of these groups are only several years old, but they are already functioning to help members establish personal relationships that could lead to promotions and better jobs. Members give one another advice on corporate problems, on how to handle men, how to get ahead, how to cut red tape and, perhaps most valuable, they provide a meeting ground where women can talk and share experiences.

But the groups are new, still relatively powerless, and thus at a disadvantage. Their members may not hear of the big jobs opening up, and they won't necessarily be chosen for the top-level slots because their "friends" in high places, who are still mainly men, still don't want them. But women are succeeding —usually because a company needs a figurehead or perhaps because the men with whom they work have finally come to realize how good they are. In a few cases a man's attitude is influenced by a feminist wife. One woman reportedly refused to go to bed with her husband until he hired and promoted more women.

But viewed topographically, the businesswoman's situation today is like a flat valley with a few tiny foothills here and there, and very few high peaks. It is a tough climb for anyone, especially someone burdened with the current load of female handicaps—old sex-role prejudices and ignorant assumptions.

Welcome to the Top

They used to say that the real power behind every man was a woman. What is it like for the female today who is her own woman, who utilizes her own mind and good counsel to promote her own power? I spoke with a number of vice-presidents, a former vice-president who changed her career, a top management executive and a manager. All except one are married. Amusingly enough, the women whom I interviewed in their offices were all wearing what seems to have become the standard uniform, the equalizer between men and women, the current female version of the ubiquitous gray flannel suit of the fifties. The women all met me wearing navy blue suits with white blouses.

Having gotten beyond the outer vestments, I noticed other similarities in these executives. They were all middle-aged; the national average is fifty. When asked where they found the confidence to keep pushing up, how they got to believe in themselves, those who had been to women's colleges mentioned the premise alive in the atmosphere of these campuses, that women are supposed to work and succeed. But all stressed the influence of their fathers who were perfectionists, who wanted them to go to law school or be engineers and do something useful with their lives. This confirms what other investigators who have looked into the backgrounds of women executives have discovered. It is primarily the fathers who gave their daughters the conviction that they could be whatever they wanted to be, who constantly encouraged them, and scratched their feminine reticence enough so they learned to speak and think for themselves.

Given their confidence and belief in themselves, how did the executives I spoke with—Evelyn, Claudia, Marian, and Lorna —get to the top? Evelyn is the first and only female manager among twenty in the research division of one of the country's major pharmaceutical corporations. She is the first woman to have power in a formerly all-male area of this giant company. Surprisingly, Evelyn is a mere five feet tall and weighs only ninety-five pounds. She appears dwarfed by her large desk and almost engulfed by oceans of pleated curtain draping a wall of windows. "When most men see me," she says, "they think I'm a pushover because I'm small." They find out otherwise.

She got her promotion by doing two things. First, she became expert in the scientific testing of pharmaceutical products and the government regulations controlling them. Secondly, she left companies that didn't promote her; and where she did finally stay, she asked for what she wanted. "I had been to seminars for women in business and I decided that I wasn't going to stay in any dead-end job. I told my supervisor that I wanted more responsibility, and he was trying to arrange something."

Asking is vitally important because it informs the company that you want to move up, and it shows you whether they intend to let you. In Evelyn's case, the manager's job came open at this point, and they needed someone with her background. They interviewed five men and her. She got the job. "If I weren't qualified, they wouldn't have considered me. But of course the fact that I am a woman helps their equal opportunity profile."

Claudia became the first woman vice-president of a research

organization at forty-five and rose to senior vice-president, the only woman among four, at age forty-nine. "This is what we're all about," she says in her soft but firm southern accent. "I love being a senior vice-president. I like the sense of power. It's better than being just a vice-president, better than being a division director, better than being anything else I was. I like the chance to see ideas carried out that I've pushed."

She also got to the top by perfecting each job she had, then moving on. After one such accomplishment she said, "I kind of decided I wanted to branch out and do new things. I wasn't bored. I wanted something that was my own. I wanted full responsibility for something. If I had a success I wanted it to be mine. Or if I failed, it would be my failure." After several successes, she asked to run one of the company's regional offices and convinced them that she was the person to do it. Once she had them convinced, she asked for a promotion. "I told them I'd only go if they made me a vice-president. I said I'd need the prestige to run the office."

It probably took a lot of nerve to set this situation up and ask for a vice-presidency, more nerve than a father would have instilled in her. Claudia explained, "I just got old. I was forty-five, and I'd gotten rid of the sillies along the way—like worrying too much about what others might think, like not wanting to displease men, like wanting everyone to like me."

Marian worked her way up in the same corporation and is now director of a division with 85 people working under her. She expects it will grow to 150 in two more years. She got her position by jumping from a "staff" job as assistant to an older woman in public relations who gave her a lot of responsibility to a "line" job as associate director of the division. In a line job she was on the career ladder on her way up.

Being an executive for her is exhilarating. "When I was made a director, I saw how this area could grow. I saw what I could do if given the power. I don't mean telling someone what to do. That's not my style. I mean I get a kick out of the corporate scene. Being involved with what's happening—the big corporate problems. You have to be in the upper levels to know what's going on, and to help decide what will happen.''

On another day I went to see Lorna, a fifty-year-old foundation vice-president. We sat in her comfortable office with the plush carpet, the large desk, the wall of windows and the navy blue suit. I was wearing last year's pants and a sweater and felt like a peasant. I could see the point of the dress code. It hit me like the clout of a policeman's uniform. It definitely carried the aura of authority. We sat at the long conference table (a real sign of prestige), my pants hidden beneath its polished mahogany top.

Lorna told me she got to be the occupant of her office by becoming so knowledgeable in her field that when a growing foundation looked around for someone to hire, she was the best available person. She refused to come unless they made her a vice-president. She, too, asked for the title. ''This was important for me because I wanted authority and responsibility in terms of program development. I came with experience. They were buying something, and I didn't want to sell myself short.''

Like all the women I spoke to, Lorna has extraordinary energy, and a rich fund of ideas. She regrets that she has to take time off to sleep and ideally would like to work twenty-four hours a day. As she enters this new era of her life, she is looking around at her options. ''I think I might be interested in running a college,'' she says, and I can't help thinking what a great idea that is, and what an ideal opportunity for seizing power a working woman can make out of the decade of her fifties.

Can We Make Her Cry?

One similarity that is inescapable among women executives is that they all experienced similar versions of hostility from men about having their once-sacred turf invaded, and all developed a style to defend themselves when necessary, or assert themselves if appropriate. When they entered the higher echelons, despite the fact that some man had helped them get there, or at least had certainly approved their being there, they were inevitably made quite conscious by the general male population of the fact that they were not the breed or gender of person one expected to see. Awkward situations abound for any executive woman, and nothing would please many of her male colleagues more than to see her break down in anger or tears over these incidents.

Take for example the time that Virginia Radley, fifty-year-old recently appointed president of Oswego College, in New York, appeared at a Rotary Club meeting to give a talk. While she stood at the door for a few minutes observing the scene, several of the older men handed her their coats and hats as they came in. She hung them up, rather than making an issue of it.

Among the executives I spoke to, examples of discriminatory action were not difficult to find. Evelyn remembered the situation at one drug company. "Our personnel director was a conservative midwesterner. I don't think he took women seriously. They weren't stingy on salaries, and you had the same responsibilities as men. But men had the better jobs and titles. The women had no visibility. You did the work and your male boss went to the meetings and discussed it. He got the credit."

At the corporation where she is now she finds the discrimination fairly well hidden. But she has noticed a patronizing attitude from the older men. And when she goes to a meeting of, say, 150 men and a handful of women, she finds the level of men's sensitivity to women's feelings pretty low. "They get up and say, 'We need a guy who can do . . . ' or, 'We need a man who will do that . . . ' It's always a man they talk of."

She also hears men discuss women in disparaging terms right in front of her. General remarks like, "Women are pushy," Then they turn to her and treat her as an equal. It's the "You're okay, you're different, but the rest of them . . ." gambit.

Claudia said she is never discriminated against to her face. She did hear of a man who turned down a job she offered him, got drunk one night months later and announced to a friend of hers, "I wouldn't work for that bitch under any circumstances." Says Claudia, "I do think men are always aware that I am a woman, but I don't think women should spend too much time worrying about what goes on behind their backs.''

Marian concedes that there are some women who "expect to be given the sun, moon and stars without working. They have to learn they won't be promoted unless they produce. They see others move up and scream 'discrimination.' This doesn't help women. It contributes to a male backlash.''

She has also felt the sting of sex bias, but doesn't let it bother her. "The higher a woman goes, the more discrimination there is. They look up and see a woman and think, 'Whoa. . . .' '' She once had lunch in the president's dining room of the New York Stock Exchange. She was the only woman present, and the men were obviously extremely uncomfortable. Another time she was invited to a business lunch at a club in Washington with a friend. As they entered, a steward barred the way. "Sir, are you a member of this club?" When her friend said he was, he was admonished, "But . . . I beg your pardon, sir. Women are not allowed to use the main stairway." Her friend glared at the man fiercely and said, "Get out of my way. This woman is going up the main staircase.''

"This breaking ground doesn't upset me," Marian said. "It's exciting. It's not deliberate ill behavior on the part of men. Their image of the female has been there for centuries, and it's hard to change.''

On the other hand, discriminatory behavior does bother Lorna. "I believe everyone should like me," she said. "I'm one of those people. I'll move mountains either to get that person to come around, or else to get out. You need to be liked by people you work with.''

She told me she has frequently noticed the difficulties that exist when men and women have to work together as equals. Men don't like the intimacy, sharing the conference room. They are sensitive to the presence of women. "They think it's inhibiting to their behavior, and it is. They enjoy the privacy of their own quarters. I can understanding this feeling," Lorna said smiling, "but that's not where the world is.''

Men Versus Women

Surely it will take men a generation or two to get over their shock at suddenly having to work with women, as well as go to bed with them. And discrimination in one form or another will linger for some time, especially from the older men who find readjustment to change too formidable a task for their already ossified ways. But I can't help wondering if there really are basic differences in behavior that are common to women. If there are, it is certainly the result of how they were socialized into a world that made everyone feel that women were genetically different. Are women really weaker emotionally? Or, on the other hand, are they more understanding than men?

I asked Evelyn, the scientist, if she noticed any real differences between how men and women approach their work. "I feel if I let myself go, I could be more emotional than a man. But I purposely don't get excited and yell. I won't scream and bang the table. I stay calm although I may be seething inside. Otherwise they will say, 'There's that hysterical woman.' "

Claudia, however, felt that the whole concept of a woman's being different from a man is wrong. "I think it's a myth." She described how it had recently been necessary for her to fire an employee in their Puerto Rico office, someone who needed the job but had been goofing off for years. She had no trouble doing it, nor did he try to appeal to her sympathies or emotions.

"One always thinks of women as being weepy and emotional, but that's a stereotype that's not true," agreed Marian. "If anyone gets upset among the people I work with, it's the men." She does a performance appraisal every year where she writes reports, which the individual sees, on how well he or she is doing. "I do this for the senior staff who report to me. If a man gets a bad appraisal," she said, "he is apt to sulk for three months. Women accept it." I assume this is because women are more used to being criticized. Whatever the reason, Marian feels it is the women who handle their emotions better.

Lorna found men and women different in several respects.

"Most women, unlike men, don't understand the personal decision process," she said. "The 'what will happen if . . .' They just let things happen to them. I really believe that is the basic problem for women." She said women make an awful lot of decisions without realizing it. For example, "When you sleep with a guy . . . that's a decision. You are no longer a virgin. You may get married, you may get pregnant. You are no longer solely in charge of yourself. You can lose or gain something. But when it comes to examining options and making calculated decisions, they simply don't go through the process."

She also remarked that men take it for granted that they will support other men. I suppose this comes quite naturally after having grown up spending afternoons involved in team games with team spirit. "Women," Lorna observed, "are used to being jealous and competing for men. They are not used to helping each other. There is jealousy where there ought to be support."

Words of Executive Advice

Having arrived so close to the top, the executive women I spoke to seemed genuinely concerned with helping other women. Their discussion not only included criticism, but also many words of advice aimed at any middle-aged woman who is working. They uniformly urged women not to be afraid, to learn their business well, perfect what they know, and then be aggressive. They find women too lacking in confidence.

Evelyn made a statement that could be construed as a call to arms. "A woman must be aggressive," she said, and then stopped herself. "No, that's not the word we are supposed to use now. We must say 'assertive.' Because assertiveness in a man, which is considered good, becomes, when it is exactly the same behavior, aggressiveness in a woman, which is considered bad." But whatever the word, the message is clear.

Claudia too said, "I think a woman should stop worrying about promotions, learn her craft, practice and do it well. If she knows more than anyone, it won't matter that she's a woman. Just set some goals, learn your business so you can reach them, and then be aggressive as hell. Your personal motivation is more important than waving banners about liberation.''

She believes that family life and social life come second for men, and women in business have to have it that way too. ''If you are going into business,'' says Claudia, ''that has to take priority. Women complain they don't see their husbands. Men know what it's like. They've been there before.''

When women are dealing with men, there are bound to be some disappointments, not because they are men, but because that's business. ''You've got to know you will have battles you have to fight,'' she says. ''You win some and lose some. You can't fracture easily. If there is something you really want that you are not going to get this week, don't let it get to you. Next week there will be something else you want that you will get.''

As far as moving up is concerned, Evelyn cautioned, ''How you behave in your company is tricky. You have to be able to gauge the water. If you start making a lot of noise about positions being open for women, you can make a name for yourself as a pariah, a troublemaker.'' She beseeches timid women to get out. ''Don't sit back and wait until someone makes you do it. If there's a closed door, if you can't advance, move to another company.''

There were also exhortations for action, risk taking and aggressiveness from Marian. But how you do it, and say it, is important and might make the difference between complete success and failure. ''In a large meeting with mostly men,'' she told me, ''you really have to assert yourself. But when the men are talking, don't try to break in. They are not rude, but they will go right on with what they are saying. Wait for a real pause, and then say it, and they will listen. Some women tend to chatter, which is bad. They may be brilliant and capable, but they won't get anywhere because they talk constantly and laugh a lot. Men conclude that if a woman does that, she's not smart. Some women resent having to change these habits.

''Sometimes in a meeting a woman may be saying something

intelligent but saying it with too much detail, with trilling laughs here and there. It doesn't work. For a woman, that's bad style. Don't babble at a high pitch, and do come to the point.''

I asked how else she perceives women's problems. What keeps them from moving up the corporate stairways to the offices with the big desks, the thick carpets, the plants and the large windows. "Women are timid," she found, as had so many others. "If I interview a secretary, I'll say, 'What do you picture yourself doing in two or three years?' And she'll say, 'I hope I'll be a good secretary.' I ask her, 'Would you like to do such and such (a better job)?' And she'll answer, 'No, I don't want that much responsibility.'

"Women have an image of themselves as girls who are supposed to get married and have families. It's a self-stereotyped role. They don't realize, if they are intelligent they can do anything. The sky is the limit.

"Women often don't have enough confidence, even the ones with experience and enough educational background. This lack makes them hang back and have difficulty dealing with men at their level and men reporting to them. It's trite but it's true. To compensate for the missing confidence, some women become 'masculine,' and that doesn't work. If you go to any male executive who is above you with a women's lib attitude of, 'I'm as good as you are,' you'll get nowhere at all."

On the other hand, she finds that using the fact that one is a woman can be helpful. "A woman now has a tremendous advantage if she knows how to work it. If I want something from an executive vice-president, I can say things to him, as a woman, that a man could never say, something like, 'I've a problem, you've just got to help me' or 'Oh come on now, Bob, don't be nasty.' And he'll respond. Don't get cute or feminine. It's just that a man has had this relationship with his mother, wife and sister, and you can take advantage of it. A male who said those things would be thrown out.''

I asked Lorna for her suggestions for upwardly mobile working women. She believes that the main thing the successful executive needs is to be strong and well informed, whether it's a request for a new desk or a whole new program. She has to be able to give them all the data. She must have analytical training. She just can't ride by the seat of her pants.

"Women also have to develop some balance in their seriousness," says Lorna. "We are too serious. We fool around less than men. We have no humor. Men are often very funny playing with an idea, but they get to the point.

"Lastly," she advised, "women have to learn how to compromise, to negotiate. Men know the ground rules. Since it's a man's world, it's been all laid out for them by various systems they travel through as they grow up. Very few women have had the opportunity, or taken it, to enter into debate, or compete in sports on the basis of skill."

And she reiterated what I had heard from almost everyone, in any field that I spoke to during my research. "Working women do far less than they should in planning their lives. Whether working with men or not, they appear to wait for opportunity to strike, and if it doesn't, they wonder why in the hell it didn't. You have to make your own opportunities. And you need to have a list of priorities, so you know what's important to you. Like family, job, salary, place, professional colleagues."

She called women unrealistic about what they might do. They don't have a broad enough perspective in managing career, children and husband. The organization the young woman executive works for also has to adapt to women's having these multiple lives. "Every woman in a professional job should try to get as much adjustment to her work at home as well as in the office. It must be decided in advance whether she will have shorter hours, do some work at home, or even sometimes bring the kids to work. I think in the future people are going to work shorter hours, anyway." Women, she thinks, should understand that they will have many conflicts in business because society is not yet ready for their multiple roles. "They must understand where society is. It doesn't mean they shouldn't be out there fighting."

Lorna strongly believes women need a support system to help them discover where they are in life and where they want to go —or else they don't see any of the options. "You might as well be in a hollow in the Appalachian hills. You need someone to dream with you. Books did that for a lot of people before television. They gave people reassurance, a way to think about problems. With television, women have lost the habit of talking. They have to get used to sharing their ideas.''

She says it is important to have someone in your life to talk things through with, either for an adversary response, or for a shot of therapy. Women must have someone to tell them they could be great, or that they need to correct a certain fault. They need someone to criticize and help. A mentor with enough experience who will be kind and patient.

For a forecast from the top, Lorna predicts that the future is going to revolve around managers who can deal with people successfully. She thinks women are the ones who have this capacity through their nurturing role. If this is true, women should continue to be even more in demand than they are now.

The executives I spoke to were full of boundless energy, fertile ideas and ambition. But they also had this strange restless quality. They were never satisfied to sit back and let life roll over them once they had achieved some status. This does not mean they lack concentration. These women concentrate to such a degree that they master what they set out to do and feel a need to attack new problems. Lorna tells me, ''Restlessness is not a bad thing. People should look at themselves, find out what they want. One has to be in a growing stage, to be evolutionary. When you get static, if you are on to yourself at all, you feel restless.''

The Vice-President Who Changed Careers

Women who have been working all their lives, like men, sometimes reach another transition where they sense a desire to move on. Sometimes they decide what they want is not to move higher but to find a completely new kind of objective, a second career. And often this new career will have more humanitarian aspects or will involve dealing more with people than the previous one.

Jackie left college at nineteen to get married and had two children. She went to night school and worked for a marketing research firm during the days. When she applied for the job they asked her if she had a doctorate. She said, ''No,'' which was the truth. ''I answered only what I was asked. I didn't tell them I hadn't even finished college.'' She worked on such things as product tests, effectiveness of advertising and how to make products acceptable to changing tastes.

Later on she moved to one of the world's major advertising companies and finally became a vice-president. How she got the title was not unusual. She asked for it, as the other vice-presidents I interviewed had done.

In her company there were a number of women copywriters who became vice-presidents, but there were none in marketing. (Women could write, but they couldn't sell?) ''That bugged me,'' she said. ''I was doing work that would have made me a vice-president if I were a man. I wanted the title because I was as good as they were. When I asked for the promotion, they said, 'That's silly, it's only a title,' with the intention of trying to make me feel small for asking.

''I told them, 'If it is important, then I should get the title. If it's not important, you shouldn't mind giving it to me.' The time had come for it. But they said they were bothered about giving it to me because I'd have no place to go after that.'' (That doesn't stop them from promoting men.) ''Actually, being a vice-president in advertising is no big deal. It's only important if you are not one.'' She got the title.

Why, I wondered, did she ever want to leave such a successful career? Jackie was imbued with that same restless quality that other successful women have, of needing to grow and learn new things. She always knew when the time came because she would ask herself a certain question which inevitably provided her with the answer. ''If I had it to do over again,'' she would ask, ''what would I want to do? Looking at life from the cosmic point of view, I wasn't sure I wanted to stay in advertising. I had fallen in by the back door when I was young and needed a job.

''So, when I asked myself what I would do, my answer was that I would go to law school. My husband said 'GO!' I needed twenty missing college credits. 'God,' I thought, 'think how old you'll be when you get out of law school.' Then I decided, I'll be that old anyway!

"I finished college and worked in my advertising job three days a week. Then for the next two years, I went to law school and continued working. I had a very flexible employer. But finally they wanted me for a forty-hour week, and I couldn't manage full-time. So I had to leave.

"I guess I really left advertising because I'd been doing it long enough. I wanted to do something different. I thought law would be fun and interesting." She said that every once in a while during the time she worked in advertising, she had the sense that selling products was a kind of game, though sometimes they were things that were too important to be a game. However, her reason for going into law wasn't idealism. "Law is a good discipline you can use in business and government. A combination of my marketing experience and law would be invaluable."

She now works for a firm where she has become a partner. She does advertising law, general practice, corporate law and has begun to get involved with matrimonial law. "There are aspects about matrimonial law I like. It's not elegant law. It's law other lawyers look down on. There's lots of hand holding. Sometimes when I spend the entire day reading, working on esoteric points, there's something nice about dealing with a client. There's a great deal to be said for actually doing something tangible for another human being.

"It's good to give nurturing and love when people need it, otherwise divorce can be like mill work—turning out sausage. My age and vintage are a help. I'm more willing to be in touch with their emotions. I know I'm approaching middle age. On one level I feel rich, deep, multifaceted. Middle age has a certain kind of ripeness, using that word in the positive sense. I don't have the feeling I've climbed up one side of a mountain and now I'm climbing down. No sense of that. Things are rich, ripe, complex. A great place to be. I couldn't have such a variety of experience to draw on if I were younger. I don't have the innocence now."

Thinking so much about her life during our talk, she finally concluded that she really hadn't changed careers from advertising to law, she had built on the old one. Then she restated the now familiar concept of restlessness. "It's my idea of heaven. You want a certain amount of constructive change. With each new thing you do, you can feed in what you've done all your life. It's not so much changing as it is a sense of evolution. It keeps you lively, young, interesting, all that people value."

Demystifying Power

I found my discussions with these five executive women enlightening. The whole mystique that has surrounded terms like "corporate," "executive," "vice-president in charge of . . ." "senior vice-president" had seemed impenetrable to me, and undoubtedly it is to most women. Meeting the president of AT&T, if that unlikely situation ever occurred, would, in my mind, have been something like shaking hands with God.

But being an executive, as Jackie said, "is no big deal." It's only a job. You see that it is attainable, and the people who are doing the attaining are far from gods. They are even women!

Those I spoke to were not afraid to try. They had confidence and the knowledge that they could be inspired managers, superb organizers and experts in their fields. They did not try to put men down, but neither were they afraid of them, and they certainly weren't afraid to ask for a salary or title they thought they deserved. They see themselves more as people than as women, although men often see them as females, creatures who have invaded their masculine territory. These women enjoy breaking ground for future female executives, enjoy the money and power and ability to see their ideas carried out. Regardless of their success, they are restless, constantly looking for new goals, responsibilities or even new careers.

This is a world where a secretary who gets an MBA can ride the executive elevator to the top. And it's not unthinkable for a newcomer to the business world to work twice as hard and catch up on promotions. Anything is possible. There are so few women who are really ready for business that those who do prepare themselves should find many options opening to them.

It's not easy to finally reach the status of the blue-flannel-suit crowd, but it's getting easier. It's obviously worth the effort. And middle age is the best time to shoot for the top. By then, if you have been working, you are ready.

The Marine Corps just named its first female general, forty-seven-year-old Margaret A. Brewer who rose from colonel to become one of eighty-seven Marine Corps generals on active duty. Why not?

13

Politics and the
Mid-Life Woman

Politics is one occupation that not only has more middle-aged people in it than younger ones but also no retirement age. In addition, it is a burgeoning field for women, one in which they are desperately needed and in which their numbers are destined to multiply dramatically in the next decade. Despite the frequent uphill struggle to gain the necessary financial and party support, politics remains, without doubt, one of the most significant careers a mid-life woman can follow today.

As many as 88 percent of women in public office are age thirty-five or older. Interestingly enough, according to a paper by Marilyn Johnson of the Eagleton Institute, Rutgers University, prepared for the House of Representatives' Select Committee on Aging, "The middle-aged woman currently serving in office reflects a tendency to *enter* public office in middle age, rather than a tendency to commence a political career in young adulthood and subsequently to age in office." In a 1977 survey done by the institute's Center for the American Woman and Politics (CAWP), the main source of information on female political office holding in the country, it was found that 82 percent of men and women entered their current office at age thirty-five or older, and that service in public office tends to be a phenomenon of middle age rather than of youth.

Politics, except for all those notable female monarchs here and there in history, has, like business, been totally a man's profession. Governments stood or fell, laws were enacted or squashed, leaders were made and broken, we went to war or we didn't, all because of the whims and beliefs and the influence that men exerted at the polls and in Congress. Women, not very long ago, of course, weren't even allowed to vote. They fought for this right and won it, only to slip back into the female life of housework and lethargy that had been preordained for them. Now as they break out of all their domestic cocoons into new fields, some of them are beginning to show a strong interest in politics.

As Marilyn Johnson says, "If the talents and energies of more than one-half the population are not used in the conduct of public affairs, then the quality of life potentially is diminished for all." She points out that women bring their "special needs and perspective to public life," and their absence deprives women of a voice in government."

The Scoreboard

Women have received 14 percent of the appointments in President Carter's administration. He is the first President to name two female Cabinet members: Juanita Kreps, Secretary of Commerce, and Patricia Roberts Harris, former Secretary of Housing and Urban Development and now Secretary of Health, Education and Welfare. According to the CAWP report, before 1977 only three other women had ever served in a federal cabinet. And no woman has ever been appointed to the Supreme Court.

One hears a few names of women elected to office who have become stars, like Elizabeth Holtzman, Barbara Jordan, Governor Ella Grasso of Connecticut. Not many. Women hold roughly only 7 percent of elective offices, yet they account for as much as 52 percent of the adult population. After the 1978 national elections, we now have 1 lone woman (out of 100) in the Senate and 16 women (out of 435) in the House.

On the state level, the report finds that, as of January 1978, 11 percent of state cabinet-level jobs were occupied by women and almost 10 percent of state legislators were women (101 state senators and 601 state representatives). This figure is up from 4 percent in 1969. The percentage has thus doubled, but by no means soared.

According to the CAWP report, the largest gain for women in politics since 1975 has taken place on the county and local level. The report notes a striking increase in women in mayoralties and on municipal and township governing bodies, an increase of at least 36 percent over 1975. They now hold 8 percent of such offices.

What Kind of Women Run?

The investigators from CAWP took a look at what kind of woman is in office. The average profile reads like this: She is married, has children older than twelve and is less likely than a man in politics to have another job as well. She sees her husband as being supportive. (Actually it was found that more men approve of having their wives in office than wives do of having a husband in office.)

Women in office, according to the study, are imbued with positive as well as negative images of themselves. On the plus side, they rate themselves as being people-oriented, conscientious, with a sincere interest in public service. They say they feel a strong responsibility to alleviate social problems and a genuine responsiveness to their constituents.

On the negative side they rate themselves as having less confidence than men in their ability to argue persuasively and make important contacts, less influence and prestige with colleagues and less financial, economic or political judgment.

Discrimination

Women were asked by CAWP researchers what difficulties they experienced as a result of being a woman in office. "In the minds of women officeholders, discrimination—especially discrimination from colleagues and party leaders—looms far larger as a difficulty of officeholding than conflict with family responsibilities or deficiencies of background and training." In the survey, women complained that they are not taken seriously, are stereotyped, are regarded as sex objects, excluded from the old-boy networks, are not consulted on pending issues and are discriminated against in committee assignments.

Women politicians also complained that they are asked to do clerical work, take on an unfair share of the workload and are subjected to opposition to their programs and ideas *because* they as women have initiated them. Whereas a man's competence is taken for granted, the woman politician has to prove hers, and she is sometimes avoided or ridiculed by her male constituents.

Such complaints sound familiar; they are the same ones that women in business make. The ways most men perceive women are not changing quickly enough to keep up with the new roles women now have taken on.

Any woman going into business or politics will have to develop a thick skin and expect shabby treatment at times from certain people. Perhaps if she expects this kind of behavior, it won't be so traumatic, and she will be able to handle it or ignore it, while hoping that it will eventually disappear.

Men, apparently, either don't realize how discriminatory they are being, or they pretend it isn't true at the same time that they do it. Men were asked in the survey what they thought women's special problems are in holding office. They were less likely than women to name sex discrimination, and more likely to mention conflicts with family life and officeholding, or a woman's "inadequacies of personality and qualifications."

Women are also up against resistance from voters, 10 percent of whom say they will not vote for a woman under any circumstances. I think if people were cornered at the polls in the act of voting and queried, this figure would certainly be even higher.

Women claim that male party leaders try to keep them out of leadership roles, don't nominate them for office or give them financial support, and that this is more common than any voter reluctance to back them. Male politicians, on the other hand, blame more of a woman's problems on voter resistance. Women also find it difficult to raise money from other sources because they are not part of a network of people who stand ready to help one another. A 1976 poll found that only half the women who were running for major offices had campaign managers, and even fewer had funds for polling and other campaign techniques.

A survey done in Wisconsin found that women candidates suffer from other handicaps. Shy women felt inhibited about campaigning in taverns and other male hangouts, they complained about long night auto trips on the campaign trail and said they needed a "wife" to help coach them for appearances and care for family while they campaigned.

Because of this several organizations have sprung up to help would-be women politicians. One, for example, the National Women's Educational Fund (NWEF) in Washington, D.C., sponsors institutes in campaign technique around the country; another, Eagleton's CAWP, conducts workshops in advocacy and campaign technique at Rutgers University. Marilyn Johnson points out in the Eagleton CAWP report that "A substantial proportion of women already in public office express a need for technical assistance in the areas of government, finance, federal programs such as revenue sharing, and advocacy techniques. Women who are considering running for office would do well to take courses that would give them a background in these subjects. Particularly, as Johnson points out, those women who did not finish college because of marriage and child rearing need counseling and courses to fill in the gaps.

Women Versus Men

In their political roles, women are quite likely to approach their jobs by stressing other things than men would. This is not because they are biologically different, but because of their experience. They are the ones who have spent hours with children, with animals, with monthly budgets, checking prices of food in stores, listening to consumer complaints, dealing with hurt fingers and upset emotions. When it comes to understanding their constituents the survey found that women place more importance than do men on discovering the public's view of issues at hand, educating them about what's going on and what the possible outcomes could mean. They seem more concerned with helping the individual constituent with his or her problems. A woman's concept of political office is to deal personally with the people she represents.

Women also appear to be more liberal than men in general, Eagleton's CAWP investigators found, and, not surprisingly, more feminist on issues. "Majorities of women in every type of office endorse ratification of the Equal Rights Amendment, oppose a constitutional ban on abortion, and favor extension of Social Security to homemakers."

They also differ with men on other human issues. Higher proportions of women feel that severe punishment is not the best way to deal with the crime problem, that mandatory retirement should be prohibited, and that busing to achieve racial balance in schools will benefit the country. They seem to be, because of past roles, more compassionate and more understanding of the human problems involved in decisions.

It struck me in talking with both women executives and women politicos, that businesswomen were more apt to underscore the fact that they were *no* different in feelings or behavior from men, whereas in politics, women seemed to feel there *are* differences in attitude that should be capitalized on, and that women had their own special virtues to bring to the political arena. Women in business, for example, feel that crying at an angry meeting would be the kiss of death, the end of a career. In politics, emotion is more rampant, and some women are perfectly willing to let the tears flow when they need to make a point.

I spoke to five middle-aged politicians whose jobs stretch from local governing bodies to the White House.

Alice of the Township Committee

Alice is thirty-five and recently became active in township politics. It took her three years to decide this was what she wanted. Now she knows it is. "I like working with people and problems, and I feel a sense of responsibility. If one wants to raise a hue and cry about things that should be done, I think you should commit yourself all the way, rather than from the sidelines."

She feels strongly that her town should have housing for a spectrum of economic groups, have enough open space and good recreation sites. She wants to help plan for future growth. "I've enjoyed my political role because I have learned more about the area I live in. The world isn't all like my town. I've met union members, blacks and whites who live in the center city nearby, blue-collar working people with lots of common sense."

Alice feels that more women don't go into politics because it's difficult on families, for either the man or woman. But one of the main reasons women involved in local politics don't aim higher and run for Congress must also be money. "It's probably the rare woman, at least at this stage of women's activity," she said, "who can make contact with power brokers and get their political and financial backing." Alice feels that although getting elected to township committee isn't all that difficult, there is a demanding time commitment. There are an incredible number of night meetings, some of which run past midnight. "To go up another level would require an awful lot of sacrifice. I know from treading the streets of my town, it takes a lot of time. It's a question of priorities, if you can juggle all the balls, family and political career, then fine. But with a young child, it's a little more juggling than I can manage. I put my family first, but it's a conflict. My husband and I have had several quarrels about it when he's thought I put politics ahead of him. Congress would mean splitting and uprooting the family.''

I asked Alice what, judging from her experience, she thought a woman needed to have to be good in politics and what the pitfalls might be. "I think a woman needs a strong ego and a tremendous amount of objectivity," she said. "The one thing women have a harder time with in politics than men do is that they take things personally when they shouldn't. A disagreement on a woman's position," says Alice, "is often taken as a criticism of her. There are very few fields where you expose yourself as much as in politics." However, this sensitivity to criticism seems to be a characteristic of women who are novices in business as well as politics.

Moreover, Alice believes, getting up on stage and fielding questions is not a customary role for women. "You see it often at meetings. Women sit there and don't say anything, and the conversation is carried on by the men." Another problem for women is expertise. Alice pointed out that most men who go into politics are usually trained in some other profession like law or business, fields women are just beginning to enter. They often simply don't know enough to strengthen their positions. However, Alice pointed to the large numbers of women who are mayors of cities or who sit on councils. "Women are far more active politically than they have been. Their next step is to run for state legislatures and then Congress. I don't think it's such a quantum jump for a woman to run for governor after having been mayor. It's unquestionably something women have been backward in, but I think we are entering a new era."

Barbara Sigmund, the County Freeholder

Here's a woman, now forty, who grew up in a political environment. Her father, Hale Boggs, was a member of Congress from Louisiana, and their house was always filled with politicians like Lyndon Johnson or Hubert Humphrey. But Barbara never had any expectations of a career for herself. "I thought I was going to grow up and be a Mommy. We weren't brought up to think we were going into politics."

After college she worked for President Kennedy for a year, doing such things as writing messages to old ladies who were celebrating their one-hundredth birthdays. One of the things that impressed her about Kennedy was "his fantastic ability to concentrate on what was at hand at the moment." But Barbara never took her job seriously, spent days "giggling in the halls of power" and eventually married and had three children.

Finally, something in her life changed. She and her family went to live in Mexico for part of a year. "I'd been looking forward to living like the queen of the plantation, having a nice house, help, and royally entertaining friends. In the back of my head I had this vision of myself doing that forever. I did it and discovered it wasn't enough. I loved it for a few months. I had a good time mañana-ing it up. But it was a seminal period for me when I realized I wanted to do 'something.' I think you have to have both family and a career. We were all astonished that it didn't work—just the family alone.

"When I got home a friend told me they were looking for a woman to run for borough council. That kind of clinched it for me. The moment and the woman had met. I was ready. My husband always said he wanted me to go into politics sooner or later. He'd have preferred later. My mother, who had always been my father's campaign manager, tried to discourage me. She said, 'You've got a nice, balanced life, a home, friends, a job teaching.' But Daddy said one word: 'Run.' We were going to have a good old-fashioned campaign parade for me, and then his plane disappeared in Alaska." (No trace of it has ever been found.) But she won her first primary and the election and received the glorious sum of $750 a year for the job.

"Then it became obvious that my past experience with my father was relevant, but not as much as I thought. Local politics is more local, more intense. People are dealing with smaller issues, but ones that are closer to them, such as their property, or their neighborhood. They can see what you're doing, like building a bike path in front of their house, and they hug and kiss you in the supermarket, or tell you off. It's not as though you were off under a dome in Washington." She enjoyed the borough council but found having young children at home made it difficult. Her kids were seven, six and two, and she felt she should have waited three more years. She later ran for county freeholder ($12,000 a year) and won again.

Aside from her young family there were other things about being in office that she found difficult. "People feel free to say things to elected officials they don't say to other people. Women in particular find it hard because of the insults and slights. Your motives are constantly questioned. People are at you all the time asking 'What have you done for me lately?' " She found that it takes time and persistence to get anything accomplished, and women are not trained in persistence, toughness, seeing a long, drawn-out project through. Barbara's background, though, gave her "an internal fortitude" about that kind of life. Her father had taught her that there is one thing that makes the struggle all worthwhile, "the results."

"My dad once helped sponsor a liberalized trade bill and I was with him when he was talking to someone in big terms but using blue cheese as an example. I realized it's all a matter of dealing with one piece of blue cheese after another."

Barbara finds her job as county freeholder important. The federal government is using counties as channels for their money more and more, and counties are becoming the main instrument for the delivery of services, because municipalities find it too hard. They don't have enough money and can't deal with day care, senior citizens, transportation and recreation. For example, using federal funds, her county recently set up a home for battered women and their children.

When we talked of how men and women operate on the local political level, Barbara said that women find the question of compromise a difficult thing. For example, she noted that men seem able to work better with men whom they don't like personally. If the woman doesn't think the person is trustworthy, or honest on the personal level, she can't get past that.

She also finds that for men, if something gets to be a public

controversy, the issue itself becomes secondary. The man has
to save face, blame defeat on someone else no matter what went
wrong. The man thinks of whom he can blame for its happening,
rather than how we can prevent it from happening. Says Barbara, "I think the public could use a little more emotion and
softness. I think women should stop being ashamed of their
attributes. They're needed. A woman's cultural training is more
to mediate, as they do with children. 'You're right, but let's do
this.' Men play it rough and tough. They want to see that their
team doesn't lose points. They play to win, not to solve a situation. Women are not culturally like that."

She admits that at a particularly heated meeting with a lot of
fighting back and forth, she has wept. "And I didn't mind. It's
about time someone cried for the poor people caught in the
middle. I'm not ashamed of the female characteristics of mediation and compassion. The best male politicians have this too.
Senator Humphrey always cried in public when he was sad or
touched—when you're supposed to cry."

As so many other women in business and politics continue
repeatedly to point out, Barbara adds, "You'd have to be deaf
and dumb to think that male politicians don't treat women con-
descendingly. You either put up with it or slap them down.
There are sexual jokes and the opinion of an older professional
man, like a lawyer, counts for more. A woman has to prove
herself," though sometimes she is ridiculed when she speaks
out. The mayor of a nearby town once called her a "witch" in
public, and others speak to her as though to say, "Come on,
dolly, what do you think you are doing in this business?"

There are the personal satisfactions, though, which make it
worthwhile for a woman. If she is able to persuade her colleagues to do something she feels is important, such as developing low- and moderate-income housing, the effort has paid
off. Barbara is drawn to public life for this reason. "You are
beguiled by the good works you can do, and the people you
work with and meet. They become almost like comrades-in-
arms. You go through so many things together. You really get
close to people. It's exhilarating."

She sees middle age as an advantage for a woman in politics.

"Say it loud and clear," she insists. As a mother and a teacher, she may not have the usual background for politics, but she finds the experience of the middle-aged mother just as useful. "Women who've been in a community and raised kids in that community know more on a practical level about that community than anyone else in it.

"For example, if you know how lonely and isolated young housewives are today and you see in a housing development that there's no common room, and no place for day care, and no place where a woman can look out of her window and see kids playing safely—you can say, 'Come on now, fellas . . .' These are the little things that can make a community a pleasant place to live."

To be the right person for a political career, Barbara advises that a woman has to be community minded, have the time, be active in a local political party and get support. She has to have stamina and learn not to cringe if criticized. She also has to be able to make decisions. "When you have to vote," says Barbara, "there's no 'maybe' button. You have to be prepared to make decisions and face the consequences, face the hostility."

Barbara Sigmund would like to run for Congress someday. She feels women have been the support system for men for a long, long time, campaigning, volunteering, licking envelopes. Now they want to do more. President Carter's sister Ruth Stapleton has been quoted as saying, if she were voting for President and had to choose between two equally qualified people, a man and a woman, she would choose the man, because there are certain times of the month when a woman doesn't function well. Says Barbara, "Well, at least we can predict those times. Men have had periods they can't predict. Don't you think?" And aside from a very small minority of women who have menstrual problems, most women are not in the least limited or controlled by their monthly periods.

Millicent, the Pipe-Smoking Congresswoman

Millicent Fenwick received more national publicity when she was elected than any other freshman Congressperson. And not only because she smokes a pipe. She is very outspoken. Now sixty-eight, she went into politics in her forties and behaves as though she were still middle-aged. Her background is not typical.

Millicent never went to college. In fact, she never even finished high school. She married and had two children. Then, when her husband deserted her and she needed a job, she went to work for *Vogue* magazine.

Around this time she also became interested in politics because of Hitler's growing influence and was turned on in the way that younger women later were activated politically by the war in Vietnam. She says, "Suddenly one could see across the ocean legalized government cruelty. It was a perversion of institutions which were supposed to be designed for the welfare of people." She joined the National Conference of Christians and Jews, made some speeches, got herself knocked down and kicked in the back.

A lot of what was going on around her bothered her. She heard about a returned black Tennessee soldier who had come home after serving in World War II to find that he couldn't get served in restaurants and shops in his hometown. She promptly joined the NAACP. When she saw things she didn't like, she would try to correct them, and the best way was through politics. When she reached the age of forty-two, she had at last gotten herself out of debt and was able to use some family money to live in the suburbs of New Jersey. She became a member of various town committees, became interested in prison reform and civil rights. She was elected to her hometown borough council, then the state assembly. "I loved it. It was glorious. I got thirteen laws passed in three years."

When a newspaperman suggested in his column that she run for Congress, she decided he might be right. She ran and was elected and reelected. A virtual dynamo, although she weighs only 112 pounds and has a pacemaker, she gets up at 4:45 A.M. to make breakfast, carries it to bed, leaves her apartment in Washington at 6:15 and walks to her office. She sometimes works until 11 P.M. with a hot dog and a cup of hot V-8 for lunch, and a dinner of spaghetti and a cup of yogurt. Her diet is hardly what one would consider ideal or nutritious, but she thrives on it. She has been on congressional trips to Cambodia, Russia, China and Yugoslavia.

We spoke of the advantage of being a woman in Congress now when there are so few. "We are noticed. People want to know what you think. It gives you a kind of prestige." It also is an advantage to be older. "Unless you are an absolute dope, you do learn something by living." For example, out of the experience of visiting her brother in a nursing home came a bill to change nursing home regulations. She also proposed giving elderly people a tax-free stipend equal to half the cost of nursing home care, so they could live with friends.

Women politicians have a personal concern for the people who vote for them. "There is no use passing all this grandiose legislation," Millicent says, "if you haven't sat down with the people involved, like the woman in the kitchen over a cup of coffee, and talked about such things as housing. Not the macro-economic view or the demographic statistics, but what she thinks. I talk to women," Millicent said enthusiastically. "I have their views at my fingertips.

"I went up and visited a day-care center. The women told me how they felt. One said, 'If I'm late, they don't make me feel small.' Another said, 'It's got the kind of people I like, people like my grandmother in North Carolina.' And a third said, 'I don't want my baby to be brought up by starched white people.' I learned," Millicent went on, "that you must pay some attention to the satisfaction of the people for whom the bills are designed. You can't just pass bills that won't satisfy the people they are intended for." She prefers firsthand learning about a situation to reading impersonal studies full of statistics.

Her assistants read the printed material that comes to her office, but she looks at all the handwritten letters. Take the issue of the rise in taxes. What should her position be? Well, it was no doubt partly influenced by one letter she received that read:

> Mrs. Fenwick:
> What do you think you are doing down there? They gave me a $20 raise. I got five children. There is $8.67 left in my pay check out of that raise after taxes.

"If that doesn't show the problems—" Millicent said looking at me, not needing to finish her sentence.

Comparing characteristics of the male and female political mind, Millicent points out that, first, women are honest. "It may be an element of our newness. But we have not been bribed, not even by a cup of coffee. On the Korean investigation, no women were bribed."

Second, she finds that women are more practical. "Our bills are more directly addressed to the practical problems of living. We are not addicted to charts to explain things that can be done straightforwardly. We don't think about the tax-deductible dollar. We deal with the ultimate dollar—what's left."

During her campaigns, she never encountered problems because she was a woman. Many men told her, "I'm glad to see a woman running. You couldn't do worse than those bums." The only criticism she ever got was from another woman who said, "I wouldn't vote for a woman, even for dogcatcher."

Why go into politics in view of such negative remarks? This Congresswoman believes, as other women in politics have said, it is the hope of being useful. Useful even in small things. As for when to go into politics, she says women tell her, "When my kids get out from underfoot, I'm going to try politics too." Says Millicent, "It's never too late."

The Senate's First Elected Woman

She is only 5 feet 2 inches tall and her name is Nancy Kassebaum. She was elected in 1978 as a Republican Senator from Kansas, and so becomes the first woman ever to win a Senate seat on her own and not because she was the widow of a male politician. However, her victory is certainly the result of family ties. Despite the fact that she has been a Kansas housewife and mother of four children for at least half of her forty-six years (not the usual preparation for the Senate), the thing that clinched her election was the fact that she is the daughter of a politician. Her middle name is Landon. Her father, Alf Landon, was a former governor and Republican presidential candidate in 1936, when Nancy was four years old.

In the past, Margaret Chase Smith was appointed to a Senate seat in 1940 after her husband Clyde died in office, then was later reelected several times. Lindy Boggs took the place of her husband who disappeared in a plane flight while he was in the House, Muriel Humphrey filled her husband, Hubert's, place when the senator died of cancer, and Maryon Allen replaced her husband, James, in the Senate.

Now, at last, one woman has done it more or less on her own. I spoke with Nancy shortly after her election, and she insisted that her father had not given her any political advice. Her campaign manager concurred. "He told her such things as, 'Get some rest,' 'Don't overdo.' " As difficult as that is to believe, it may well have been her ninety-one-year-old parent's prime concern.

However, Nancy did not hesitate to exploit her father's name and the obvious affection some voters still felt for him. Coupled with her own drive and a first-rate television promotion job done by a New York firm, this Kansas housewife made it all the way. Whatever the reason for her victory, she has broken new ground.

Nancy grew up in a political atmosphere. "She's been campaigning since she was born," says her manager. She told me she studied history and politics in college and thought she might be interested in the foreign service. But she did nothing about it. After graduating she went to work as a receptionist for Hallmark Cards. She was elected to the school board and recently worked for a year as an aide to Senator James B. Pearson (whose seat she has now inherited), but she had no special political ambitions. She never thought of being a candidate herself, though she has volunteered in many campaigns when others ran.

Her only other work experience has been as owner of a radio station in Wichita and part-owner with her father of another station in Topeka, which must have given her some knowledge of business and organization.

But politics has always played a part in her life. She remembered, "I was interested in politics while growing up. There was a heritage of interest. That was part of the reason for my being involved. I always kept up on current issues."

Two things made her decide to run. One was her legal separation from her husband. "I would have been just as content staying home, but my separation provided me with an opportunity. If not for that, I wouldn't have left home. My youngest child is still a junior in high school." (One shudders to think that the United States Senate has its first independently elected woman because of a case of marital discord.)

The second factor was the urging of friends who thought the time was right in the country for a woman to run, and that she had the personality to do it. They were right. It's not only hard to believe that her father stayed out of her campaign, it's just as incredible that a housewife, even with her political background and experience in business and political volunteering, could have pushed through her own campaign. For one thing she had to participate in fourteen debates, seven of which were televised —a total higher than any other Senate candidate. She had no debating, television or public-speaking experience.

"I had to prepare myself for the primary first, so I read a lot on the issues." (There were nine candidates in the primary, eight of whom she had to annihilate.) "And the questions were fairly similar, not that detailed. You just do it," she said. "You get better as you go along, like with any skill. The first few speeches I gave must have been frightful."

There were serious questions posed as to whether this petite woman could be aggressive enough, or tough enough, or whether any woman could do the job. "But I got respect from people, even those who were opposed to me." She attributes her having won to three things: her name, good TV coverage and honesty. "I didn't promise a lot."

She received quiet support from women; it seemed to her they were usually the younger or older ones. Those of her own age appeared to her to be less enthusiastic. Although she says she experienced no discrimination as a woman running a campaign, she recalls some women telling her, as other female candidates have also reported, that they would not vote for a woman. "Women are our own worst enemies," she said.

The prospect of being alone in the Senate chamber full of men doesn't scare her. "I don't know why it would be any more difficult than facing a roomful of women.'' And being a former housewife now sitting in the nation's highest governing body doesn't frighten her either. ''The qualifications are the same,'' she says. ''I think being a housewife is important, and I think being in the Senate is important. You have to do a good job wherever you are.''

Nancy Landon Kassebaum is one housewife who discovered she had a lot of talent she didn't realize she had: a clarity of mind that enabled her to make speeches, debate in public, perform on television and campaign over tens of thousands of miles around the state of Kansas. She told one interviewer, ''Unless I'm willing to change my tire when I have a flat, I'm never really going to get there.''

Whether the political drive is in the blood through heredity or interest, it does seem, as Nancy's friends urged, that now is the time for women to make their move and start running their own campaigns for Congress, rather than stuffing, licking and voting for others. They ought to be where the action is.

Anne Wexler, the President's Special Assistant

I arrived in Washington for my interview with Anne Wexler on a hot April day. I presented myself at the West Gate and the guard asked for identification, then retreated into his glass cubicle to verify my appointment while I waited outside the black iron gates feeling like an intruder. At last he appeared, handed me my orange badge which I had to wear clipped to my dress, and the gate swung open.

I entered the West Wing doors and the guard announced me and asked me to wait. I asked if there was any part of the White House I could see in the meantime. I was disoriented and not sure of where I was in relation to all those famous rooms. He motioned me quietly (everything is hushed as a library) along the thick carpet, and I found myself suddenly standing at the entrance to the Oval Office. The office was lighter and larger than it seems in pictures and managed to be both extremely cheery and elegant. The President's heavy desk sat in front of the tall bay windows with their two-inch-thick bulletproof glass. Across from where I stood were French doors leading out to a terrace, white garden furniture and flowers. Opposite the desk, at the end of the room, was a working fireplace and a couch in front of it. A wonderful vanilla-colored rug with a blue border covered the floor. I stood there stunned. There is no other word for it. It is an extraordinarily impressive room. I tried to visualize Roosevelt, Truman and Johnson behind that desk, and the voice of John Kennedy in that room. It is a room that breathes power, but more than that, responsibility.

I thanked the guard and looked into the Cabinet room and the less-formal Roosevelt Room. By the time I was called to the second floor of the West Wing (this wing is for the President and his staff, the East Wing is for the First Lady's offices) I was pretty overwhelmed. Outside Anne Wexler's office her secretary told me how great she is to work for. "She's fun, smart and gets things done." The secretary went on to say that she ordinarily finds women harder to work for than men. "They are unpleasant and demanding. They forget they started down at the bottom."

I found Anne Wexler, forty-eight, special assistant to President Carter, to be a warm, dark-haired, shiny-eyed woman who exudes friendliness, confidence and competence. I sat on a yellow couch, and she chose a nearby chair and put her feet up on the couch. She made me feel comfortable.

How did she win the office on Pennsylvania Avenue and the salary of $56,000 a year? She is as thickly involved with politics as anyone who has ever been elected, but she has taken the other route to power. She arrived by being appointed rather than elected, and she is in an administrative job rather than a governing and lawmaking job. The incredible thing about Anne Wexler is that a little more than ten years ago she was simply a Connecticut housewife with an ophthalmologist husband and two children who often tried her hand as a political volunteer. Today she sits in the White House advising the chief executive. My first question to her was "How did you do it?"

Anne was the oldest child of a New York architect, and it was he who developed this self-confidence. "My father always made me feel I could do anything.'' (There is that paternal influence at work again.)

She told her story quickly, efficiently. She began by joining the Democratic Women's Club in her town. Rather than social occasions, the gatherings there were issue oriented. She took part in campaigns and found she was always interested in ''process systems,'' how things work. She was elected to the Democratic town committee and devotedly addressed envelopes. ''I was also doorbell ringer and stamp licker. It took a long time for local people to realize that women knew more about getting the job done than the men. A man running for office would pick a friend to handle his campaign, someone who didn't know a goddamned thing about it, and the women had to do the work. But they weren't allowed in the back room where the decisions were made. Local politics is still a man's game,'' she said. ''On the state level it isn't much better, but it's just beginning to open up. On the national level women are taken more seriously.''

She went from one campaign to another until finally she had done everything there is to do in a campaign. Next she tackled state politics and issues relating to the war in Vietnam. ''I thought the only way to attack it was through the system. Burning buildings didn't help. I didn't have any idea how naive I was. I found out how much the cards are stacked against the ordinary person who wants to use the system to change things. That was the genesis of my work in parliamentary procedure, changing the rules.'' As an example of the kind of changes she meant, she said, ''Some delegates to the convention were picked two years before the convention met, and their point of view on current issues couldn't be known at the time they were chosen. I got very involved with the rules things.''

Anne was on the Governor's Commission on Election Law Reform in Connecticut in 1969, delegate to the 1968 and 1972 Democratic National Conventions and a member of the Convention Rules Committee. By this time she had a reputation for being a parliamentary expert and a skilled political operator. She was a floor leader at the 1972 convention and spent her time organizing votes and influencing people.

By the time she met Jimmy Carter in 1974, she had worked

for Eugene McCarthy's campaign in 1968, Edmund Muskie's primary campaign and George McGovern's presidential campaign in 1972. In a very few years she was amassing an impressive list of political contacts. She was also involved with several groups of the Democratic National Committee. During that period, Carter initiated a system of "support mechanisms" for candidates which is still being used. It involves a series of books which the National Committee publishes that advise would-be candidates on how to raise money, register votes and develop issues. She remembered, "We worked together that year and developed an informal relationship."

Hamilton Jordan and she stayed in touch and, after the Carter-Mondale campaign, which she of course worked on, he called and asked her to come to work during the transition. He has been quoted as calling Anne "tough, strong, straightforward, a can-do kind of person." Others call her one of the country's most competent women in politics. "She knows which macho buttons to push with the people she has to deal with. A real pro."

She has also been called "abrasive," as have so many women who are unusually competent. A White House official commented in an interview that he would phrase it differently. "Abrasive is a word that is used for some women, while phrases like 'dynamic,' 'hard-charging,' and 'take-charge,' are used for men who act much the same."

Anne was assigned to the Commerce Department, and finally in 1977 became deputy under secretary of commerce. "Juanita Kreps and I hit it off. She's a terrific woman." A little more than a year later, possessor of a breathless series of successes and appointments in only ten years, she was given the large office in the White House in which we sat.

That is how she got there. Now, what does she do? She quite simply galvanizes support from the public for specific Carter programs, such as urban policy, civil service reform, natural gas pricing and so on. She also confers with agencies to develop policy issues for the President, and she picks up legislation from Congress to see if the votes can be gathered to get it passed. She points out, "There has never been a constituency building from the White House to get enough support so Congress can feel the pressure." There is now.

Mayors, governors, urban volunteers, labor unions, civil service and tax groups, any organization connected with urban life, are her targets. She sees labor, women's and ethnic factions. "I tell them what President Carter is doing, what he's about, and get their input. When the White House drafts legislation, I work with all the constituent groups. We go over the legislation line by line. By the time the bill is sent up to Congress, there is already this constituency for it."

She deals with lobbies. "I have road construction people in here because they are concerned about the size of the highway bill. Once we explain what we're doing and why, we have no trouble getting their support." She is credited with helping to push through the administration energy bill.

I pointed out that there are a lot of women who began working on the local level, and they didn't all end up in the White House. I asked her what it was she had that made the difference in her case? She attributes it to a "confluence of events that really got me going. I found the process—the conventions and voting—was so unfair, I had to get involved. I'm a natural organizer."

I wonder how it feels to be working so close to the top, where everything of importance is happening. "I think that everyone who works here feels it all the time. I feel very special when I walk through the gate every morning. I'll never be blasé working here. There's a special quality about seeing the President of the United States at such close quarters. It really increases your motivation." When he takes her advice, she said with modest restraint, "I feel good, I am happy."

The only thing she doesn't like is the goldfish-bowl aspect of the job. "I don't have a private life. It's unfair. People think they own all of you."

But Anne feels something overwhelmingly positive about her role as the President's assistant. Is it a sense of power? "No, that's not it. It's the privilege of being able to care deeply about your country and being able to do something about it that is important, not the manipulation of power. It's the idea that you can have an impact. You gain credibility from how much you can accomplish rather than what power you might have. That kind of thing ended with Nixon.''

Speaking about whether women make as good politicians as men, Anne, who has been around and worked with politicians in many places and at many levels said, ''I don't necessarily think men make such good politicians. Politics is a craft like any other. Some are good at it, some are not. I don't separate them by gender. There is politics at every level of life, in business and in the university as well as in government.''

People often ask whether she ever intends to run for office. As a candidate, she would benefit from all her unique experience. ''People always ask me if I want to run because of the stereotyping. Women think the ultimate goal in politics is to run for office. There are lots of other roads to political success, such as policy development or organizational management. I don't want to be elected to any office I can think of running for. If you win, you may have to be a Congressman, and who wants to be *that*,'' she says with emphasis. ''It's not the kind of life I'd enjoy. I'm not a public person. I don't want to work seven days a week and give speeches.''

We discussed the dearth of women in politics, and Anne described enthusiastically what other observers also sense is happening. ''There are a lot of women out there in the state legislatures. I think the lack of women politicians in Congress is temporary. As time goes on, you'll see more women at the top. In the past, women got there by a fluke, such as the death of a husband. Now we're in a time lag. There are a lot of women working their way up. I think they will burst into national prominence in five or ten years. They're doing their homework. It's a time warp,'' she said. ''The vacuum is being filled at the bottom. By the time they get to the top they will be very good, like the men who paid their dues.''

When women do get to the top, what will they have to offer? It's the old question of whether men and women are inherently different or merely behave differently—if, in fact, they do even that. Anne said, ''Sometimes I think women have something special and sometimes I don't. But the differences will be blurred more and more. I do think that women are less competitive, not so turf conscious, willing to help others. It's very refreshing. Women try to help each other more maybe because there are so few of us.''

At this point we heard the sound of a helicopter coming closer and closer, and we looked through the sun-splashed window. Anne Wexler said, ''There's the President.''

There was silence again, and we moved on to talk of the burst of middle-aged women who are working now. ''All my friends who were suburban housewives have jobs. I'd go nuts in twenty-four hours if I didn't work. I think we are seeing this phenomenon in middle-aged women because of the way they started life, as I did. I married two weeks out of college. My kids would no more do what I did than fly to the moon. The bridge and Mah-Jongg games are over.''

Anne is a very businesslike woman, and I pushed her to try to get her to explain, in more personal terms, what having this job does for her. ''There is no lofty, grand, cosmic thing I get out of my work. I just like to do a good job for this President. I believe in him. I see myself as being his instrument. I'd be gratified if I could do that.'' She told me how exciting it is to participate in strategy sessions, to see ideas brought up and then discarded, rightly or wrongly. ''I feel an awesome sense of responsibility. When I go home I sometimes say to my husband (her second), 'God, it's hard to run the country.' She is aware of the high level of decision, the impact on the country these decisions create, the crisis management necessary at times.

Women have often wondered whether and when a woman will run for President. Anne says, ''I know a dozen women who would make good Presidents. What is a good President, though? A serendipitous coming together of events that make it possible for that person to be good.''

As I walked through the halls again after our interview, I saw the door to the Oval Office closed. The President was already at work (no cumbersome unwinding after a tiring trip), and people were gathering in the Roosevelt Room for a meeting. I turned to leave, stepped out into the sun and headed toward Pennsylvania Avenue reluctantly giving up my pass to the guard who came out of his glass cubicle for it. He buzzed the iron gate open, I stepped onto the sidewalk and once more I was part of the mass of citizens looking in from outside, I'm a million miles from the center. But one thing is different now. I feel government is accessible, and more than ever before, accessible to women who want to work for it, especially those of middle age who want to take the jump.

The Egyptian President's Wife

Not long afterwards, in early May, I accompanied my husband on a business trip to Egypt and, with some effort, was able to arrange an interview with Jehan el-Sadat, the wife of Egypt's president. She is a woman whose political power is not the result of having been elected or appointed, but of having married the man who succeeded to the office. The interview was memorable, to say the least.

Outside the presidential villa, Cairo was hot. The sun glared white against the sand-colored buildings, the streets were sandy, and piles of sand and lay here and there on the broken sidewalks where they blew in on the Khamseen, the desert wind. Cars zigzagged, their horns blaring constantly, their brakes screeching as they stopped short of hitting people who walked in the road, or colliding with each other.

Inside the villa, all was quiet, an oasis in the noise and heat. I looked through the tall windows watching the gray Nile slip by. As the wife of her country's president, Mrs. Sadat certainly could enjoy the duties of her official role, greeting other first ladies, visiting hospitals, thinking of nothing more weighty than menus for state dinners, or staying completely in the background as Nasser's wife had. But something within her made this limited role unthinkable. Not content to be simply an appendage of her husband, she strives to realize her own potential, make her own mark. She believes passionately in Egypt, its future and its women.

I therefore felt both honored and excited about including Mrs. Sadat in a book about American women, because her experi-

ences and beliefs are so strikingly similar to those of our
women. Some of the things she said, in fact, astounded me by
their similarity to what Americans had been telling me. At
forty-seven, Mrs. Sadat is not only Egypt's First Lady, she also
juggles many other lives: wife, mother, grandmother, teacher,
and poet (she publishes under a pseudonym and toured the
United States reading poetry in Arabic and English in the spring
of 1980). As a continuing student she is completing a study of
the influence of Shelley on modern Arabic literature for her
master's degree. She is also president of her local political council, and a strong advocate of women's rights.

Trying to raise the status of women in a country like Egypt,
which is still deeply embedded in conservative Moslem tradition, is not easy. This is a land where a man looks upon a woman
as his social, legal, and moral inferior. Polygamy is legal (a man
may have four wives, though few do); a woman cannot inherit
more than half her husband's estate; a man can divorce his wife
without her consent; and child custody, alimony, and other such
rights benefit the man. In addition, the custom of subjecting girls
to clitorectomies still exists. In this brutal operation which is
said to date back to pharaonic times, the clitoris is removed in
a rite of circumcision which leaves the girl permanently without
most or all of her primary erogenous zone. In rural areas and
traditional quarters of cities, women are still veiled in black
from head to toe and are not allowed out at night to visit their
friends without their husband's permission. This First Lady has
a tough uphill battle ahead of her.

Five minutes earlier than the time set for our interview, Mrs.
Sadat walked briskly into the elegant reception room where I
sat waiting. Waves of perfume (American, she later told me)
followed in her path. She is short, a little overweight and beautiful. She had on a blue-green long-sleeved shirtwaist print,
"sensible" high-heeled shoes, a thin gold necklace. Her skin is
unusually fair, her immaculate short brown hair seems high-
lighted by a hint of blond across the forehead, her eyes are
brown, and her features extremely delicate. Like many Egyp-
tians, she is warm with a winning sense of humor. Unlike many,
she is organized, efficient and dynamic. Her English is very

good, and she tended to punctuate thoughts she wanted to stress by saying, "That's a fact."

She sat on a couch under a lovely Gobelin tapestry; I took a chair beside her. There were voices of playing children in the background. She ordered the usual coffee and we both declined sugar, making comments about losing weight. She told me she had met Anwar el-Sadat at her cousin's house when she was sixteen, though she had admired his revolutionary career long before that. They were married one year later. She had not finished high school at the time and was dismayed to suddenly find herself at home while her friends were still in school.

"I was divided between continuing my education and doing something for my husband. I thought, I must be a good wife, he was one of the revolutionaries [who overthrew King Farouk]. But something in the back of my mind kept knocking, 'Why don't you continue your education.' " She tried being wife, and mother to her four children, then after fifteen years of marriage, she began studying at home. She kept at it and finally got her high school degree when she was forty. "I had to take all the exams over again because I had passed some of them so long ago. When I think about it I can't believe what I did."

Her husband encouraged her but advised her to study something fairly easy when she went on to the University of Cairo, like history or geography. "To get some knowledge without any problems," she smiled. But she chose Arabic literature. "I am always giving speeches and it helps me to express myself better." She received her degree in June 1978 at age forty-six, first in her class.

One might assume that she would naturally be given top grades because she was the wife of the president. But she assured me that, no, the professors couldn't possibly have known which exams were hers since every student had a secret number, rather than a name, and her professors did not even know her handwriting.

Why would such a busy woman as the First Lady of any country want to make room in her life for the rigors of study, exams, writing papers, in addition to all of her official functions? What was she looking for?

Even her children wondered. They asked "Why don't you sit as the wife of the President, mother? Why choose difficult things?" But Mrs. Sadat is driven. Since getting her degree, she spent one year as a substitute teacher at the university and began teaching regularly three days a week the following year. At the same time she continued working on her master's. "Once I start," she said with her winning smile, "I never stop. I will go for the master's and Ph.D. (There are only about a thousand women in all of Egypt who have Ph.D's. The country is 65 percent illiterate, another 20 percent have not finished grade school, and only 3 to 5 percent of women have gone to college.)

I began to ponder what motivates this Egyptian woman. Where were the seeds of ambition and success so firmly planted?

As a child, Jehan used to read a lot. When she was ten she was reading books that American girls choose, biographies of Mme. Curie, Florence Nightingale and Helen Keller, whom she later met.

"I was fond of reading about women who suffered until they reached something. It didn't come to them easily. Women who set a good example and helped humanity in some way."

Mrs. Sadat told me, as so many achieving women have, that her biggest influence was her father. He was a young Egyptian medical student who went to Sheffield, England, to study and there fell in love with a schoolteacher. He returned to Egypt with his English wife rather than his medical degree. (Her seventy-six-year-old mother now lives with the Sadats in Cairo.) Jehan was very fond of her father. "He was warm and loved my mother very much. He always brought her chocolates—a small thing, but it gave me the image of a faithful father. Because of that I felt there was no one else like him. It made me also want to do things for people, and he encouraged me. He always told me, 'You can do it. You can do something.' "

One of the important things she did was to return to school, to improve her mind and to show Egyptian women that it was not too late to get an education even if they were older and had children. She fashioned a rigorous schedule of getting up every morning at five and studying until eight before starting the day.

And she organized herself. "During the October War, I was preparing for exams. Instead of being a lady in a car rushing places with lipstick and perfume in my bag, I had lecture tapes I would play or notes I would read. I had to concentrate, to learn how to make use of every minute in my life, instead of wasting time. I also had to learn to be patient."

I asked her if she wasn't scared going back to school in mid-life, and whether as the wife of the president of the country, she wasn't afraid of not doing well enough and embarrassing both of them. She smiled and admitted, "It was a risk. Every professor was expecting too much from me because of my age and experience. But I put all my effort into it."

She felt her age had helped her succeed in school and, as a woman in mid-life, she feels she has had more experience and is stronger than ever in her beliefs. "This is a fact," she told me. But she quickly added, "Women should not wait until they are middle-aged, my age, to do things. They should start earlier."

She goes out in the countryside and tries to help. "I thank God it is very easy for me to convince people. I have this gift. It is very rewarding. In the villages I talk to women and say to them, 'Don't think you are nothing in this society, everyone is important.' I always encourage women to do something." And she encourages them to have fewer children. "Family planning," she explains leaning toward me, her warm voice obviously concerned, "is the main problem we have here. I don't have to convince educated women, but other women I do."

She is a proponent of the IUD for contraception. "Pills you will forget. I encourage the loop. I tell them my children are putting the loop" (as she phrased it. Although she has an English mother, the family spoke Arabic at home, and she has had to learn English as an adult). Mrs. Sadat's struggle to help cut Egypt's growing population which threatens to strangle the country (it is so crowded in places like Cairo that people are living in the graveyards) will be a long, hard one. The estimate is that only about 5 percent of the population uses contraception.

But Jehan Sadat doesn't give up easily. She asked the minister of health, education and insurance if there was anything against family planning in the Moslem religion. He said no. Her idea is to get the sheikhs who preach in the mosques to convince people. "I told them we must have these men with us. Involved with us." She also studies the Koran to know more about what it says. "I couldn't answer people's objections to what I say if I didn't know more than they about the Koran."

She tries to promote ways for women to learn to help themselves. "Let's start small industries in the villages, even in one room, like sewing machines in one village, weaving looms in another village. Let women earn money. I can't persuade a peasant to have fewer children. She wants children so they can earn money for the family. But if I give her a handicraft, she can depend on herself. She won't have kids." Her main problem is finding the money to buy the machines, and she has asked the World Bank for help.

Mrs. Sadat told me that working women are slowly becoming more acceptable. "The majority of peasants are already working in the fields between having babies," she said, "but recently women in the upper middle class have begun to work in middle age. They are opening boutiques, selling ready-made clothes, making cookies at home and selling them. They used to be ashamed to work like this, but no longer. It is now practical to earn money."

Raising the standard of living by urging women to work and have fewer children is one of her priorities; another is getting women into politics, in positions of influence. "We had only 4 women in parliament," she explained. This she felt was not enough representation. "I called my husband on the phone and said, 'Anwar, I'm not talking with you as your wife, but as a woman. We appreciate what you are saying, but I want something concrete, something practical for women. Give seats to women.' There were 350 seats in parliament which men and women could run for equally, though men almost always won, plus 10 seats appointed by the president (he would appoint two women). Now there are 30 extra seats which have been added, which are reserved for women and for which only they can run. "They did not want to antagonize men by usurping their seats," Mrs. Sadat said with a smile. "Several other women will be nominated by my husband, and we will have at least 35. It's a good base for women in the future. Such a push for women," she said with enthusiasm.

Her fervor for women's success goes beyond her own country. She led the Egyptian delegation to the International Women's Conference in Mexico City in 1975 and recently watched with growing interest Margaret Thatcher's success in England. When Mrs. Thatcher won the election and became Britain's first woman prime minister, Jehan Sadat sent her a cable of congratulations even before her husband had time to. "When she won, I felt very proud, not just for Mrs. Thatcher, but for all women."

At this point in our conversation, I asked Mrs. Sadat if she influenced her husband's political decisions, as does Rosalynn Carter who sits in on cabinet meetings and is her husband's acknowledged partner. She said, "In the United States you are very open. Here I must be more careful or they will think I am imposing myself and not like me. I want to reach the people, but it's difficult to do it here. They are too conservative. I move slowly but surely. I don't want to lose them. I want them with me. I want them to accept women."

It is said in Egypt, however, that she is a strong influence on her husband, that she has awakened his awareness of women's status and the need for family planning (though it is not as high on his list of priorities as it is on hers).

I asked about her part in the Camp David negotiations. When her husband went to Camp David the second time during the difficult meetings with Menachem Begin, she did not go with him. She was in Paris but phoned him often. "Every day he would say, 'There is no news.' I would say, 'Anwar, don't feel upset.' I encouraged him."

They are both strongly adamant about securing peace with Israel so the country's resources can be used for development rather than armament. There is little doubt that Mrs. Sadat tells her husband what she thinks about most things. But she implied that he has a strong mind of his own. "He is open, clear, says what he thinks."

She is, however, not above questioning him in public, or expressing her independent point of view. On a television program once, the president was speaking about what great progress was being made in education. She broke in and said she thought her husband was exaggerating. "We still have far to go," she said, "and we must bring these things out, not be ashamed of them."

A 1978 Public Opinion Research poll in Washington found that a quarter of the people surveyed said they thought Rosalynn Carter, Betty Ford and Lady Bird Johnson would have made better presidents than their husbands. I asked Mrs. Sadat if she thought that if she and Mrs. Begin had been at Camp David instead of their husbands, they might have reached a peace agreement sooner.

At this point the color rose in her pale skin and she said slowly, "I've never thought of that." I had the feeling, however, that perhaps secretly, even subconsciously, she may well have thought of that. "I like Mrs. Begin," she added.

And when I asked if she thought women had any characteristics that men don't have that might be politically useful to the world, she said something which led me to believe that whether she had thought of it or not, perhaps she and Mrs. Begin might have been able to solve their differences more easily.

"Maybe women are for peace more than men," Jehan Sadat feels. "First they have to bring peace at home between children and the father. Women are peaceful. They think. They are not emotional. People say women can't be judges because they are too emotional. That's not true. The world will be better with more women in important positions." And perhaps remembering her own experiences she added, "And women are more efficient than men. They can stay up all night, then work the next day. If a man doesn't sleep one night, he is terrible the next day."

She herself is active in politics and takes part in local government. Egypt has twenty-six governorates, like states, each with a governor, mayor and city council. She is a member of the city council of Menoufia, her husband's home governorate, was elected chairperson in 1974, and reelected after four years of service.

I asked how all this frenetic activity impresses her husband, whether he perhaps objects to her speaking out on subjects which are delicate ones in Egypt. She has been criticized for her westernized liberal ideas. "My husband would prefer me to stay at home, like many husbands, but he says nothing."

Jehan Sadat is no Jackie Onassis or Margaret Trudeau whose efforts to find themselves have led them toward lives of frivolous activity, of great expenditure, of frantic liaisons with men. Jehan is a serious, totally dedicated woman who believes she can help free her country from its backwardness, illiteracy and poverty.

It's a horrendously difficult job for a lone woman to be influential in any country, especially an Arab one with its still traditional attitudes toward women. But Mrs. Sadat seems to have the energy that it takes. At one point in our conversation she bent down and ran her fingertips up and down her leg. "Sometimes I have pains in my legs," she said, no doubt from her incredibly demanding routine, "but I am never tired. I am only tired when I have nothing to do."

Our coffee had long since been drunk. The late afternoon sun was streaking the Nile with a tinge of gold, her grandchildren's voices sounded closer. If she could broadcast a message to all women, I asked, what would it be? Again she leaned toward me and spoke with her hands as well as her voice, cupping her fingers together as though to hold the core of what she was trying to say.

"Let women feel the importance of themselves. A woman can live without a man. A man cannot live without a woman. Discrimination is always from men. Women don't discriminate. A woman is important. She must feel her own value, do her best to fulfill herself, reach what we want to reach.

"I can reach where I am going with fighting, but if I stay calm I will gain. Men here are very sensitive. But at times I must say what I think."

Jehan, in Persian means "the world." It is not only women but the social conditions of the world's women that interest Mrs. Sadat. She is turning the position of president's wife into one of strong political influence in her effort to help catapult Egypt into the modern developed world.

There is a growing belief in the quality of what women have to offer and an obvious need to urge them to open their eyes to the opportunity of being part of government. Not everyone can arrange to be a president's wife, but any woman can run for office and many can win. The country can only benefit if women do take a strong and active role. Just as they have been frightened off by lack of outside support and a dearth of self-confidence in the business world, they also have assumed that they could not possibly understand the workings of, or help run, a government. They are so wrong. How more than half of the adult population can placidly agree to exclude themselves from determining the policies of the country that governs their lives and those of their children is difficult to rationalize. Some of us do remember to vote. But there is an urgent need for a lot of us to do more than that.

14

My Own Way

Women go back to school, get jobs, start businesses, and go into politics. But it is also possible to react to this middle period of life in a very private way.

For example, one woman, who spent her life bringing up five children and putting off her dreams until the time when the children were grown, now yearned to travel and find the continuity of life through history. She developed a ten-year plan according to which she and friends (her husband had recently divorced her) hope to visit such places as the Valley of the Nile, Australia and Mexico. She has already been to China.

"We saw a Neolithic village dating back to 6,000 B.C. There were egg-shaped ceramic containers, fairly large ones, that held the skeletons of children," she told me, tracing the shape of an egg in the air with her hands. "The Chinese people at that time wanted the spirits of their dead children near them and placed these containers around their houses. I feel a kinship with these people when I find a detail like that."

Other women find they have the chance now to nurture artistic talents that have been slumbering for decades, or discover abilities they never knew they had. A teacher from Great Neck, New York, started writing poems when she was forty-five and now cannot imagine not writing. She admitted that she harbored dreams of glory, of being discovered, of winning prizes. But she also said she really didn't expect that to happen and feels even if she never published she wants to continue to write. "It's too much a part of my life. It's a thing I have to do now. I have to get it on paper." Many women—surprising numbers in fact—feel this same desire to write. And many others want to paint or sculpt or even act. This is the time when whatever aspirations or talents have been suppressed emerge into the light.

Portrait of the Artist as a Middle-Aged Woman

There are men who believe they must submerge their hopes for a creative life because of their obligation to support a family. They give up ideas of writing the great American novel, or painting the ultimate masterpiece, and stick with the advertising job. This has its advantages. There is absolutely no risk of failing, and it's always easier to be an undiscovered writer or artist than a failed writer or artist. The disadvantage is, of course, that you never know the extent of the talent you are repressing.

But by middle age, the woman with too much free time and the nagging remnant of her dreams has little to lose by giving it a try. Being supported by someone else may keep women at home during the long early years when the children are young and there is no real necessity to get out and work, but now that child-rearing is over, such support offers women an enviable freedom, a veritable grant-to-the-arts, a private Ford-Rockefeller-Guggenheim of their own that many men wish they could have.

I am sitting in the sunlit studio of a middle-aged, slender, intense woman. This studio is an extra bedroom in the house, and there are clay sculptures standing on tables, lying on a bed, resting on the floor.

"Don't use my name," she says. "Call me Fran." She sounds like almost every woman of her age I have spoken to when she says, "I had in the back of my mind having kids. I never thought of a career." Just out of college she married, then went on to graduate school. A year before she would have gotten her degree, she gave up the idea of being a professional and has never had any desire to return to it. She got a job as a nursery school teacher, enjoyed it, but had to give this up because she was continually ill. "I caught everything the kids brought in. I had one strep throat after another."

In rapid succession she had a child, divorced and remarried. Now there were a total of five children to be cared for. Some belonged to her husband, one was hers and some they had together. "I spent the next eighteen years as a mother, a wife, a manager of the house and all that entails. I never regretted having the family. I was never yearning to do something else. But I also never stopped going to art galleries. I'd liked art since college." Fran admitted, "There was no plan to my life. It just unfolded. I never said, 'When the kids are older I'll do this and this.' No plans were there at all. Except a grinding building up of life experience."

Then one day she reached a point, perhaps of saturation or desperation, a point when her life changed. As Fran says, "One fine, beautiful Saturday when I was forty-six, I decided 'I'm going to have to say some of the things I feel.' I was going through a very difficult and emotional time. It had been a difficult summer. There were emotional problems with the children. I sometimes felt I was at the end.

"I didn't want to say what I felt with words. I'd read a lot. I didn't want any more words. I was washed out with words. All those kids and words. All that child rearing. Their change from children to teenagers was not very rewarding for me. I wanted to get what I felt into my hands. Anything with words was— yuk! I didn't want to hear anything." So she turned to clay. She had known potters and seen them work.

On this hot Saturday in August when the art stores all over town were closed, she went to a friend and got some clay, sat down and did her first piece. Without any formal training or grand design, she began to sculpt. "It was an inside explosion —inside of me. A way for me to let off steam. I didn't even known how to work with it. I pushed tinker toy sticks up in the clay to make it stand up. I made what I called 'shrieking' figures. A wail that comes from inside of me. I hear it all around me from men and women and mothers in agony who never say anything." Her "shrieking" figures have their arms flung out, their heads leaning back, their mouths open.

She worked at the kitchen table with just her hands and the clay. At mealtimes she'd clean up the mess, and her family would sit down to eat. At the beginning she worked three to four hours a day. Then it got to the point where she became so engrossed, she would have to yank herself away to make dinner. Her art became her new life. She began to work six or eight hours a day but insists that "It's not more of an accomplishment than bringing up kids. That was my monumental accomplishment. I think of them as my enduring contribution."

Her children, however, did not react to their mother's new work. The youngest child was twelve at the time, and none of them said anything. "They might have seen all this as competition for my attention," Fran surmises. "Also, my work is different and scary and sad for young people. They might have thought, 'Oh my God. Is this the way mother feels?' "

After taking workshops, learning more and working in clay for her own personal satisfaction, she was quietly seduced into the public, commercial side. "You think you are not interested, but suddenly you are." Exhibiting her work and having it bought made her feel like a public personality, and problems crowded in. "Shall I make what sells? Or what I want? How do I set a price? Up to now I think I've gotten too little, $150 to $250 for the better ones."

Fran intends to sculpt "forever." She confided, "Sometimes I stupefy myself when I see my works exhibited. I think, 'Did I really do this?' I surprise myself. I hear other women say they want to do things. They make noises. I say to them, 'If you really want to do something, do it. Never mind, 'I would only if—' There are no excuses."

She considers herself incredibly fortunate in having a husband who encouraged her work and who sometimes even set aside his own work. "If I needed clay he'd go get it, drive an hour each way for it. He goes to art shows and lectures with me. He was totally appreciative. If supper wasn't ready he'd start getting it. He'd never say, 'Where's dinner?' He also enjoyed developing an interest in art."

I carefully touch one of her clay figures admiringly. She feels they are emotional and moving, and they are. Again she emphasizes, "I think if women want to do something in art, they should go ahead and do it! Never mind the paraphernalia or teachers. Never mind—you don't have this or that or a potter's wheel. Just do it, and be quiet." For Fran it was the advice that no one gave her, which grew out of her guts, that she knows has to be right. She takes one of the clay figures in her hands and looks at it. "I have to be doing something wholly, with my whole self. Now my whole self is doing this."

Andrea's Affair

There are other women whose personal reaction to middle age leads down different paths. These women sense that they are at last experienced, liberated and old enough not to care what others think about them, and to admit that they want more out of life, and especially out of marriage, than they are finding. They may be working, they may be in politics, they may have their own businesses, they may be writing or sculpting, but these activities do not necessarily satisfy a deeply felt need for a more intense intimacy, perhaps real, perhaps a romantic and idealized dream of what love and marriage should be like. Or it may just be that old hunger for variety that women are developing a taste for too. Their sexual appetites are far from satiated at this age. For whatever reason, these are the women who have affairs.

Now that so many middle-aged women are out of their houses, they are encountering the same opportunities for multiple human relationships that have always made it so easy for men to meet women and have extramarital experience. Women stuck at home with children either don't dare look for other relationships for fear of publicizing their actions in the small community environment, or they don't have opportunities other than the local delivery boys, some of whom, no doubt, were pressed into service. But now that women work, and work with men, they have real opportunities for these secondary intimacies, if that is what they want. Obviously affairs are not limited to the middle-aged woman, but her casual, perhaps even gleeful acceptance of this type of experience runs so counter to the way she was brought up, it seems more surprising, even to her. One can safely assume that more married, middle-aged women than ever are having affairs, though exact percentages remain a mystery. (Despite the well-publicized sex surveys, the problems of securing representative samples are formidable.)

Whereas a younger woman who has an affair may just be enjoying herself, the middle-aged woman may have several motivations that make her different. Because she is older, having an affair means she is once more saturated with the sublime reality of feeling very young again, feeling wanted, needed, loved with a passion. Romance, which had probably become only a dim memory in her past, is once more bursting around her, and she feels incredibly happy, pursued, admired. In a way she feels regenerated, reborn. And it is obviously a much nicer feeling that she has, a much happier image of herself that she sees, than the way she feels when her husband comes home at night and the first thing he says is, "The bed's not made!" Even if he is the perfect husband, the mere fact of having lived together for years has dulled the fine edge of romance, and it is very tempting to experience it again.

There are many middle-aged women today who leave marriages that aren't satisfying, but sometimes all the woman needs to complete her marriage is an affair. As Andrea confided one day eating a grilled-cheese sandwich in a diner near where she works, "By having an affair, I'm having my cake and eating it too."

She explained, "My husband's a great guy. We've been married for more than twenty years, but he's not enough. I need an immense amount of intellectual stimulation which I don't get at home. He's a decent guy and I'd feel rotten if I walked out on him. I don't have the guts. And in a weird sense I have a strong sense of loyalty to him. We have bonds of companionship and we share things together.''

Then she met someone who filled in all the missing parts. When she began her affair, this friend and she agreed they would just have a good time together. Her husband doesn't suspect. "If this kind of extramarital relationship is handled judiciously," she said, "it can enhance one's life. My affair has been going on about a year. It's pleasurable and rewarding and adds a dimension to my life and my knowledge.

"If you have a sense of humor about life, your grand passions can end in practicality. But I love this man. I'm not just after the physical aspect." She said her friend thought he was impotent until he met her. Now he knows he's not. "It's amazing what it has done to his creativity. And I was over the hill. Nothing like this could happen to me. With all those gorgeous girls around, why would anyone go out with a forty-five-year-old woman who's no blond bombshell. I've put on weight, my breasts sag, I have jowls, I'm short-tempered." (Andrea has obviously bought that masculine image of what makes a woman worthwhile.)

She finds the concept of an affair flattering. They go around together, and no one suspects. "I have a daughter in college. I've wanted to tell her about the different aspects of love that I've known, and I can't do it. I know it would help her, but I can't. She'd think I betrayed her father. Since my lover and I sometimes work together, I have been able to invite him for dinner without creating suspicion. I get so much pleasure out of this love for him, I wanted my children to know and share him, if only for a moment.

"In four years I'll be fifty. My mother may be dead. My lover may be dead. One has to accept age philosophically, come to grips with one's natural life span. I've had it up to here with car pooling and worries about kids. I feel justified in enjoying myself and doing what I'm good at. This may be my last affair. I find it difficult to believe I'll find anyone else, or anyone will find me attractive. I'm not alone in this situation. I can think of a half dozen of my friends having affairs.''

Because Andrea works, the logistics of the affair are tricky. Sometimes she takes an afternoon off and borrows a friend's house. Their ''honeymoon'' was going to a meeting in Chicago. But she has other worries besides how they can meet. She worries about his dying of a heart attack and people finding them together, or that her letters to him will be found by his wife whom she respects and likes. ''I get away with a lot,'' she says, ''because I don't look the type who would.''

Sex with her husband, she told me, isn't too good. But that's not the main point of what she's doing. Without this affair her life would be duller. She has learned compassion and understanding; she is more tolerant of people. She has learned to share an experience and bring all those emotions to bear on dealing with her children. ''I don't mean I have the wisdom of the world between my legs.'' She laughs. ''But it adds a great deal to my life.'

There are women like Andrea who at some point live the same kind of double life men have lived for centuries, adding richness to whatever their primary commitment gives them. If she were found out, however, she would probably still be judged more harshly even today than all the married men in the world who are doing the same thing. But Andrea takes what she considers a small risk because she has found a way of venting the tensions created by an imperfect marriage, without giving up her husband. She has found a very personal solution to a problem that middle age made more crucial.

The Woman Who Turned to Religion

The search for some profound means of explaining life may lead to the classic art of sculpting or the human art of having an affair. Or it may transcend the flesh and find the answers to be spiritual. We have heard many stories of men and women who embraced God on their deathbeds. Today it seems to be happening increasingly often a long time before death, often in middle age. The evangelical movement is growing, even as some religions are losing members. There are an estimated 45.5 million people in evangelical groups in the country. Certainly President Jimmy Carter's born-again religion is typical of the movement.

Some women have embraced religion in middle age to find peace and to help them interpret the remainder of their lives. I spoke to a forty-year-old California woman who told me that her interest in religion came as a result of growing older. ''I had felt God was what I needed at this point in my life, but I didn't know how to learn about Him. I began to realize that we are here temporarily, and whatever we have and want, we better work for and enjoy. Ordinarily we never think of death. I had always taken everything for granted. I got married, I had kids and they were driving me crazy. There was no way out of the diaper pail all those years. Now things are different. I no longer take life for granted.''

She began to study religion, joined a Bible study group for a year, then joined a five-year Bible-study fellowship. She finds, ''The main result for me of becoming more interested in religion is that I just became a happy person. I don't try to be the perfect mother any longer. I'm not always finding fault and being critical. The bickering stopped. I feel happy, at peace, at ease. I'm a more positive person. Religion has improved my relationship with my husband. I can give to him more easily.'' Religion has also become the support system to help this woman cope with her daily life, whatever problems middle age has brought with it.

The Woman Who Became a Priest

Daphne Hawkes, forty, married to a surgeon, mother of four children, invited me into her cozy office in the Episcopal church where she is a priest. The wood paneling gave off a warm glow in the afternoon sun, and the churchyard outside was neatly laid out with weathered white tombstones, some with flowers placed beside them. On the wall was a framed statement, ''I found God within me, and I loved Her fiercely." I had come to find out what made the Reverend Hawkes become the first woman Episcopalian priest in New Jersey when she was thirty-nine years old.

Daphne was an English major at college. Her parents were divorced when she was eight, and her mother worked as a saleswoman to support the family. Her father died when she was fifteen. When she was twenty-one, six months after becoming engaged, her fiancé was killed in an automobile accident. She says she was never very religious, but "had the usual questions about death and the meaning of life." In fact, the church had never fit into her social concerns. "When I was younger, I thought the church was hypocritical. People worried a lot about what they were wearing, rather than helping others. I dreamed of being a strong woman like Katharine Hepburn, or I was Ingrid Bergman leading the children across the China border."

What she actually did was marry a man in medical school and have two babies. But there were two church experiences that awakened her interest in theology. In one place where she and her family lived the rector's wife developed cancer. There were five children in that family, and they would all come to church on Sunday with their mortally ill mother and sit there while the rector, with tears creeping down his face, preached about death and funerals. Daphne was impressed. "They dealt with that so beautifully. It was a community of people that grew. They were honest with each other. No facades. There was just this amazing bravery. He asked the questions and faced the grief."

In another town where they lived they belonged to a church that worked for the reconciliation between the races. Says Daphne, "It may have been the first completely integrated congregation. I had never seen both together. The theology and the social action."

When she and her family moved to New Jersey, Daphne audited a class at Princeton Theological Seminary. Later she became a part-time student and finally went full-time. "They had no prejudice against a middle-aged housewife, and I didn't think I'd ever be ordained. I really didn't come up against a mid-life crisis period until I was in the door. The focusing happened in my mid-thirties. I thought, 'Hey, you ought to start focusing in one area. See if you can put a lot into it. Take yourself seriously enough to do it.' "

She finally decided to be ordained at the seminary. "I felt a growing awareness that I was as qualified as all the men in the class, and I could do it. I didn't have the sense that *I* had to do it, break women into the priesthood, but I knew it had to be done. And it felt right for me. I didn't have to struggle. If I had had to fight to be the one, I probably wouldn't have done it, (it's so like a woman to feel that) but people encouraged me, and it fit." The rector in her church believed in her. And he believed the church was wrong in not allowing women. He probably felt he could push her through.

"I worried about being a symbol rather than a person," said Daphne. "That's a lonely, alienating feeling, to be a symbol for women's lib. I wondered, 'Do I want to buy into that?' He encouraged me in a challenging way. Yet at times I felt like an impostor. I wondered if I really had it underneath. When all the issues are won, can I do the job?"

Looking back and thinking of herself she feels that women are too timid. "They need to celebrate themselves. They are too unbelieving in their own strengths." She pointed out that most women who have made changes in their lives had to find their own strengths, but for her it was more like being part of something that was growing. Even so, she acknowledged that she needed support. "If I was honest, I had to realize they wanted a woman priest, not especially me. You know, 'She walks, she talks, she crawls on her belly like a snake.' I felt like a traveling liberal symbol."

While the rector was encouraging her to be ordained, her family was discouraging her. Her mother and mother-in-law thought she was stupid. "No one will invite you to parties," they told her. "You'll be in church all the time." When she would come home from a seminar, her husband would complain, "There are never any clean clothes." Daphne remembered, "I'd always feel guilty. Finally I said, 'All right. The guilt is so bad I can't handle it. I'll quit.' And he'd say, 'You can't do that,' even though he was hurt and afraid. On the adult level he knew he wanted me to succeed. But on the child level, there was the little boy who wanted attention."

There were times when she doubted herself and felt despairing. Instead of giving up, she would react in anger at the ludicrous arguments against women priests, and the anger would make her feel braver. She also was sustained by her feeling that it was right for women to be priests. The church, she believed, could not speak to women if there were no women priests.

There was criticism in the form of ugly incidents from the outside world even after she was ordained. Once she was attending a conference and some of the male priests put notes under her door saying she was "a witch," and "a vehicle of the devil."

When she gave Communion one Sunday, several men in the congregation came up, "and when I came to them, one turned his back on me, and another showed his fist to me as though to punch me and said, 'I will never take wine from a woman.' "

Now that she has been a priest for several years, preached sermons, been sought out by members of her congregation, I asked whether she had observed anything that was bothering the middle-aged women to whom she gave counsel. Did she notice a discontent? The Reverend Hawkes smiled at me and said, "I see women going under and struggling to be fulfilled, and it doesn't mean they aren't successful in terms of the world —married, kids, jobs—it's not correlated to their success. Women are not told it's all right to feel good about themselves. They must learn to say, 'I don't have to feel guilty about what I'm doing in terms of husband and kids.' They are always feeling guilty. They think they have to play down any of their gifts. Women need to find something that fulfills them. But it's going to be a long time before it becomes expected for women to feel good about themselves." She says the general sense of helplessness, and inadequacy that women have is much more pervasive than we know.

She continued, "I see middle-aged women having terrible difficulty letting go of their children, finding their own identity. There is lots of depression. Many women in their mid-thirties and forties are dealing with their parents. Parents may be needy, senile, break hips. They may have the responsibility of these parents. It's a Crisis of the Parents. They were the stalwart ones who now need care. And the children—maybe your kids are in California living with someone. Kids are doing things their parents didn't do. One worries about kids' safety.

"And women are drinking too much. Trying to cope. The relationship with the husband has grown weaker. He's successful, maybe traveling a lot. They struggle to balance husband and kids. They almost have a feeling of doing something bad. Women don't want to leave their husbands, burn bras, desert their kids. But that was the picture of women's lib. You could not be successful *and* be married. Women felt guilty about choosing. One of the aspects about being a woman today is she has to be guilty. Lots of it is unjustified."

She turns to me and says, "I wonder—if you think of depression as anger turned inward, I wonder if women are depressed and self-destructive because they feel angry at being trapped, of being a victim, tired of doing, of caring for kids. It's been so long. Women don't even know what they'd do if they were free to do something. They put so much on the marriage relationship. They are so lonely."

She tells me she thinks it is essential for women to have a place where they are doing something that's theirs, being creative. Otherwise the drive that is a part of being alive, and is as necessary as food and air, gets bent in a way that's destructive —like living vicariously through one's kids or husband. That's how women get off balance.

"You're supposed to make kids so strong with love that they don't need you," Daphne says, "then cheerfully separate. If you put all yourself into children, it's psychologically impossible to separate. It's like an amputation. Women should not put all of themselves into any other person. They should learn to be separate and independent before giving themselves to another. Otherwise they become the martyrs. They demand things back. Doing things you need to be paid back for all the time can be sick."

The Reverend Hawkes asks someone to bring us tea, and we sip it in the waning light of a summer afternoon. I wonder if she feels her age a positive factor in her new work. She finds middle age an advantage because she doesn't have as strong a sense of right and wrong as when she was younger. She's not so judgmental. "Young people can be very self-righteous, holier than thou. That's not how people get the courage to change. As you get older you realize we all have our story dealing with pain, our problems. I have more a feeling that we're all in this together," she says. Daphne also thinks that having children certainly has taught her humility. She remarks that the young priests are so sure of everything. "Their idealism is exciting," she adds, "but it can also be insufferable. It's important to have gotten to the stage where you are not young, because authority coupled with youth can be dangerous, especially in dealing with ethics and morals."

What would Daphne Hawkes be doing if she had not been encouraged by her rector to become the first woman priest in her church? Would she be home with her children who are fifteen, fourteen, ten and nine? As it is, she works only part-time at the moment. Would she be sitting home being a proper doctor's wife and baking cakes for picnics? "If I didn't have this work," she says, "if I weren't a priest, I'd be doing something else. I have to have a meaningful life doing something that I really feel challenges me. It's very important to be stimulated as an individual. I've always had a need to do something of my own." She flicks her blond hair away from her stiff white collar and says, "I can't imagine living without that."

PART THREE

Telling It from All Sides

15

Backlash–What The Other Women Say

Any social movement that is as sudden, as demanding, and as disturbing to accepted tradition as the women's movement has been, is bound to generate its detractors. Some feel personally menaced by what is going on.

As the doors open up and masses of women stampede out of their small worlds to try their luck in the larger universe, those who simply throw another log on the fire, or sit down to another round of bridge, or an extra cup of tea, begin to feel uncomfortable and unimportant. There has been such a transformation among middle-aged women that many of those who don't want to change their lives have become extremely sensitive. Some even fear going to parties where the threatening "And what do you do?" question may come up causing an awkward halt to all conversation.

Not surprisingly, there has been a protective counterthrust among women who want it plainly known that you can work if you like, but they think being at home is beautiful and important. They want it made clear that they see their work as a legitimate choice that should be respected.

Do they have the right to stay home and contribute no more to society than raising their children, repairing furniture, making bedspreads and improving golf and tennis scores? They think they do. They consider their families first on any list of priorities and feel they can give both children and husband more care in such forms as homemade bread, hand-knit sweaters and vital attention. Some also do volunteer work.

In trying to justify being a housewife, one woman from California told me, "I used to be uneasy with other women who are making strides in their lives, who are such great achievers. It bothered me that I didn't go to graduate school and have a parchment or a job. I felt I wasn't as smart as they, that's why I wasn't doing what they were doing. But I realized if I wanted the degree, instead of just sitting home and regretting that I didn't have it, I could go get it. It was then I decided I really didn't want it. It was just a status symbol that I didn't need. For example, I have a friend on a board of directors who asks me for advice. I may not be as smart, but now I can say, 'So what.' I'm learning that I'm pretty important too."

This housewife's "I'm as good as you are" defensive response is necessary for her self-esteem. She was right when she said she felt uneasy. The new opportunities for women are making those who don't take advantage of them feel the need to prove that they are not inferior, lazier or less intelligent. Some react to the point of anger.

One such housewife told me, "I don't object to women's working as long as they don't object to what I do." Another said, "I consider being a housewife a paying job. I think of myself as a professional housewife, not *just* a housewife." Then she turned to me in real annoyance. "Why can't I just sit home and read and rest on my laurels? I've set the scene, launched the family, which is what I set out to do. I created a home and got the family started. Now I want to relax. I resent the pressures to have a career."

All housewives I spoke to agreed that a woman should be home at least for the first five years of her child's growth. Some would say even longer. After the children are older, the housewives split direction. Some favored a career. Others preferred staying at home which, whether career women believe it or not, gives many people a satisfying life. It's the matter of doing what you are good at. Some really enjoy success in the housewifely arts. Or if their husbands are interesting enough, sharing his career may also be fulfilling.

She Gave Up Business to Be a Housewife

The first time I met Janice she was living in bachelor digs with a German Shepherd. She wishes she had had some idea of where she was headed when she grew up, but women simply didn't then. Janice did not go to college and she did not get married. From the age of eighteen, she made work her life. She started by helping her father in a small business and learning about bookkeeping and finance. By the time I got to know her, she was managing a dance company. Then Janice shocked everybody by getting married in middle age and leaving business to become a housewife. Recently we sat in her newly decorated living room and talked.

Fear appears to have been one of the main motives in determining the decisions of her life. She didn't go to college because she was afraid of failing, she explained, and she didn't want to marry because her parents' marriage hadn't worked and she was afraid of forming a permanent relationship with a man. Falling in love as she did in middle age seemed like a miracle. Janice stopped working and got married at age thirty-nine for the first time.

Her husband, she says, is the one who gave her the confidence she needed to get married. "He was the first person who saw me as me. He brought everything out including my emotions. He saw all my weaknesses and strengths. All the curtains fell down. I never had sex till I met my husband. I never thought I was sexy. People looked at me and said, 'What the hell is that?' I think I'm an affectionate person but I held back. All of that was released by Peter. For once in my life I let all the barriers down. I took the risk that it would lead to something. I've always liked people but was afraid to get too close."

Why did love happen then? "Don't ask me why," says Janice. "I guess it was approaching middle age. I was finally ready for a permanent commitment." Now she is enjoying everything about being in a big house of her own, decorating and learning to cook. "When I got hungry in the past, I used to go out to eat. I was like a kid that didn't know frozen orange juice comes from an orange. I didn't know radishes grow one at a time. I thought they grew in bunches." For her, marriage has opened a whole new world. She feels it is special and wonderful being at home. "I feel very content. It's the most marvelously secure and happy feeling. I can't tell you what it does to my insides."

But Janice too has been made uncomfortable by her decision. "Women's-lib talk gets on my nerves," she says. "At the moment I'm not making a huge contribution to the world. To me society is built around the family. One's first responsibility is there. Next comes the environment, then your work, then your community, then the state, nation and world.

"Some can cope with all that at once. I can't. That's the funnel in which I exist. I worry about being happy in my own individual, personal world first. Being in harmony within my world. If I can't be happy in my immediate environment, what the hell am I doing worrying about the world? I'm aware of it, yes. But I can't contribute to all of it."

Janice says she gets so angry sometimes at some of the women interviewed on television "for degrading me and what I'm doing now. They are downplaying everything that I cherish at this point. My husband worked hard in his life and I want to do things for him now. It's a privilege doing his laundry, getting the ice cubes ready. It's an important function to make life easier for him. I think a lot of people today who are doing housework think they should be doing something else. I'm in a reverse position. I think I should be doing housework. Washing windows in the spring takes me a week. But I'm accomplishing something. I don't have to pay for it. I get a sense of importance and accomplishment from cleaning the oven.

"I get angry about people I've known before saying, 'Well, what are you doing?'

" 'I'm married and taking care of my house.'

" 'Why aren't you working?'

"I resent that. Why are they questioning my happiness? What is their problem about work? Why should I feel guilty about being happy? Like going to a cocktail party and having people say, 'What school did you go to? Where do you work? Who are you?' And I don't like having to explain why I'm not working while I'm standing out on the street talking to people. For God's sake. I'm me. And if people don't like me, tough beans!

"Occasionally I go through periods of guilt about having a good time and maybe not earning it. But I figure what I'm doing for my husband and our life together is a hell of a lot of work. I spend one day a week keeping our full set of double-entry book-keeping on household accounts. It helps with taxes. Everything's ready at tax time. I know how many kilowatt hours we spend each year. I clean upstairs, I painted upstairs, painted furniture. I work in the garden, clean gutters, I do all the laundry. I enjoy it."

Whether it's fashionable or not, Janice enjoys being the support system for the person she feels very close to. Because being a housewife is a second career for her, and she'd had the work experience all her life, it may even be a more intense experience than for the average housewife. "If I didn't like it, I wouldn't do it. There are lots of people not doing things like housework that I think plumb don't want to do them, and they use woman's lib as an excuse. It's funny," she says, "I can make a business decision—yes or no—right away. I have more difficulty going to a cocktail party and just making chatter. I feel just as insecure in this social world as housewives are now feeling in the business world." Janice is just as defensive about becoming a housewife at thirty-nine as are others who have been doing it all their lives. When that's what they have chosen, these women don't want their choice derided, they don't want to be looked down on and made to feel inferior. They are ready to fight to stay home, if necessary.

Rachel, the Washington Housewife

Rachel is the wife of James Schlesinger, our former secretary of energy. She made headlines a few years ago when she and several of her children went up to Alaska to help her husband, then chairman of the Atomic Energy Commission (he has also been director of the Office of Mangagement and the Budget, director of the CIA and secretary of defense), prove that an underground atomic test would not be catastrophic.

"It was his idea to go up. I took two daughters and we flew with my husband in Air Force One to Anchorage, then took a commercial airliner to the island of Amchitka. Environmentalists were afraid the explosion would crack the world right open, there'd be a tidal wave or an earthquake. My husband was sure of what the scientists were doing. I thought of it as a great adventure, and only very secondarily as being useful to a cause." She also christened a nuclear submarine in 1977. "I knew I was asked because of Jim. I was just a symbol, a stand-in. It was an honor, of course, not a personal triumph." And in 1978 she accompanied her husband on an official trip to China.

Usually, though, she and her husband and their eight children, the youngest is seven, live the way many suburban families do. Rachel is a housewife, despite her Radcliffe education and all the obvious power connections she might use, and strings she might pull, to get any number of jobs.

I decided to go to Washington to find out why she chose to stay at home and what she gets out of it. I looked forward to seeing her again. At one time, just out of college, we had shared an office as editors at *Mademoiselle* magazine.

My train is late and Rachel, who has come to pick me up at the station in an old blue station wagon, is waiting patiently, thinking maybe it is the wrong day and I will never appear. Once I arrive, I join her in the front seat of the wagon and we drive to a typical two-level red brick suburban house near several similar houses on a cul-de-sac in Virginia, fifteen minutes from the White House. We lunch in the kitchen on bacon, lettuce and tomato sandwiches while four of the eight children pass in and out looking for their various belongings or pausing to listen to us. There is a mouth-watering banana bread made by daughter Emily cooling on a wooden board.

Many women would have lived life differently, I am sure, had their husbands held, in succession, so many of the nation's most important jobs. But Rachel has responded by remaining herself and doing exactly what she thinks she wants to do. Perhaps because of her husband's high-powered life and fame, she has reacted by choosing a simple life, and being primarily a mother. Says Rachel, "You have to compromise if you are going to take on a career. I don't want to have to compromise my time with my family. Some women feel insignificant if they're not out there doing what their husbands are doing. Women I think have to derive sense out of their own experience."

On the other hand, Rachel admits that she is not interested in being a supermother: in playing games, sharing her children's hobbies, or having endless conversations with them. They have been brought up to be self-reliant.

Rachel herself came from a family of five girls who lived on a cattle farm in Ohio. "We are farm people," she tells me. "Those women were strong. Life was very close to survival." Nevertheless, Rachel went to college and after graduation got the job on *Mademoiselle* magazine. "I didn't like some of those older women at *Mademoiselle*. They had no dimension as family women."

She also reacts against the attitude of her Ivy League college. "They imply that you are not living up to your education if you aren't involved in a public, tangible career. They give you the mental furnishings, tell you that learning is better than applied research, then they backtrack and give all their coverage to utilitarian achievements. A utilitarian woman with a utilitarian career is what I don't want to be. I really don't give a damn what they learn as professionals. Women are under pressure from these deans, these utilitarian 'lovelies' to do something they can write about in their alumnae weekly. You're supposed to write a book, a pamphlet for the Food and Drug Administration, anything you can get money for. I don't care how paltry.

If you wrote a dental bulletin, you'd get mentioned in the *Radcliffe Quarterly*. They think it's more important to write a child's book than to have a baby, so they can list it in their bulletin.

"I feel I'm helping my husband because I'm not neurotic. He doesn't have to hold my hand and tell me I'm his helpmeet. I'm independent. Every woman in middle age gets to feel on top of it. They feel psychologically they understand themselves, or accept themselves. I'm self-propelled. I run my own life. He doesn't know too much about it because he's gone all day. He never felt I was an adjunct to his professional life. We don't feel we have to entertain. They tell me I was the only wife at the Department of Energy who didn't come over to pick the furniture for her husband's office. When he comes home we talk things over, but the last thing he wants to discuss are the endless complexities of getting an energy bill through Congress."

She tells me she thinks a family is more interesting, more rewarding and more secure than a career. It's something she feels she can count on. The career can decline, the job can be dull and dead-end, you can be fired. "You should not put your values in such a shifting situation. I'd feel incomplete without a family." Like some housewives, Rachel thinks that spending time with children and then having a career later on makes better sense. "Goodness knows, we women feel we have all just begun. Why leave our children? I wonder how those who have struggled and juggled the two time schedules to get a Ph.D. and bear children will view the subject after six or ten years? Why not do this when you are forty-six, gerontology promising what it does these days?"

She goes on, "Women's lib made a certain kind of thing gel. But what we're faced with is to try to keep open the idea that women should not be forced into a new conformity. The household is a microcosm in which life can be more fun, a refuge. Not everyone is cut out for the marketplace." Rachel says she used to think that certain low-level jobs like a five-and-ten-cent-store clerk would be fun and she could be creative in them. But now she imagines herself less and less working outside the home.

"You couldn't pay me to work. I do some volunteer work

and enjoy it." Among other things, she was president of the high school PTA; and she has come to believe that school politics is "just as interesting and twice as dangerous as national politics. But I have to do something that suits me. I plan to do some writing, but the waters usually close over, I don't do it, and I find I don't miss it. My husband's attitude has a lot to do with it. If he wanted me to perform professionally and felt I was a dull hen, that would be different. But he wonders why a woman would want to do all the dull stuff he does.

"I have come to believe in the value of specializing. We didn't set out to do it that way, but I think as a family we got ahead faster because I was the wife and mother and he was out there working. Could he have had this super career of his if he had to be home when the kids had the flu, living this meatloaf life with its mixture of things?"

Part of Rachel's attitude toward the importance of a woman's being home to raise her children may come from her rugged farm background. Part also certainly comes from the same situation many Washington women share. Their husbands' lives are so intense, their men are so influential, that there is a certain vicarious excitement and emotional satisfaction in sharing them simply as wife.

As Rachel sees it, "One of the advantages of my life is having a husband in a crucial spot. You're at the nerve center of the world. You hear the straight poop. I'd rather have that than the substitute kicks. You become sensitized politically. Nuances. Gossip. The daily paper becomes more interesting."

She has not only traveled to Alaska and China and crashed a bottle of champagne against a nuclear sub, but she is also involved in a steady stream of other activities. She has visited Saudi Arabia, Korea and Japan with her husband on official business, and she sometimes was invited to lunches with wives of visiting dignitaries. Not long ago, for example, she was able to get the woman's point of view on the kibbutz children from Mrs. Begin, wife of Israel's prime minister. Another time she and her husband were invited to help entertain former Canadian Prime Minister Pierre Elliott Trudeau when President Carter was busy at Camp David.

Going places with her husband is not only fascinating but it gives her an identity in addition to the one she earns in the community. "You're observed. You're identified with an important person. You see things and places and ceremonies you wouldn't ordinarily see. I got a ringside view of Watergate. I get vicarious feelings of importance and success from my husband. I know I'm not married to someone who is just plodding along."

Although many Washington wives work, and some have fascinating jobs, Rachel finds that many women whom she knows agree with her. "Women here are too sophisticated not to know they are living exceptional lives, and they won't bargain that away to hang a shingle on the door. If I worked, I'd have the feeling I was sitting on an absolute volcano—things would be undone, bills unpaid. I don't want to have to budget my time to stay on top of two or three different jobs. I like to do the cooking, gardening, painting the house myself. And I don't want to feel that I'm losing touch with survival by hiring people."

The sandwich and banana bread are long gone and I must leave. I get a tour of the casual and roomy house, the children's rooms downstairs and the fish pond outside. While looking at the pond, Rachel suddenly turns to me and with a quizzical expression on her face says, "I don't think I'm dissatisfied with my life, but I do wonder why I've been turning this subject over in my mind." The pressure to conform is tremendous, and as satisfied as she is, she cannot help but remark, "I've felt uneasy because I didn't want to rush out and do things." With other women pouring out in droves, today's housewife has to keep reminding herself why she doesn't want to follow along.

Who Is Happier—the Housewife or the Working Woman?

"There is nothing intrinsically fulfilling about going to an office and sitting at a desk. Some of it is drudgery, just as staying home is," a middle-aged psychiatric social worker and mother once told me. "Part of every career is drudgery. For me there is lots of stress in the job from other people's problems. But I get rewards. There are also rewards for women who stay home, in watching their kids grow. But I think the quality of the reward from the job is greater.'' Rachel and others would disagree.

Who is right? Is the woman whose time is spent producing for an employer happier than the woman who works alone, whose time is her own, who can write a poem or clean the floor or save money by making her own bedspread?

The liberated women say they are happier. The housewives say they are happier. But although the number of women who work and those who do not is split nearly evenly, the percentages of those who work are increasing every year. And who is happier continues to be a subject of professional debate.

In a 1976 study John A. Clausen of the University of California finds that women who are now working are by far the happiest and that those who once had jobs but gave them up seem the least happy and the most likely to be dissatisfied. Dr. Clausen also asked women which was the most satisfying period of their lives. Both women currently working and those who were housewives agreed that the most recent period was the happiest. Women who said they couldn't make up their minds about whether to work favored an earlier period. He concludes that life satisfaction seems to depend less on whether or not a woman is working than on whether or not she is doing what she wants to do.

Other evidence, which differs from Dr. Clausen's conclusions, appears in two studies by Dr. Myra Ferree, also in 1976. She interviewed 135 married working-class women in the Boston area. All had at least one child in the first and second grades but no pre-school children. Half the group had outside jobs, the rest were full-time housewives. Dr. Ferree found that full-time housewives were much more likely to be dissatisfied with the way they were spending their lives than working women. She points out that housewives "pay a considerable price in personal happiness." They also experience feelings of social isolation, whereas the working woman has a sense of competence and self-esteem. Dr. Ferree concludes that "despite the strains of carrying a double role, the woman with a full-time outside job is happier and feels herself to be better off than the full-time housewife.''

Even though most of these women were in nonglamorous, rather routine jobs and worked for economic reasons, even though they would have young kids to contend with after a full day's work, and even though they were married to blue-collar men who might have traditional ideas about where the wife ought to be spending her days, the working women still turned out to be happier. Housework was seen as a ''prison,'' but the burden of the working woman's ''double role'' was easily lifted by her enjoyment of being outside the home.

In a recent article on this subject in the *Journal of Marriage and the Family,* James D. Wright of the Social and Demographic Research Institute, University of Massachusetts, also considers the question of who is happier.

Dr. Wright cites a 1971 Quality of American Life survey done by University of Michigan researchers and five National Opinion Research Center surveys which contradict Dr. Ferree's results and seem to show that housewives and working women are both equally happy with what they are doing, and this applies to both middle- and working-class housewives and women in the labor force.

Why the contradiction? How can such different conclusions be reached, and what does it mean?

Dr. Wright concludes that ''for large proportions of housewives, full-time housewifery is preferred to outside work, and moreover, that housework is a genuine source of satisfaction to them . . .'' He goes on to say that ''. . . working women and housewives simply do not differ in the degree to which their lives are interesting . . . or rewarding . . .''

He points out that both roles have costs and benefits. The working woman has an income and some increase in independence, but she also pays for it with ''a more hectic pace, and a more complicated life.'' The life of the housewife is easier and less hectic, he says, but housework is possibly less satisfying. Neither the myth of the happy homemaker nor that of the isolated, lonely homemaker are true. Nor is the idea that women in the labor force necessarily have rich and meaningful existencies, when most jobs are boring and routine lower-echelon jobs.

The answer to the puzzle may lie in looking a bit further into the Quality of Life Study than Dr. Wright did and differentiating among women according to educational backgrounds.

Housewives with a grade-school education were happier than those with a college education, whereas working women with a grade-school education were less satisfied with their lives (only one half were happy) than the college-educated ones (three quarters were happy). The crucial difference seems to be education. The happiest women of all seem to be college-educated women who are working, according to this study.

Interestingly, they also seem to have the better marriages. Housewives and working women, both with college degrees, were asked whether they think their husbands understand them very well. Only 28 percent of the housewives said yes, whereas 50 percent of the working women did. These figures don't speak well for marriage in general, but when a woman has a college education, she seems to be better adjusted in every way when working.

The future will certainly see more variety of choice. With shorter work weeks and more staggered working hours including shorter working days, men and women will probably think of home more as a base for recreation and leisure than as a source of full-time employment. There are women who will continue to make magnificent housewives, but there is no doubt that the full-time raising of children and devotion to housework is a fading goal in women's lives. Economic and peer pressures always win out.

16

Views from Both Sides

The response of men to working with women has ranged from enthusiastically positive to downright negative. The main criticism that even many of the most positive men seem to have of women is that they want everything. They want the advantages of equal opportunity with men, but when things get rough, they want special consideration. The main compliment paid to women who work is that they bring an enviable quality of enthusiasm and excitement to the job. They are said to be less competitive, less prepared to be Machiavellian, more objective, open and honest.

The Husband's Perspective

But to look beyond the tug of personalities that governs a strange, new situation, one wonders how the men in their *other* role, not as business associates or employers, but as husbands, feel about women in *their* other role. How do husbands react to their wives who go out to work? What do they say about late meals, dull meals, sharing household chores or taking them over completely when their wives travel?

The husband of a middle-aged woman who suddenly has gone out to school or work has to relinquish some of his authority in the family, give up expecting his wife to devote herself primarily to managing the home and helping him along in his career. Now that she is as tightly scheduled as he, her husband will have to adjust to frantic time constraints and new obligations. Many men experience surprise, incredulity and annoyance at dealing with this new person. The partner they have been married to for twenty years is no longer the same person. Her middle-age transition has catapulted her into unaccustomed interests and behavior.

Understanding the demands of someone who has never demanded anything, except perhaps a new dress, is not easy for them, and they don't all succeed in renegotiating their relationship with a wife who has just joined the labor force. Many men are afraid and hurt when they are no longer number one, and now that their wives earn money and could support themselves, they do not feel as secure in their marriages.

There is little doubt that many husbands miss the sense of being the dominant male and of living in a world of clear, comfortable differences between male and female. They are irritated at being forced to accept compromises they never expected to have to make and to pretend an equality they don't fully believe in. The habits and expectations of centuries are not easily relinquished. Even the husbands who accept the changes because they understand their wives' need to develop their potential will nevertheless often find it impossible to ignore many of the inconveniences. They can be sublimely understanding when they say they want their wives to work and then stoop to the ridiculous when they add the caveat—as long as dinner is ready on time, the house is clean, the shirts are ironed and she continues to do everything she always did around the house. Anyone who assumes the dual-career marriage begun in midlife is going to be easy is mistaken. In just about every case, there are frequently going to be days when it's damned difficult, and even a few others when it all seems completely impossible.

The fact that he is burdening her with a double or triple load, if children still live at home, doesn't seem to faze him. It is only fair to say, though, that although some men are not able to readjust and look for various routes of escape, most others are more understanding, even though they have notable lapses.

The Lawyer's Husband

The forty-year-old husband of one of the young women lawyers I interviewed is very supportive of his wife's working. He finds her career interesting, but he also admits he is more annoyed than he thought he would be about the compromises he has to make.

He could see that it was a good idea. "I knew she was frustrated, and it made sense economically," he said. "Jobs she could get paid little and had no status. She'd have become increasingly unhappy if she hadn't done this. She had to do something of her own. And she felt it important that our three girls have a role model, that they see a woman doing something in a structured way. I can't conceive of being married to someone whose interests are house and kids. If my wife said, 'I want to sit home and make sure there is no lint on the floor,' I just couldn't accept that level of ambition."

So, with his wife in law school, they hired an au pair girl to help. "It was always tense finding the right girl, but once we had her, she took a lot of heat off." He pitched in and shopped for some of the food, cleaned up afterward and did the dishes. He washed bathrooms and gardened. But there were limits to what he would do.

"My wife went to school and still did a lot around the house. We shared work, but I'd get impatient if things were a mess. I knew I could have unmessed it, but I didn't. If we were choking on dust, I'd finally get the vacuum."

When they both came home tired in the evening, two people with all the problems of their careers, each with a different set of tensions, it was difficult. He admitted, "At times I could be hostile, withdraw myself, get pissed off. I don't have much patience. I'd bitch, hassle. Complain about the money we spent. We'd disagree on what the kids should be doing. And she over-committed herself. That bothered me. I'd nag and pester. I'd pout. I can be a lunatic, a madman. I get hostile, childlike."

As for money, they never seem to have enough, but his wife's salary makes a large difference, especially with three children to send to college. As an extra bonus he finds himself becoming interested in law. His wife's career, in fact, has taken on some of the fascination his own career no longer has. "I don't see myself going anywhere for the next twenty-five years. I'm al-ready as far as I can go in my career. Now I'm interested in where her career will go. I find I get vicarious pleasure out of it." The sum total of his reaction, which seems typical of most middle-aged men, is a heady mix of annoyance and pride, which can balance out either way, depending on how the winds are blowing at any given moment.

The Restaurant Manager's Husband

Marvin is forty-nine and the father of two teenage sons. He's a security analyst for a banking house. His wife, like some men, has a job that takes her away from home for long periods of time. How does he feel about it? The question here is more complicated, because it not only involves having a working wife, but one who is often absent. The combination puts him to the test and results in a strong sense of ambivalence. "I get almost schizophrenic about it," he admits. He constantly sees the pros and cons of the situation.

He is happy about her doing something she likes, but it seems like centuries when she is away. He enjoys the extra freedom, but he misses her. "She's educated, intelligent, a talented per-son," he says, "and it would be a shame to bury that in the role of housewife for so many years. But on the other hand, it would be a tremendous convenience to me if she didn't work."

Her being away a lot has resulted in several radical alterations in their life style. They don't entertain, and consequently don't get as many invitations. Their lives have contracted. Her absence has taken time from his leisure activities, "keeping the household from being smothered." He spends one day a week doing all the shopping, which he doesn't enjoy, but now he is more aware of the cost of food. "Last time I went shopping as a bachelor, sirloins were 69 cents a pound. I knew what prices were in the abstract, but it's been a shocker." And last, his sex life "is put in the closet for a while." But on the plus side he has gotten to know his sons more intimately than before, and they are closer to him.

They have a woman who cleans every other week and one who comes twice a week to cook. He does the laundry, they eat out once a week, one son makes spaghetti and he makes steak dinners. "It has made me aware of the tediousness of what my wife has had to put up with all these years."

The strain begins to show. "I get annoyed when there are things I'd rather do but have to put off because there are chores. Things pile up. I get ticked off having all this burden put on my shoulders because my dilettante wife wants to indulge herself in what seems like a mere pastime to me. When I feel that way I can't quite bring myself to recognize that this is really a serious endeavor for her."

Marvin admits that the children were growing and "didn't need their noses wiped for them," and didn't need a full-time housewife and he didn't want to keep her "imprisoned" in that role. He realizes that he has had an exciting life of his own that she has had no part in. "How can I possibly resent her having a whole other life, when for our whole married life, I have had one?" A reasonable question he poses to help convince himself that everything is all right. He resents her nevertheless.

She has found a great deal of discrimination in her field of hotel and restaurant management, and he ends up on the receiving end of this struggle. "At times she appears to heap all the blame of male chauvinism on me. Damn it. I understand, but I didn't invent it. She takes her negative feelings about men out on me and treats me as though I am responsible for them. She has changed. She can't throw a switch and immediately become a wife and mother when she comes home."

He says his wife is more interesting now, she has more confidence, but sometimes she appears to him to be pompous and trying to act superior to him. He also sometimes detects in his wife the characteristic that many men who work with women are noting. "She wants both worlds. She wants to be treated equally as a jobholder, but also as a woman. She wouldn't think of mowing the lawn because that, to her, is man's work, though what she does in her job is also man's work and that doesn't bother her."

But having to balance all the positive and negative aspects of having his wife away, Marvin decided she should work and, he reasoned, if she made enough money for both of them, then he could work part-time, which he said would make him very happy indeed.

Marvin's thoughts whip back and forth between pride in his wife's work and the annoyances that result from it, what he thinks he should believe, and what he really feels. He is buffeted by his negative traditional response to the situation and the logical sense that it makes. He has traveled and worked so why shouldn't she, he says. Very logical. But a hell of a lonely inconvenience. He finds his wife more interesting, but things around the house don't get done unless he does them, and cooking his own meals is not what he contracted for. For Marvin, having a wife who works is a mixed bag which is aggravated by the fact that she very often isn't home.

The Divorcée's Former Husband

Bill, a black teacher of English, was married to the black lawyer I described earlier (page 147). They were divorced shortly after she finished law school. Was her breaking out the cause of the breakup? What kind of tensions were involved? Talking in his bachelor apartment, not far from where his wife and children live, he said he was in favor of his wife's going to school. When she was afraid to apply for fear of being turned down, he was the one who filled out the application.

When she began school, he started doing a lot of the cooking, cleaning, washing dishes. But the logistics never were properly worked out. "We were never able to divide our total responsibility. Either she did everything or I did everything. I'm sure she must have cooked some meals and done some washes, but it seems I did it all. She did spend a lot of time with the children."

He felt his wife had been supportive to him as he worked his way up, so now it should be her turn. (There's the logic. And next comes the reality.) But he resented the fact that she couldn't do enough of the housework as well as study law. He says, "I didn't feel she was willing or able to give to the extent of supporting the household. The daily maintenance. She gave emotionally, she was loving, we had a good sex life. She was good with the kids. The one thing she wouldn't give was her labor. Maybe," he surmises in all seriousness, "her energy level was low."

Bill admits that he is a stickler for neatness. "I like the salt to be in a certain place. If I put something down, I like to be able to find it two weeks later." He says he thought his marriage was fine, yet he was aware of a growing feeling of discomfort. For whatever reason, he took up tennis for the first time, and during the last year of his wife's school, he had an affair with her best friend. "At the time it seemed that I was drawn into the affair because the woman was physically attractive. In retrospect, I see it wasn't different from my tennis. In a way the routine at home was very confining. The affair and the tennis were a way of having something that belonged to me." With remarkable candor, he admitted, "I needed someone who was not threatening to me, someone who could be supportive and not question me."

He still feels that law school was not the cause of their breakup, though in fact, it seems to have brought about changes that did affect the marriage. Despite all their personal problems in arranging a satisfactory way of handling a new schedule, the house, and their relationship, he theoretically believes, "It's impossible for a woman to fulfill herself as a person, as we define it, through the role of housewife. It's like having your feet bound so they stop growing. Identity is closely tied to work. That housewife identity is for the birds. It's shit. For a person with imagination and intelligence who can see beyond that narrowly prescribed role, it's debilitating. Some women like it, but I can't understand it. It's important for women to work, to find their self-worth, to share the social reward that comes from the public recognition of what one does.''

Bill laughs and tells me that men are considerably weaker than they are given credit for being, and you can have a better relationship with your wife if you recognize each other's weaknesses. His problem may have been that he never recognized or accepted his wife's weaknesses. Or it may have been her problem in not accepting his. In any case, it is very difficult to separate trouble areas that are basic to a marriage, those that are aggravated by the woman's role change and those that are directly caused by it.

I never met a man who said it was easy having his wife work. Whether the man, the woman and the marriage can grow and remain flexible enough to absorb new conflicts, some of which will be only temporary, may determine whether they can survive. This marriage wasn't built that way. Instead of feeling that he was being supportive to his wife, Bill felt that her routine was limiting him. Listening to him speak on the subject of women's working, it seems to me that he will be better able to handle such a marriage if he tries again and both partners understand the terms from the beginning. Sometimes, it is simply too difficult for the man to accept new rules in the old context.

Those who try to revise their marriages in mid-life must understand, before the wife even begins to work, that life can never be exactly the same again. Some things will be better. They will share new fields of interest, she will be more interesting, they will have new friends, there will be more money, she will feel better about herself, he will feel proud. On the other hand, the husband will have to do some of the dirty work or pay someone else to do it. Even if there is help, his wife will be more tired, there will be less time for the house, less interest in a social life, he will often be irritated and some things just won't get done, ever. The husband of a working woman has to realize that mother doesn't live here anymore. The marriage has become one of two adults.

The Wife's View

While the men are fidgeting in their new relationships with their wives, the women either realize with relief that their husbands are making serious efforts to be supportive and help them on their way, or they discover with chagrin that these men are weighty millstones around their necks. I do not know one successful married working woman whose husband is not supportive. And I mean support in the form not only of encouragement, but also actual help with children and household work. The man either has to grow with her in a parallel direction, or it's not going to work. His support, however grudgingly offered, however ambivalent, must be present.

How do you make a recalcitrant husband back your ambitions to work? Usually the need for the second salary check solves the problem. But otherwise, you plan a well-organized campaign. First, the motivation. You explain your desire to do something you have always wanted to try, or your need to discover new strengths at this juncture of your life. You point out your wish to make money, to have something of your own, to prove you can accomplish things, to keep busy after the children are in school, to make yourself feel more important, to do what other women are doing.

Second, you assemble the troops to obliterate any objections. You have names of people who can baby-sit, house-sit, or come in and cook for several days if you are away. Students, neighbors, friends, a housekeeper, a mother-in-law, no matter what, these people should be lined up at the ready so that when your first business trip coincides with his out-of-town conference there will be no acute crisis. You also present some scheme for how things in the house will operate when you are in town. You may suggest, for example, cooking all the weekday dinners on Saturday afternoon and freezing them so they can just be pulled out and thawed as they are needed. There are very few husbands who will veto a well-thought-out plan.

Third, you should impress upon him the fact that you will be a more interesting companion and that you are looking forward to his help and advice as you begin your entry into his kind of world. You want him to share this new adventure with you.

And last, and perhaps most important, you make him feel loved and secure. Make him feel that your marriage is going to be even stronger once you are both busy people. And with more money coming in, you will at last be able to take those exotic vacations and do many of the things he has always hoped to do someday. He might, you suggest, even be able to use this extra financial cushion to try a change of career, part-time work or early retirement.

How Women See Their Husbands

Many of the women I have spoken to in the course of this inquiry into the vicissitudes of middle age have offered more than one spirited comment on their husbands' reactions to their new activities.

One woman found two sides to the male response. On the one hand she thought her husband was nervous about what would happen when she went out into the world. On the other, he was relieved that she was no longer totally dependent on him financially and emotionally. He both wanted the dependence and didn't like it. He also had a split reaction to certain behavior, depending on whose it was. He didn't mind being out for the evening, but when she was out he would say, 'How come you're not home more?' When she was home he expected her to reconstitute herself completely and be involved only with him.

When wives travel, it is often upsetting for men. All the little jobs women do effortlessly from habit become for them time-consuming, complex tasks. They panic even before you are gone. One of the executives I interviewed said if her husband traveled it was expected. She helped him pack, took him to the airport, then kept the house running. But when *she* traveled, he never got used to it. ''He complained, and the children lectured him which made it worse. They said I had every right to travel and wondered why he was being selfish. This put a strain on our marriage. He had to shop, get things cleaned, and he resented it. He'd blow up over something unimportant, but it was really about the trips. I would be about to leave for Chicago and he'd be screaming because the steak was cooked too much."

Some men, though, learn quickly. A woman who has her own business said, "When I travel, my family gets along fine. My husband is an excellent cook. I just make sure there is food in the house. If we both travel, my mother-in-law moves in. I think it's good training for the kids to be independent. My being away gives them a good opportunity to work things out. They decide who will cook, who will clean up. It's valuable family time for them without mother around."

The woman who owns an advertising agency confessed that things have not been completely smooth in her marriage. Her husband went through a rough period when the person he thought he knew was changing. While the excitement of building a new life kept this woman involved, her husband could only stand back and watch their lives undergoing major alteration.

She explained, "To build my business I had to work twelve to fourteen hours a day. I read five newspapers. I worked on Sunday, frequently to 9:30 at night. It began to affect a good relationship. I had to make conscious choices which he had to accept. He'd have been happy if I brought home $15,000 a year and weren't so involved. He finally accepted it, but I'd occasionally see him looking at me in a sad way.

"He misses the time we had. There's no jealousy. It's never a question of who's the star. My work simply changed the marriage. It is more equal, more interesting. I realize how important having a good marriage has been to my success. I've not had to waste emotional energy or time on personal problems. He made it possible because he said I could do it. I went through a period of saying, 'Should I or shouldn't I do it?' He said, 'Do it. I know you can do it. Go ahead and do it.' Or I'd say, 'You know, that machine I need for the office costs $63,000. Should I get it?' and he'd say, 'Go ahead. Do it. Buy it.' He advises me and has taught me a great deal.

"If a marriage is strong, it can stand this kind of change. All things human change. If I had a potential that I didn't realize,

I'd be the less for it, and the marriage would be affected on my side. The marriage is still good. He still takes care of me, wakes me to be sure I make my plane or train and even makes sure I eat breakfast.''

But a former housewife I spoke to told me that going back to work was the big factor in the breakup of her marriage. Her husband could not adjust. As she saw it, ''I'd been patient during his different jobs. I resented the fact that he didn't want to help me. My husband, though, felt cheated. To him, his career was the most important thing. He wanted the house spanking clean, the meals on time and hot, and the kids were my responsibility. He felt threatened by my new routine. He was losing some of his domestic services. It is nice to have a mother in the home providing all that warmth. He wanted my time to go to him or to the support system.''

Another difficult situation for men is having a wife who makes more money and has more status. There is obviously a lot of male ego involved in accepting any women in high positions, but having one's wife there can make it harder. A woman who had a job at the top commented, ''I'm not sure my husband could take it if I earned more. He's joked about it over and over. I think we'd have a real crisis. He couldn't handle it and I couldn't refuse the raise.''

Daphne Hawkes, the woman who became a priest, found that having an exalted role of her own created some temporary problems in her marriage. And in her discussions with women who seek her advice these and other problems have repeatedly emerged.

Rev. Hawkes says, ''Men can't admit the little boy in them. They're feeling hurt and miss their wives if they are away. If they told us, we could understand and want to be there more. But when a woman is asked to hold herself down, not to be so successful, not to be the center of attention at parties, then the wife feels anger.

''The man should say, 'Hey, I need you. I miss you.' Instead the man also shows anger—the primary emotion a man is allowed to feel and not be emasculated. As the woman gets stronger, the man gets angrier out of fear. A woman will be first in her law school class, but when she comes home, her husband will tell her she's stupid for not putting the detergent in the machine the right way. The woman will end up thinking, 'Who needs this?'

"Few husbands can come out and say, 'I'm the one who hurts. I worry that maybe you won't want me if you keep growing, or if you earn more money.' In the long run, somehow, men believe as a woman gets strong and independent enough, she won't need them. They never talk about it. It's subtle, but a factor."

Daphne's own husband had a combination of feelings. On the cerebral level he was very supportive in many ways. On an emotional level it was a marvelous thing in terms of growing, but sometimes very painful. There were times when he had to do all the motherly things when she studied. "He didn't complain while he was doing them," she remembered. "But after the fact he was angry about the reversal of roles. Now, five years later, he's grateful for the change and is much closer to our children. There is no way I could force him back to being the way he was.

"My husband and I are now at a new level of relationship. So much more exciting, so much freer. Our kids leaving home is not scary. Growing is the most vital thing in life. Things change all the time. You have to learn to embrace change. It's exciting to know I have something I can always grow in. It's important all your life. In a relationship you have to grow."

Sometimes, though, a wife's working can be the element that actually improves the relationship from the beginning, particularly when the marriage starts out in mid-life with both people working. In talking about her second marriage, Presidential Assistant Anne Wexler said she thought their equally demanding careers may be one reason their marriage has been so harmonious. "If one of us were busier than the other and constantly waiting for the other to come home, there would be problems.

"My working improves our marriage. All the tensions that go along with only one partner having the responsibilities are missing. There is no problem about what time you are coming home, how much you have to use the telephone, or working on weekends. All the anxieties are missing. We have so many interests in common, we can almost talk in shorthand. I have a sense of sharing everything from doing the laundry to probing discussions on all kinds of issues.''

The Problem with Men

Now that the two-career couple is becoming the normal, expected way of life for growing numbers of people, the problems of how to manage each career separately, plus the family life, demand some complex plotting out for most of us. For young people beginning the post-college stage of their lives, each with a job, the decisions of how to manage with children, or how to take care of food and house even if they remain childless, can be worked on little by little as the need arises. ''You do this, and I'll do that,'' is a very simple code to follow if you begin with it.

But when an already established family of teenagers and a fifteen- or twenty-year-old marriage begins to undergo radical change, there are usually crises, and the solutions read like intricate exercises in deployment. Although men think of themselves as adventurous creatures, they do not seem to respond to this kind of adventure at all easily. They noticeably lag behind in doing their part to make the two-career couple work. Logistics may be minutely planned, but at times the effort overwhelms them and leads to the mixed attitude that most middle-aged husbands of working wives seem to have today.

Even my own husband, Charlie, who, intellectually, completely understands the need for women to have careers and independent lives of their own, and wants me to have one, who insisted on hiring the first tenured woman professor at Princeton in 1970, nevertheless wants me at home to give him dinner and take care of him when he arrives from work.

Once I arranged to interview Congresswoman Fenwick who was coming to my hometown for dinner at a secret conference of heads of state. We decided to meet an hour before dinner and talk. Because my husband and I were going to another dinner right after the interview, he agreed to drive me to the conference center, find a comfortable chair and read his paper until I was finished. We passed through the police barricade, parked and went into the main lounge. I had purposely arrived early to find a quiet corner for the interview. But my wandering around looked suspicious and the obvious fact that I was no head of state led the high security command to order us escorted back outside the center. Henry Kissinger had just left when we drove to the barricade again, and while I stayed there waiting and freezing, my husband was ordered to park on one of the outer drives. Finally Mrs. Fenwick arrived and, folded under her protective wing, I went back into the sacred halls of top-secret diplomacy. Charlie, curled somewhat uncomfortably in our compact car, opened the first section of a Saturday *New York Times* and began to read. While the Congresswoman and I chatted and munched whatever sat on the table to be munched, the fall sun began to set and my husband grew colder and colder. He quickly finished that section and went on to the second one. There isn't much of a second section on Saturdays, and he soon finished that one too. He sat there growing more and more impatient. Three times police cars aimed their searchlights at his face and asked him what he was doing. No lurkers or lookers were tolerated. "I'm waiting for my crazy wife who's in there," he said, pointing to the exquisitely modern conference center.

Inside, time went by very quickly and when I looked at my watch I was fifteen minutes late for our dinner date and rushed to leave. At the door I met dear Charlie being escorted back in out of the now black night by a sympathetic policeman who was afraid I would never show up and my husband, in frustration, would attack the building.

Once on the road Charlie complained, "How could you be late? How could you keep our friends waiting? How could you leave me outside freezing in the dark?" It was unforgivable.

I was frankly shocked that he simply did not wait for me submissively as I had for him at airports and train stations for years. Why didn't he know that my work at that moment was more important than his comfort? Why wasn't he asking me about the interview? Why must men always try to beat woman back down where they belong, doing what is best for men at every conceivable moment? Why are they so stuck in their middle-aged ruts?

I have long ago learned that if you are going to work and be your own person, you've got to continually remind those men you live with that it's your right, it's no longer something they can direct. You are no longer asking to be allowed to be you.

17

The Wisdom of the Middle Ages

There have been many surprises for me in talking to the scores of women I reached in writing this book. The first, quite unexpected, realization is the enormous range of response that women have had to middle age, from searching for who they are at a transition weekend, to working, getting a degree, or a face-lift, starting a business, sculpting, taking continuing education courses for the simple pleasure of it, going to medical school or becoming an executive. Once they were out on their own as individuals, these women allowed their pent-up emotion, talent and energy to pour forth.

Many who were helped and supported in their quests became successful and astounded even themselves as well as their husbands and employers with their capabilities. Some of those who still were not listened to or allowed to express themselves, whose anger still raged deep within, resorted to alcohol or drugs, ended up in mental clinics or divorced their husbands.

Mid-Life Surprises

As a middle-aged woman, I was surprised that in the middle of her life when she might be expected to want to relax, a woman would, for example, even consider going to medical school and facing the rigorous discipline of study and the difficult hours, much less actually do it. I was surprised that all the women who returned to finish college did as well as the best of the younger students. It was a revelation to see how quickly many women are jumping from initial efforts to important jobs, from research into management, from neighborhood political clubs into the Senate and White House, from secretaries to office managers, from staff members to company vice-presidents, from students to lawyers and doctors, from housewives to real estate executives, owners of advertising companies and advisors to corporations on human relations. For the first time, they climbed to the summit of Annapurna, and a woman commanded a U.S. military ship. A forty-four-year-old woman became Chicago's first woman mayor; a fifty-two-year-old woman became the European Parliament's first president; and a fifty-three-year-old woman was elected the first woman Prime Minister in the history of Britain. They started their upward push around middle age, they are still middle-aged, and they are successful.

Another surprise was to find such a different rhythm in the life stages of women compared to that of their husbands. Couples are no longer two people who sail through life as one (if they ever were). As Daniel J. Levinson, the Yale psychologist, has pointed out in his study of the male life cycle, after reaching age forty men are either waving farewell to youthful ambitions, finding out that the dream wasn't so great after all, or looking around for some young person to help along and play mentor to. He describes the middle-aged man as deep in a mid-life crisis where he accepts the fact that what he has done is all he is ever doing to do. (I have seen many exceptions to this thesis among some men who launch themselves on a second career at this point, and others who find they enjoy what they do enormously and are very pleased with their lives, who have no sense of crisis at all.

In contrast, it appears that the woman has been passing through a continuous series of transitions, which do not necessarily arrive at specific ages, and in each stage—marriage, divorce, remarriage, children, work—she deals with new sets of problems. While the man in mid-life is approaching a slowdown of his career, settling in, resigning himself, she is now oreaking out into new ventures.

A male friend I have, who didn't get the final higher promotion he wanted, now knows he will never get it. Whatever he is doing, he knows is *it*. On the other hand, his wife keeps moving ahead because she started later. Her life now is one of discovery, not resignation. She is, in effect, living the life her husband lived at thirty. He is beginning to act like an older man. She is beginning again to act like the younger woman she once was. Even if she doesn't work, she feels in control of her life, her capabilities, on top of it in a way that has passed most men by. She is not thinking of being a mentor, a role Levinson calls, "One of the most significant relationships available to a man in middle adulthood," unless she has worked all her life as men have. At mid-life when he is ready to play Professor Higgins to some Eliza Doolittle, she is ready to be Eliza.

The enormous amount of frustration that the average housewife has harbored shocked me. So often her exposure to higher education made her too aware of the richness of alternatives to be content with devoting herself to the hausfrau role of dishes and dust. Caring for husband, listening to his problems, never having time to talk about her own problems, finding no one interested in them anyway, ferrying teenagers, cooking, cleaning, often criticized or nagged, never properly appreciated have provoked many women to the boiling point. The extent of hidden discontent is incredible. There were so many women who, until recently, were afraid to express themselves because there wasn't much they could do about it, who were afraid of losing their husbands and their economic support, or afraid of being alone, that they tamped themselves down into the small space they were allotted in the world of marriage and family and squashed their real desires. And all the time they were hurting deep inside like a slow-bleeding ulcer. That the current generation of middle-aged women could be so deeply thwarted without the sounds of pain being heard is truly amazing. They had learned mute acceptance too well.

It wasn't just a woman here and there who felt defeated. It was large numbers of women. And it was particularly in middle age when they had accumulated years of frustration, when they could see the wrinkles and imagine their own mortality as friends or parents died, that the reality of their position really hit them. They had had children but had built no monuments of a more personal kind to their own immortality. Their moment was passing too quickly and inconsequentially. And that, I think, is why women's lib has affected these women so dramatically. They were sitting there at the breaking point when it all happened. A whole generation, who grew up with the idea that they would marry, have children and probably never work because it wasn't encouraged, were suddenly finding the rules changed. And they started expressing what they needed: "I need that bedroom for my sculpture," "I need that room for my writing," "I've got to get out of the house and work or go crazy."

The universality of desire expressed by women I interviewed, to establish a new identity for themselves as they reached the middle years, was staggering. The woman at this time is often in search of a basic rebirth of her psyche. If she can't make the transition into a purposeful life after early retirement from the career of mother, she may even become physically ill. A spate of aches and pains that drive a woman to bed or to the doctor at this age, or even culminate in an early death, often originate because the person is worried, unhappy and suddenly bereft of any reason for living. They are very real physical symptoms, but they originate in the mind.

So women began to bridge the way to this next transition by asking, "What is the most important thing in life to me now in the new structure of things? Is it still my husband? My kids? My job? Myself? How much of myself shall I give to each and still retain the sense of ME?'' When they found the answers, they discovered that it was not just getting out of the kitchen and back to school or into a potting studio or an office that was so fulfilling. It was the discovery of the individual essence of "self" in every woman that has been so liberating, particularly for those of middle age who by now need self-definition from the bottom of their guts to the top of their muddled heads.

It is ironic to note that though women have become so independent, men continue to be extremely important in their lives. If the woman is part of a couple the attitude of her husband toward anything she wants to do is still crucial. His support continues to determine in large measure whether or not she can follow her plans and certainly whether or not she can enjoy her work and succeed. Husbands have got to help their wives in the same way women have automatically aided men in their careers, or else the job and marriage are not going to make it together. The willingness of many men not only to encourage their wives, but also to learn to cook and clean bathrooms, is surprising too —but only because the assumption has always been, in the sex-role order of things, that they could never possibly concern themselves with such banalities.

On this list of surprises is the fact that women are demonstrating that they are able to deal with situations rationally. Stereotyped as being prone to emotional displays and tears, they are proving that they can control themselves when necessary and think logically. They are surprisingly astute at business, math, engineering and statistics, fields that only men were supposed to be able to master. They enjoy buying, selling, being competitive and problem solving. They find after years of managing household accounts that they are really good at it, and they get the same kick out of clinching a deal and making money as men always have.

Considering the fact that men and women both have been brought up to see women as wives, mothers, and sex objects, I have been amazed at how well they have adjusted to working side by side. Neither has been quite certain of how to treat the other in this transitional period. For a man used to thinking of women in various nonwork roles, seeing her become an integral part of his once exclusive business world cannot be easy. For a woman who is used to expecting all men to be the domineering, decision-making member of the relationship, learning how to use her new independence or wield her new authority has not been easy either. Each has had to test the other, probe, spar, find out how far each could go. I was astounded that women at work have been so successful, though their acceptance has by no means been universal.

Detesting housework, I was surprised to observe how many skills are brought to bear in the domestic chores that women routinely perform. Most women and their employers did not recognize that such a large amount of what they lump under the title of "housewife" can go under a more pretentious name in business—and that by borrowing these same principles and skills women can fit into many jobs quite easily. The housewife, I found, is also a management consultant, an executive director, a dispatcher, a chef, a senior placement specialist, a sheet metal worker, and many, many other things.

I was also impressed by the importance of the second salary check for families today. It enables couples to send their children to more expensive colleges, to buy houses, cars and afford vacations. And in this period of economic stress, possible unemployment and the likelihood of eventual illness, the new income keeps the family going and, in many cases, lifts them above the poverty level. It is fast becoming an economic necessity for most women to work.

I might also add that in our youth-centered culture, it was no surprise to me to find that women were reluctant, regardless of how old they were, even to admit they were middle-aged. If you feel young and act young, by God you *are* young, regardless of how old you are. Although it is now fashionable to admit to being forty, because forty is still okay and beautiful, the push among women who are older is to want to make fifty equally fashionable. Once that is achieved, can sixty be far behind?

Being conscious of the fact that many women went to college, I was quite surprised to see how many in this generation gave up their education after only a couple of years, in exchange for a man and marriage. On the other hand, as a devotee of coeducation, I was also surprised at the significant part women's colleges played in the lives of those who did stay in school, by making their students strong, giving them female role models and instilling in them confidence that they could have families *and* work *and* succeed. Now that feminism carries the torch once entrusted to the women's colleges, I assume these institutions no longer need to play the role of women's advocate to the extent that they once did. But what an important message they carried in their day to so many women—a message unknown to those of us who went to coeducational schools to find husbands.

And finally, I was surprised at the ultimate nature of women as it kept unfolding for me. I had not been aware of how firm and substantial women can be versus how soft and ineffective they have been. Nowadays they are smarter and stronger, more adaptable and more creative than anyone suspected. Mentally, they had just become used to taking the lazy way. Aroused in vision, talents, abilities of all kinds, they have at last revealed their true potential.

What They All Said

I have listened to these women describe with justifiable elation what they have been able to accomplish and discuss with candor what some of the obstacles have been. Many have talked about some of the specific personal qualities they feel are holding women back. And they have noted certain other more general characteristics. When more than one hundred women all repeat similar observations, I think they are worth noting.

Here is a short sample of what may be called the new truths of middle age:

—Women are too timid.
—Women have little self-esteem.
—Women have trouble finding their identity.
—Women usually do not know what they want. They do not plan their lives adequately. Most say some accidental event or circumstance got them into a job or career.

—Women look at their jobs as static. Men view their situations as developmental.

—Women entering business are imitating the worst behavior of men because they are unsure of themselves. Later on they will develop their own personal style.

—Many women prefer part-time work until their children leave home. Their many responsibilities make it harder for them than for men to achieve.

—Jobs that require judgment, mediation, organization, attention to detail, patience in dealing with problem solving, the ability to manage an office or a situation are especially suited to the middle-aged woman.

—Some women resent their husbands' success, prestige and interesting lives.

—Many men get upset when a woman puts her new interests first. They want to be first, to be constantly listened to about their work and problems.

—Women could not have done what they did without some support from their husbands.

—Breaking out inevitably changes a marriage. But not breaking out will change it too.

—Women in mid-life try harder. They feel obliged to do well as part of the first wave of older women to go back to school and work.

—Women in power don't want to wield that power as much as they want to see their ideas used, have an impact on business or politics.

—Women realize at this point in life that they are no longer going to *feel* any older. They will only *look* older.

There are many more observations that could be added to this list. During a period of transition into unaccustomed work and marriage styles, what women do to excess or inadequately, what they feel unsure of or excel in, their mistakes, their problems—all become a public part of the learning process. They are being observed and measured with the same curiosity that scientists devote to any new species.

The Advice of the Middle Ages

In addition to the theories of mid-life women and their changing life patterns that I have suggested, and the general observations that women have made about themselves and others, I would like at this point to serve up some of the more salient bits of advice offered by those I interviewed.

By reading these warnings, women may be able to identify with a similar situation or avoid it. If you can say, "Yes, that's the way I feel," or "That's what I need to do," it makes the solutions that much easier. I have friends who visit a psychiatrist twice a week. That's the expensive way. It is to be hoped that women can find themselves and unravel their problems before they reach that point.

With a bit of advice it will be easier to insist on certain rights, like being recognized for whatever you do whether it is pumping gas, serving martinis, cooking dinner every night, writing, potting, painting, or asking for a promotion. You deserve recognition for the role you play. You need encouragement to give up your habitual meekness. The meek inherit the earth only in books. Don't allow yourself to be exploited. Don't spend the rest of your life thinking you will do everything later. Later is now, however old you are. It is time to heed advice.

These are the pragmatic details that women need to be aware of. If they want you to wear a navy blue suit around the vice-president's office, your office, by God you ought to know that, whether you intend to fight it or not. If some suggestion suddenly opens a window, touches a nerve, it's worth reading the fifty others that pass by undigested. For so many women who have gone obediently through the domestic mill and gotten stuck there, only other women can help.

Here, then, is a sampling of some of the advice mid-life women have handed out in hopes of helping others about to embark on their own adventures.

Family

—Women who want a family at any age, even thirty-five, should consider children *and* a career. Have them simultaneously, or in a series: job, children and then back to the job. Both are possible. You do not have to choose one or the other unless you want to.

—Feel good about yourself if you work. Don't feel guilty in terms of your husband and children.

—Make your children so strong with love that they don't need you.

—Don't put all of yourself into any other person.

—Family life and social life have to come second for a successful businesswoman. The career is first.

—Though husbands are happy with your extra salary, they are reluctant to lower your standard of housekeeping. Lower it yourself.

—Try to make your husband realize your work is just as important to you as his work is to him, despite the fact that your salary may be much less.

—Don't take out your hostility about any discrimination at work on your husband. He may be a male, but in this case he's not guilty.

—Make your husband feel self-confident and loved so he won't feel threatened by your working.

Personal

—Find out what you want and go after it. If you sit home and stay scared, nothing will happen. Take fate into your own hands. Don't think, "What is going to happen, will happen." It won't.

—You must believe in yourself, have confidence in yourself, so others will too.

—You must grow and change. Never allow yourself to become static. Set goals for yourself.

—Have a private place where you can do something that is all yours. Be creative.

—Don't any longer be concerned about what other people think of what you do. It's your choice.

—Stop undervaluing yourself and your abilities. Celebrate your talents.

—Reach for confidence by looking around and seeing that others who are doing things aren't any better than you.

—Be able to work because men die earlier than women.

—Be able to work so that you are more interesting.

—Be able to work because financial and career independence promise the only security that can be counted on. Marriages don't always last. You can find a new job more easily than a new husband.

—Women should try to remain as they naturally are, more sensitive to other people than men now are, more caring about human issues, more aware of others' needs.

—Learn to compromise, negotiate.

—Learn to make decisions and be able to justify them.

—Face up to personhood if you suddenly find yourself widowed or divorced. Stand on your own feet, work three times as hard for your friends and social life. Call people, go out, be more aggressive. Get a job.

Preparing

—Do something you do well, something that nourishes you.

—Housewifery does not have to be dead-end; it can be an initial experience that can lead to other things.

—It's never too late. You can get back into school or the working world after thirty-five or forty, or later.

—Never say, "Oh, school or training will take three years or five years and it's too long at my age." It isn't. The important thing is to start.

—Take courses in business, economics and statistics. Be able to read a financial report. Don't be afraid of numbers.

—Learn more about politics and logic. Be able to argue persuasively.

—Train in a field that is not overcrowded. Apply your talents in a unique direction. Fields that were formerly all male will be looking for women.

—Befriend younger students at school. They are known for helping mid-life women and teaching them the tricks and short-cuts.

—If you volunteer, try different kinds of work to get more experience.

—If you know yourself, you are more likely to find the right job. Send for career brochures, talk to other women, make lists of your skills, join women's groups, go to encounter or medita-tion sessions, visit personnel advisors at various companies or a professional career counselor. Try, in several of these ways to get to know yourself.

—Don't allow yourself to be splintered in too many direc-tions. Establish a continuity of interest in whatever you do.

—Get in at whatever level you can if you want a job and learn, learn, learn. Listen and watch. You absorb a lot by os-mosis.

—Don't be afraid to start small if you want to have a busi-ness. Small things can grow pretty big.

—Establish or join a new-girl network so you can meet with other women to exchange information, hear news of important job openings, share expertise, discuss problems and solutions and get advice.

On the Job

—Try to adjust your job as much as possible to your other roles of homemaker and mother by, for example, putting in shorter hours, working at home or looking for flexitime, where you decide your own hours.

—Move up or out. If you are working and can't get ahead because of discrimination or lack of openings, leave. Go else-where.

—You have to make your own opportunities. Those at the top don't get there by chance. They work for it. And they ask for it.

—Don't be afraid to try new things. Take risks.

—Don't type too well or you might get stuck as a typist, unless you want to be one. Say you can do rough drafts.

—If you are doing what men do and being criticized for it, just ignore this double standard. It's what makes you able to do the job well. Be strong. Be aggressive! Women need action-oriented traits to be successful.

—Don't become like certain men, hard, overly agressive, cutthroat, swearing, because you lack confidence.

—Become expert in whatever you do.

—Be efficient. It is one of the major keys to success for women.

—The importance of management and organization cannot be overemphasized.

—Know how to make decisions. Be able to understand the "What will happen if . . ." way of thinking.

—Don't giggle or chatter, but don't be too serious. Have a sense of humor.

—Don't put men down. Try to get them to see you as an equal, not a sex object.

—Don't wave banners about liberation.

—Don't wander when you are trying to say something. Come to the point.

—Don't take office joking or constructive criticism personally.

One can not only derive specific good sense from such lists, but also become familiar with a new mind-set. Women who have creative outlets or who work, and even those who remain at home who have strong interests of their own, no longer sound or think as women used to only a few years ago. Others, too, now need a new language and a new understanding of themselves. Advice will help point the way.

Middle-Age Power

"The mind is a terrible thing to waste," a recent United Negro College Fund appeal proclaimed—an observation that is painfully true. And no one is more aware of this than the educated middle-aged woman who is rotting on the vine. That is why it is so important for women in this mid-life generation to take hold of themselves and make sure that they find a creative outlet, do what they choose in a way that will not waste their minds. They must control their destinies, plan their futures, the way every successful man has always done.

There are twenty-nine million middle-aged women (forty to sixty-four) in this country. Too many are timid, deferential and afraid, behaving as though they have no choice, as though it's some primeval instinct they are acting out. They are so habituated to having to get permission from Dad, or husband, to do anything, that by the time they reach mid-life, they are mentally stalemated. It's hard to break out at forty or any other time, if you don't think you have the right to, and no one has given you permission. It is now time to give yourself permission.

Middle age for women is rapidly becoming one of the most exciting periods of life, rather than a fallow, dead-end time to be used only for comparing physical complaints, sitting around waiting for old age. The woman of this age still feels strong, capable, looks better and knows herself more accurately than she ever did. She has become a wise and very human person, a warm and understanding human being who can be monumentally effective in whatever she does. If, as one executive said, "The future is going to revolve around managers who can deal with people successfully," the mid-life woman is certainly at her peak in this capacity. It is now that she commands her most impressive power as a person. It is this power, and her talents, that have to be tapped in whatever way will lead to her success. Her only problem may be convincing herself that all this is true. If women believe they can be important in their work, they will go out and become important. And because most men are not going to convince women of this, we will have to convince each other.

Appendix

Selected Sources of Career Information

U.S. GOVERNMENT AGENCIES

U.S. Department of Health, Education, and Welfare
Office of Education
Bureau of Occupational and Adult Education
Washington, D.C. 20202

Women in Non-Traditional Occupations: a Bibliography. 189 pp., 1976.

U.S. Department of Labor:

Employment Standards Administration
Women's Bureau
Washington, D.C. 20210

Publications of the Women's Bureau. Leaflet 10. Lists publications on a variety of careers. Includes instructions for ordering the publications, many of which are free.

Manpower Administration
Washington, D.C. 20213

Index to Publications. Lists titles of various special reports and projects, as well as popular articles related to target groups in the work force and to specific occupations.

Employment Security offices in many states have prepared job briefs or leaflets describing the kinds of occupations found in the state. Inquire at your local employment office, or request the *Guide to Local Occupational Information* from the U.S. Employment Service, Manpower Administration, Washington, D.C. 20213.

Bureau of Labor Statistics
Washington, D.C. 20212

Occupational Outlook Handbook. The 1978–79 edition gives descriptions and projections for more than 850 occupations and 30 major industries. Published every two years. 825 pp. $8.00. Reprints of specific occupations available at minimal cost.

Occupational Outlook Quarterly. Reports on new occupational research results and sources of current career materials. Published quarterly. Yearly subscription price, $4.00; single copy, $1.30.

(Both publications are for sale by the Bureau of Labor Statistics in Washington and regional offices of the Bureau of Labor Statistics. They are also available for reference at local Employment Security offices, in most public libraries and in school and college counseling/placement offices.)

PRIVATE AND PROFESSIONAL AGENCIES

Council for Career Planning
541 Madison Avenue
New York, New York 10022

Job Fact Sheets. A single sheet describes an occupation. Yearly subscription rate, $12.00 for approximately 15 occupation descriptions; 90 cents for a single copy.

B'nai B'rith Career and Counseling Services
1640 Rhode Island Avenue, NW
Washington, D.C. 20036

Counselor's Information Service. An annotated bibliography of current literature on educational and vocational guidance. Published quarterly. Subscription price, $14 a year.

Washington Opportunities for Women (WOW)
1649 K Street
Washington, D.C. 20006

WOW in Washington publishes *The National Directory of Women's Employment Programs,* a book of organizations which help women. It includes 140 names of groups in the Midwest, West, South and Northeast. $7.50 per copy. WOW operates a free advisory service and information center for Washington-area women who are seeking job information, career planning assistance and education and training program descriptions. With Labor Department cooperation, WOW has been providing technical assistance to other self-help centers since 1973. Some of these are:

Atlanta Wider Opportunities for Women
161 Peachtree Street, NE
Room 310
Atlanta, Georgia 30303

Baltimore New Directions for Women
1100 North Eutaw Street
Baltimore, Maryland 21201

Jobs for Older Women Action Project
3102 Telegraph Avenue
Berkeley, CA 94705

Opportunities for Women
144 Westminster Street
Providence, Rhode Island 02903

Richmond Women on the Way
308 East Cary Street
Richmond, Virginia 23219

Wider Opportunities for Women, Boston
C. F. Hurley Building
Government Center
Cambridge and Stamford Streets
Boston, Massachusetts 02203

Work Options for Women
YWCA
350 North Market
Wichita, Kansas 67202

Working Opportunities for Women
65 East Kellog Blvd.
St. Paul, Minnesota 55101

WISE-WOW
38 South Main Street
Hanover, New Hampshire 03755

Various other organizations provide a combination of services that may include job-availability information and educational opportunities as well as counseling and career information. A member of a local Washington, D.C., metropolitan area women's group compiled a list of institutions and groups that provide such services. To see if anything similar has been done in your area, contact universities, colleges (including junior and community), adult education centers and women's organizations.

Women's Organizations and Leaders—1979 Directory, lists more than 8,000 active women and women's groups. It sells for $50. If it is not available in libraries or at chapters of women's organizations, write to Myra E. Barrer, Editor, Today Publications and News Service, 621 National Press Building, Washington, D.C. 20045.

For additional societies and associations, consult the *Encyclopedia of Associations,* National Organizations of the United States, which is found in most libraries. Also, the *Women's Bureau Handbook on Women Workers* contains a section, "Organizations of Interest to Women," grouped by various specialties.

ADDITIONAL SOURCES

How to Get College Credit for What You Have Learned as a Homemaker and Volunteer. By Ruth Ekstrom, Abigail Harris, and Marlaine Lockheed

Accrediting Women's Competencies
T 185
Educational Testing Service
Princeton, N.J. 08541

Includes a list of colleges that give credit for volunteer and homemaking experience. Price: $3.

Catalyst
14 East 60th Street
New York, N.Y. 10022

Lists centers around the country that offer counseling and career services.

Women's Career Project
Northeastern University
360 Huntington Avenue
Boston, Mass. 02115

Options for Women, Inc.
8419 Germantown Ave.
Philadelphia, Pa. 19118